# The Startup

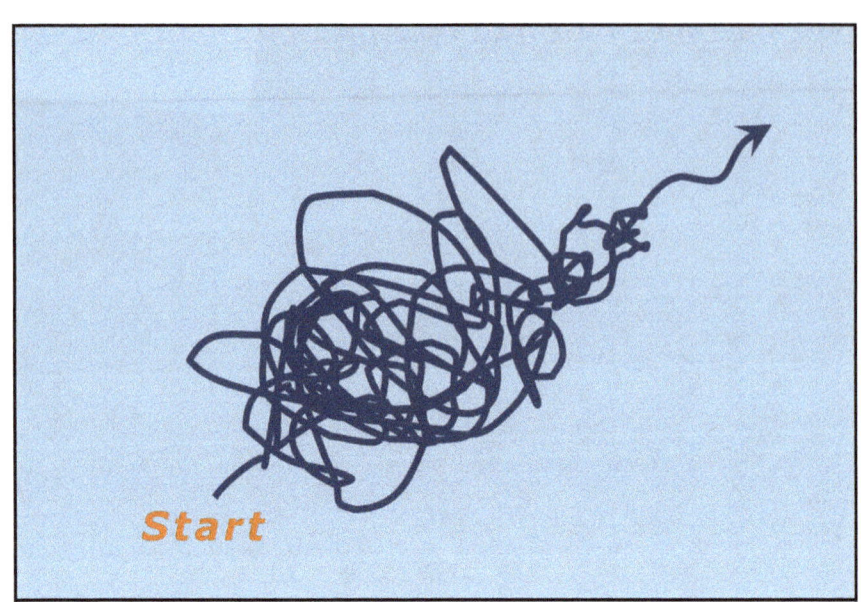

Jesko von Windheim

# The Startup

## Navigating Chaos to Elevate Your Career and Achieve Entrepreneurial Success

Jesko von Windheim
Nicholas School of the Environment
Duke University
Durham, NC, USA

ISBN 978-3-030-45077-9      ISBN 978-3-030-45078-6 (eBook)
https://doi.org/10.1007/978-3-030-45078-6

© Springer Nature Switzerland AG 2020
This work is subject to copyright. All rights are reserved by the Publisher, whether the whole or part of the material is concerned, specifically the rights of translation, reprinting, reuse of illustrations, recitation, broadcasting, reproduction on microfilms or in any other physical way, and transmission or information storage and retrieval, electronic adaptation, computer software, or by similar or dissimilar methodology now known or hereafter developed.
The use of general descriptive names, registered names, trademarks, service marks, etc. in this publication does not imply, even in the absence of a specific statement, that such names are exempt from the relevant protective laws and regulations and therefore free for general use.
The publisher, the authors and the editors are safe to assume that the advice and information in this book are believed to be true and accurate at the date of publication. Neither the publisher nor the authors or the editors give a warranty, expressed or implied, with respect to the material contained herein or for any errors or omissions that may have been made. The publisher remains neutral with regard to jurisdictional claims in published maps and institutional affiliations.

This Springer imprint is published by the registered company Springer Nature Switzerland AG
The registered company address is: Gewerbestrasse 11, 6330 Cham, Switzerland

Jesko von Windheim

# The Startup

## Navigating Chaos to Elevate Your Career and Achieve Entrepreneurial Success

Jesko von Windheim
Nicholas School of the Environment
Duke University
Durham, NC, USA

ISBN 978-3-030-45077-9     ISBN 978-3-030-45078-6  (eBook)
https://doi.org/10.1007/978-3-030-45078-6

© Springer Nature Switzerland AG 2020
This work is subject to copyright. All rights are reserved by the Publisher, whether the whole or part of the material is concerned, specifically the rights of translation, reprinting, reuse of illustrations, recitation, broadcasting, reproduction on microfilms or in any other physical way, and transmission or information storage and retrieval, electronic adaptation, computer software, or by similar or dissimilar methodology now known or hereafter developed.
The use of general descriptive names, registered names, trademarks, service marks, etc. in this publication does not imply, even in the absence of a specific statement, that such names are exempt from the relevant protective laws and regulations and therefore free for general use.
The publisher, the authors and the editors are safe to assume that the advice and information in this book are believed to be true and accurate at the date of publication. Neither the publisher nor the authors or the editors give a warranty, expressed or implied, with respect to the material contained herein or for any errors or omissions that may have been made. The publisher remains neutral with regard to jurisdictional claims in published maps and institutional affiliations.

This Springer imprint is published by the registered company Springer Nature Switzerland AG
The registered company address is: Gewerbestrasse 11, 6330 Cham, Switzerland

*This book is dedicated to my mom and dad who taught me to be bold and to embrace chaos.*

# Acknowledgements

You don't ride a roller coaster in a vacuum. All the experiences I have had, difficult or exhilarating, have enriched my life, and I feel truly blessed for all of it. But I couldn't have done any of it without my family—Monika, Tasso, Natalia, Katriana and Thilo—who, during good times and bad, have my back unconditionally.

I am also incredibly lucky to work with amazing people who have taught me everything I know: Stephen Brooks (manufacturing), John Fuscoe (legal), Karl von Gunten (marketing), David Koester (product development) and Rick Scott (finance) have been the backbone of everything I have done for the past 20 years.

When it comes to actually writing things down, I would not get very far without Wendy Graber whose patient editing smooths the rough edges and brings my stories to life.

Finally, I want to thank Karen Lee Weil, a rare "impact player" and the gold standard that I measure every chief technology officer by.

# Contents

| | |
|---|---|
| Turbulence | 1 |
| Opportunity Knocks | 13 |
| Planning to Lead | 21 |
| The One that Got Away | 29 |
| The North Star | 37 |
| Customer Call | 47 |
| Technology Overload | 53 |
| Mining for Prospects | 65 |
| Striking Gold | 73 |
| Gathering Clouds | 79 |
| Into the Storm | 89 |
| Pivot | 97 |

| | |
|---|---|
| Switching On | 107 |
| The Final Touch | 125 |
| Cash Is King | 131 |
| Pitching and Flailing | 145 |
| Closing Time | 153 |
| Going Large | 165 |
| Chasing the Unicorn | 179 |
| Epilogue | 189 |

# Contents

| | |
|---|---|
| Turbulence | 1 |
| Opportunity Knocks | 13 |
| Planning to Lead | 21 |
| The One that Got Away | 29 |
| The North Star | 37 |
| Customer Call | 47 |
| Technology Overload | 53 |
| Mining for Prospects | 65 |
| Striking Gold | 73 |
| Gathering Clouds | 79 |
| Into the Storm | 89 |
| Pivot | 97 |

| | |
|---|---|
| Switching On | 107 |
| The Final Touch | 125 |
| Cash Is King | 131 |
| Pitching and Flailing | 145 |
| Closing Time | 153 |
| Going Large | 165 |
| Chasing the Unicorn | 179 |
| Epilogue | 189 |

# Turbulence

Turbulence sucks.

At 33,000 feet in the air, we were in the thick of it, causing even a seasoned traveler like myself to grip my armrests in forgotten prayer. Ignoring the twists and turns of the plane, I leaned my forehead against the window, trying to get some sort of relief. The cold felt good, easing the headache that was about to explode, taking my mind off the nausea building in my gut.

It had been a rough, almost surreal trip—starting with the flight up to Ottawa, into the middle of an ice storm with ice thick enough to topple electrical transmission towers—and ending with… failure. There was just no other word for it. Forget turbulence, I had failed.

As we descended, I realized the feelings in my head, my gut, and even my heart weren't physical; they were the manifestations of a failing venture and the bitter recriminations that came with it.

Yes, turbulence sucks. But it's one thing if you're experiencing it on a plane, flying from one city to the next, and quite another if it's a defining characteristic of your career. Or your earning capacity. Or your life. On the plane, you're just a passenger. Turbulence is a short-term nuisance until your pilot finds a smoother flight path.

As an entrepreneur, you learn quickly that turbulence is an integral and unavoidable part of your life. The ups and downs are extreme, with the potential to cause damage that goes far beyond a bit of nausea or short-term sphincter clenching. You, the entrepreneur, are the pilot. Attempts to find smoother air are entirely up to you. And in this case, there are no fancy gizmos to help you get there—no maps, no flashing lights, no gurus at the top of the mountain. It's you and whatever you can dream up to make things better.

Most people avoid such craziness and get a "real" job. That's what everyone is taught to do.

Successful entrepreneurs learn to embrace the unpredictability of turbulence—understanding that highs and lows are a natural part of innovation. Of course you envy friends—the ones with stable career paths at McKinsey, Apple, or Google—but the corporate grind is not in your DNA. There is an element of gambling to what you do, with a unique twist because the game is your own. Success or failure is entirely based on your rulebook. Under these conditions, success is insanely gratifying and failure is particularly bitter. I know.

If you want to be an entrepreneur, you need to understand the game. Turbulence—risk, the unknown, chaos—is unavoidable. Embracing entrepreneurship, but not turbulence is the path that is least likely to lead to success. If others depend on you—your co-founders, co-workers, or family—then ignoring turbulence is worse than a mistake, it's reckless and can have a profoundly negative impact on your life and the lives of those close to you. As an entrepreneur, it is crucial to appreciate the chaos that permeates your situation and proceed with caution. Anything else may be disastrous.

When I began my career commercializing technology innovations, I learned that many people I worked with—particularly my bosses, but also technical collaborators—expected the "business guy" to magically make the chaos go away—or, at the very least, be able to identify and avoid it, just like the pilot in the plane.

But new innovations are never quite what you think they will be—they always require more development than expected and more time than you planned for. Technology rarely performs exactly like the tech team said it would. And, it turns out, customers are just as fickle! One day they like your new technology, the next day they don't, and the day after that, they go with a competing product. All of this creates chaos for your startup. A lot of chaos. Turbulence.

While you can't make it go away and you certainly cannot guarantee anything, you can work to understand the chaos and manage it, hopefully avoiding a death spiral. I never imagined that I would be an entrepreneur. No one explained to me what entrepreneurship would be like before I jumped in, not because I wanted to, but because I had to. And so here I was learning about startup turbulence the hard way.

The plane dropped sharply and I shook my head ever so slightly back and forth, as I often do when bad thoughts threaten to creep in. What was I thinking? There was no room for imagined death spirals here! A physical shake of the brain should have buried things where they belonged. This was no time for recrimination: I knew that to dwell on failure was the beginning of the end. Nevertheless, instead of looking forward as we descended into Raleigh-Durham, my thoughts drifted backward in spite of myself.

Twelve months before everything looked very different. A new job and an exciting career in a new direction filled me with hope. I was consumed with excitement and joy at being able to direct my talents and capabilities to something that could possibly—hopefully—be spectacular. I'd had a choice back then between a great job and an exciting opportunity: the job—Vice President of Business Development at a small company that produced specialty materials in Buffalo, New York; the opportunity—Manager of Business Development for a nonprofit technology center in Research Triangle Park, North Carolina. While for some, the choice of Vice President might have been an easy one, for me it was a tough decision made even more difficult because of the pressures I was under. Having been laid off from my previous job, I was currently a jobless breadwinner in a single-income family. I had two kids, a mortgage, car payments, and very little savings. I was at the raw end of the American Dream. A job with a big title in Buffalo seemed so obvious, but my heart just wasn't in it.

At the time, rational analysis and a lot of outside advice pointed unerringly in the direction of Buffalo. It was 1997. I was thirty-six years old with a PhD in chemistry and a newly minted MBA from the Kenan-Flagler School of Business. Even as I had been finishing my PhD in Canada back in the early 90s, I had known that a technical path was not for me, which is why I had immigrated to the United States six years before. I came specifically to get involved in the business side of technology in a country that really knew how to commercialize exceptional ideas. As any Canadian would tell you: Canada may have great innovators, but it's the Americans who are the experts at making money! Yet, in spite of my best efforts, my technical background kept pulling me back into technology management positions, even in the United States. The MBA was my last, desperate effort to make the shift into business. A shift that I knew was critical for my career and, honestly, for my peace of mind.

Much to my dismay the MBA *was not* the golden ticket that I had anticipated. I *still failed* in countless efforts to move from technology management into marketing or business development positions. One such attempt with Lord Corporation in Cary, North Carolina had been particularly galling. They needed a German speaking candidate—me—with a PhD in chemistry—me—and business development experience—me—to do business development in Germany. Me! Me! Me! Honestly, even today I don't understand why I didn't get that job.

It was evident in my interviews with various companies that I was talking to technical managers who knew they wanted business development capabilities, but were not very clear on what this actually meant. One interesting interview was with Allegro Microsystems, a small, specialty designer and manufacturer of magnetic sensors and power management circuits. I made it all the way to the final interviews at the company headquarters in Worcester, Massachusetts. The preliminary interviews were with engineers who were convinced that I had the skills to help them expand the market for their devices. They liked me and desperately wanted me to get the job. However, in the final interviews I faced upper management who were equally convinced they needed an electrical engineer who understood the details of device design—definitely not me!

In preparation for the final interviews, the engineering team frantically coached me on how to address the technical gap. They sent me papers and book chapters to study and guided me on who at the company would be the most insistent on testing my technical knowledge (the most senior decision maker!). I was very up front on what I could and could not do for the company. I could easily learn enough of the basics of the technology to identify new applications, new customers, and new markets. I felt confident that I would be able to sell products and product ideas and develop collaborations and agreements with new customers. But an expert in electrical engineering I was not, and I had no intention of faking it. Needless to say, I did not get the job. Today Allegro is still in business and appears to be doing well. Clearly, they found other good people for that position.

Another surreal experience I had was in an informational interview with Ben Lynch, a local entrepreneur. Ben didn't know it, but at the time he was my idol. With a PhD in electrical engineering and a pioneer in fiber optic communications, Ben had done what I dreamed of doing: He had raised venture capital and started NewCom, a well-respected company in the local community. I had heard Ben speak a few times and was enthralled. He was what I wanted to be! As I was looking for a new job, I managed to get a lunch with Ben, thinking that this, finally, was the silver bullet I needed to propel me from the technical world into the business realm. After all, we were alike; we were kindred spirits!

I could not have been more wrong. Ben tore me apart. Even today, I remember it well. Ben was an imposing figure. As he sat across from me at lunch in a patterned crewneck sweater—he had a casual, almost colorful look that contrasted sharply with my jacket and tie. I told him I was looking for advice and he gave it to me in spades. First, he asked me what I wanted to achieve.

"I have a PhD in chemistry; I just got my MBA. I want to get into business development," I told him.

"What do you mean by 'business development'?" he asked.

"Well, uh…," I stammered. I was surprised by the question and tried to think fast. Why would this guy not know what business development was? He had built an amazing tech startup from scratch. Maybe this was just some kind of test.

"Uh… Well, I'm sure you know…"

"I don't know. Educate me," Ben replied.

"Okay. I want to develop new products and markets based on cutting-edge technologies. I think I can do that for you. I'd…"

"I've got salespeople all over the world. What can you do that they can't?" he asked pointedly.

Hmmm, a very good question. And not one that I had a good answer for. What I knew intuitively, and know for sure today, is that there is a large—huge—difference between business development and sales. The best salespeople can sell anything and are highly motivated to do so. But you also have to give them a product that customers are ready for and willing to buy. With this in hand, they will take the product and relentlessly pursue any customer where there is potential to close a sale. If there isn't, they simply move on to the next target. If they are good at this, they can make a lot of money. On the other hand, no salesperson is going to waste their time trying to match esoteric customer needs to new-fangled technology capabilities. There's just no money in it, at least in the short term. Commissions drive sales people, and fact-finding conversations—also called "customer discovery"—generally do not generate commissions.

But when Ben asked his question, I had no good answer, and it went downhill from there. Ben spent the rest of the lunch mercilessly exposing all my weaknesses. How can someone with a chemistry degree possibly hope to make an impact in a company that is developing advanced networking systems? I should be in the chemical or pharmaceutical industry. An MBA meant nothing. I was naïve. Misdirected even. End of lunch.

Whew! I came out of that meeting feeling like a wrung-out dish rag. Literally, I had to roll my shoulders and work the kinks out of my neck as I walked across the parking lot to my car just to feel human again. I also had to chuckle somewhat at the verbal beating. I had to give it to Ben—he hadn't been rude, but he hadn't pulled any punches either. He had given it to me straight, something most people wouldn't have done.

Thankfully, I had already learned enough in life not to be deterred by Ben's verbal beating. Whenever someone takes an extreme position—either in your favor or against it—you need to take it with a huge grain of salt. Despite being a person I revered, Ben was also just another data point, and I was convinced he was wrong.

So, when George Keethly in Buffalo subsequently offered me the job in his materials company, and—much more importantly—agreed that I could add value in a business development role, even offering me a position as *Vice President*, it seemed like the answer to everything I had wished for. We'd hit it off fabulously over the phone, and even as I had made preparations to go up to Buffalo for final interviews, I was already packing up my furniture in my mind. This was what I had hoped for when I took night classes for my MBA. This was a fantastic step forward in my career. This was *the* job.

The opportunity, on the other hand, was with a local, nonprofit-technology organization MCNC (formerly the Microelectronics Center of North Carolina). Originally set up by Governor James B. Hunt in 1980, the State of North Carolina had funded MCNC to the tune of about $250 million to create a high technology semiconductor design and production facility and also a world-class supercomputing and networking center. At the time of its inception, MCNC was cutting-edge in everything—just walking up to the buildings (one which was even built in the shape of a supercomputer!) took your breath away.

I'd often driven past MCNC on my way to work and even knew some of the people there, although I had never set foot in any of its imposing buildings. What I had done is hire one of their leading technology managers Vera Cohen as a consultant in my previous job at Kobe Steel. When I lost my job, Vera was one of the first people I approached.

"We definitely can use your skillset over here," she informed me. "But budgets are tight!"

With this mixed feedback and no clarity as to whether there was even a job available, I decided to take matters into my own hands. Financial pressures were looming, and I could not afford to wait. I made a cold call.

It was just before Thanksgiving in 1996, when I walked into the huge lobby of MCNC's main building on Cornwallis Drive in Research Triangle Park. Much to my surprise, the lobby was full of people, lined up in a long, snaking line that eventually made its way into a room that I could not see into. I went through the crowd to the front desk of the lobby where a very nice lady greeted me. I told her that I was job hunting and wanted to speak to the person responsible for marketing or business development. Failing that, could I at least leave my resume?

"Well, Sugar," she said, with a drawl that was clearly born locally, "You are in luck! It's our Thanksgiving potluck today, and there is the President of MCNC standing in line right over there."

I looked over and saw a portly man, very well dressed in a high-quality suit, talking to a scruffy-looking guy in a plaid shirt, torn jeans, and flip flops—engineer written all over him.

"That's Dr. Clarke," the lady continued, referring to the gentleman in the suit. "Just go over and introduce yourself!"

I was a bit taken aback. I had come prepared to drop off a resume, maybe talk to someone in human resources at best, and here I was just a few steps away from the president of the company! Deep breath. Don't mess up his name! Make this count! I was suddenly unsure of myself as I prepared to approach Dr. Clarke.

Fortunately, we were close enough, and the receptionist was talking loudly enough, to catch Dr. Clarke's attention and he was already looking at me. This saved the embarrassment of trying to barge in while he was deep in conversation with the engineer. I caught his eye. Step. Step. Step. I leaned forward and shook his hand.

"Hello, Dr. Clarke, my name is Jesko von Windheim. I've done some work with Vera Cohen, and she tells me that MCNC is looking for business development skills. I'd like to talk to you about that, if you have time."

Delivered smoothly with a firm handshake, it was a perfect introduction, and done with so much more confidence than I actually felt. I breathed a big, inward sigh of relief.

Shelby Clarke was the consummate southern gentleman. Much to my surprise, the first thing he did was invite me to participate in the potluck lunch. Despite my initial nervousness, he was so kind and inviting, it was very easy for me to make this cold call. As we waited in line, he asked me questions about my background, and as I responded he went from being friendly to getting visibly excited about what I wanted to do.

"You'll need to join me upstairs in my office for lunch!" he finally exclaimed as we approached the food.

Unbelievable. As we advanced past numerous tables filled with every kind of Thanksgiving food you could imagine, my shot-in-the-dark cold call became lunch with the president of MCNC! It was an important lesson: You never know what will happen when you just go ahead and do something.

We loaded up our plates and made our way upstairs to what I later learned was called the "fish bowl." It was a large, second-floor atrium with many cubicles taking up the bulk of the space, encircled on all sides by offices. But the offices had no privacy. Everything was glass with each office having a glass wall and door facing into the atrium where staff worked. Staff were completely surrounded by executives and managers looking out through their glass walls; and of course, staff could also see everything that the executives were doing—hence the term fish bowl. It was an open, but also eerie work environment, where everything was on display, including my unexpected meeting with the president.

"You have a PhD?" was Dr. Clarke's first question once we were settled, revisiting some of the ground we had already covered downstairs.

"Yes, in chemistry," I answered, a little concerned as to what might be coming next, given my recent experiences in other interviews. "But, to be honest, I'm not much of a chemist—"

"Ha," he laughed, "I don't need a chemist! I've got a building full of them!" He waved his arm in the direction of the fish bowl. "But, if you want to do business development here, you need a PhD, otherwise you won't have the respect of the people who run our technical programs. They all have PhDs, except Vera of course, but she's special." He looked at me like everyone knew this.

He explained that MCNC had around 140 technical staff who worked on semiconductor devices, electronics packaging, micro electro mechanical systems, supercomputing, and networking. The organization generated $40 million annually in revenue, but a good chunk of that—$19 million—came either directly or indirectly from the North Carolina legislature. MCNC had a contract to manage the communications network for the North Carolina University system which generated around $13 million and then also a direct subsidy of $6 million from the State. The rest—$21 million—came from government grants from agencies like DARPA (Defense Advanced Research Projects Agency), NSF (National Science Foundation), and DOE (Department of Energy). There were also a few, small commercial contracts, but these had very little impact on revenue compared to the various state and federal government-funded programs.

"We have a problem with the subsidy, Jesko. Well, it's not the subsidy, it's the fact that it's going away," he chuckled as he dug into his lunch. "Over the years, the North Carolina legislature has poured $250 million of subsidy into this place, and, frankly, they are tired of it. So, that's it. We get $6 million this year, $4 million next year, and $2 million the year after that. Three years, Jesko, and then no more."

He looked at me as if he expected me to say something, but at this point I was a bit shell-shocked. I'd come to drop off my resume, and here I was in the office of the president in a private meeting as he, with great humor, explained the inner workings of his organization. I was later to learn that this was just who Shelby Clarke was: a kind man with classic southern charm who made fast decisions and looked on the bright side of almost everything. I also learned that, as a state-funded, nonprofit organization, financial information at MCNC was much more available to the public than it would have been for a typical business. I didn't know it at the time, but nothing Shelby told me was secret.

I'm not a poker player, but when needed, I have a great poker face. I stayed calm and did my best to follow the twists and turns of the conversation as we ate lunch acting as if this meeting and our discussion were exactly what I expected.

"Well, I'd say $6 million is quite a hole, but at least you have three years. Are you currently running any kind of cash surplus?" I asked, hopefully.

"Nope. We run pretty close to the edge. We're a nonprofit, after all." Shelby smiled at the idea, once again showing little concern for what seemed to me like a pretty serious looming shortfall of revenue.

"But, still," I said, starting to think it through. "You need to replace what is essentially a $6 million gift. Whatever work you generate to do that will have its own associated cost, so your contracts will have to be a lot more than $6 million to make up for the subsidy…"

Dr. Clarke looked at me blankly, and I rapidly—and foolishly—lost confidence in my analysis. What an idiot I was—a freshly minted MBA trying to tell the president of this company about his business! But I really wasn't so far off. It was more my host was completely uninterested in a financial analysis of the situation. It was something I learned later about Dr. Clarke: He had many positive attributes, but he was not a financial guy. To his detriment, he left such details for others to figure out.

In future years, well beyond my experience at MCNC, the indifference of scientists to finance would be a recurring challenge as I tried to commercialize technology out of the laboratory. Perhaps it should come as no surprise that many technologists, academics, and nonprofit administrators are not primarily motivated by the economics of their innovations. On one level, this makes a lot of sense. When experimenting with new science in the lab, management decisions are—and should be—focused on technology improvements, not financial viability. But, as technology transitions to commercial applications, the economics become increasingly important, until eventually they are all that matters. This gradual evolution from a research to a financial focus is one of the most significant barriers a new technology must transition to make it into the market. Many research organizations simply do not have the skills—or even the motivation—to cross this bridge. Little did I know in this first interview at MCNC, that Dr. Clarke's lack of interest in economics was a harbinger of things to come as he often pursued projects without deeply considering the financial implications.

My point that day was unless MCNC had a lot of unused engineering capacity, generating extra revenue to replace the subsidy would also incur extra cost. In the worst-case scenario, if there was no extra capacity at MCNC to do revenue generating work, then you would have to replace the subsidy entirely by generating profits. Even if MCNC could generate a 20 percent profit margin, that would mean a need for at least $30 million in incremental revenue, almost doubling MCNC's top line in about three years! To me, that seemed like a very big hill to climb, but it was also not a conversation we were going to have that day. Dr. Clarke simply pushed aside any attempts to discuss the financial implications of the disappearing subsidy. He was much more excited about the opportunities at MCNC.

"And here is the really great news!" he told me, walking over to his desk and producing a thin, bound document with a flourish. "This document is an agreement signed by the North Carolina legislature, essentially handing MCNC over to management—that's us—to do with what we will! With board approval, of course," he chuckled again, and this time actually winked at me. "Of course, we're pretty good at managing the Board!"

He came back and deposited the document in my lap. "Here, go ahead and read it."

I did, and sure enough, the North Carolina legislature, after investing over a quarter of a billion dollars into MCNC since the 1980s, was cutting the organization loose. The deal outlined in the document was to end the subsidy and, in return, MCNC would be an independent, not-for-profit organization, with all decision making controlled entirely by management under the governance of its board of directors. Wow.

The $6 million subsidy was a huge problem, but in my mind this paled in comparison to the assets MCNC had with its contracts and research potential. The fact that the North Carolina legislature was writing all of it off with the wave of a pen was mind-boggling to me, or with the wave of many pens, as there were a multitude of signatures on the document I held. As I read, I began to understand Dr. Clarke's optimism and excitement.

Most people, when they hear the term "not-for-profit" or "nonprofit" think that this represents an organization that lives day-to-day on handouts from benefactors and support from volunteers. But this is not the case at all. A nonprofit organization is certainly limited in terms of the amount of profit it can generate and how it is governed, but at the end of the day, a nonprofit can be very successful financially—and so can its management and employees. There are lots of examples out there—RTI International (a billion-dollar organization) and Blue Cross Blue Shield (much, much larger) just to name two in North Carolina.

Imagine someone coming to you and saying: "Here is a nonprofit that we've invested $250 million into for bleeding-edge technologies. We are done, do with it whatever you will." I think you would get excited too. To me, it seemed like a shining beacon of opportunity, difficult to ignore, impossible to walk away from. Shelby obviously felt the same way.

"We're sitting on a gold mine, Jesko!" Dr. Clarke exclaimed as I looked up from the document. "And I think you can help us get where we need to go." Even though he was an academic, Dr. Clarke at his core was the consummate salesperson.

I left the MCNC offices with my head spinning. Everything I had heard was so unexpected, fascinating, unbelievable… and scary. My emotions ran the gamut from excitement to disbelief. Fear was in there somewhere too, considering the financial challenges MCNC faced, but it was conveniently buried in the recesses of my mind as the potential opportunities overwhelmed me. On top of that, MCNC looked like an organization that really wanted—no, needed—my skills! Certainly, one thing was absolutely clear: It had been a heck of a better lunch than the one I had with Ben Lynch.

I walked to my car with a lightness I had not felt in years.

# Opportunity Knocks

Some people believe a bird in the hand is worth two in the bush.

An entrepreneur doesn't think this way. The entrepreneur says: "Well if you know there are two birds in the bush, who's to say there aren't a lot more? How do I catch them all? And how about when I catch one, I sell it to you—think of it: for you, a guaranteed bird in hand! Now that's convenience!"

The unknown, and even the unknowable opportunity, is what drives an entrepreneur. For better or worse, an entrepreneur strives to find something where everyone else sees nothing. Because fame and fortune are not made with the bird in hand, they are made by the multitudes to be found in the bush.

The problem is good opportunities are really, really hard to find.

When I was studying physics as an undergraduate student, I was fascinated to learn that "nothingness" does not really exist. What we observe to be the complete absence of anything—a vacuum—is at its core actually a mix of matter and anti-matter. Together, two opposing matter/anti-matter particles perfectly cancel each other out, leaving us with nothing to observe. My physics professors at McMaster University, who knew a thing or two about how the universe works, taught me that this is not the whole story.

Apparently, on a subatomic level, a lot more is happening: On an infinitesimal scale, particles of matter are constantly being created along with their anti-matter counterparts. These two ill-fated partners very briefly zip around in space before they recombine and annihilate each other. It is, in fact, a big mystery that our observable universe exists at all. Everything we observe—the stars, the planets, the earth, and humankind—is definitely matter! But, if every particle has an anti-counterpart, what happened to the anti-stars and anti-planets and the anti-humans? They are missing!

Very smart people have put a lot of thought into this question. They theorize that very, very rarely, two particles of matter and anti-matter can somehow become separated, leaving a new particle in our universe without its anti-counterpart around to destroy it—where the anti-matter particle ends up raises another mystery.

As a physics student, I was consumed by these concepts. I envisioned the universe to be a constantly boiling cauldron of creation and annihilation. All of it unobservable to us, except for an occasional, statistically insignificant event resulting in a new particle of matter coming to life that can coalesce into something bigger, like a star, or even becoming part of you or me. Even today, the magic of it astonishes me. These ideas are much more than some kind of cosmic fantasy—they are grounded in mathematics. Apparently, universal laws of physics very, very slightly favor matter over anti-matter, making it possible to do what should be impossible: create something from nothing. Even more amazing is the fact that this slight skew in physical laws appears to be why the whole universe exists today. I marvel that the universe behaves in such a way that allows for the creation of something out of nothing.

What has physics to do with entrepreneurship? Creating something from nothing is exactly what entrepreneurship is all about. An entrepreneur doesn't want the bird in hand, they want what they cannot yet see in the bush.

Fortunately, just like those matter and anti-matter particles constantly born and dying in a vacuum, there is a constant, often unseen, bubbling cauldron of innovation and opportunity all around us! Ideas, concepts, and theories are constantly being created, sometimes to be observed, sometimes not, often to disappear before they are realized or, on rare occasions, to be seized and carried forward by an entrepreneur.

Seizing an opportunity is only the beginning of the journey—one with a strong likelihood of ending in annihilation. On the other hand, perhaps—just maybe—the opportunity has what it takes to grow into something stupendous. That's what every entrepreneur wishes for: to create something grand where nothing existed before. Entrepreneurs are prospectors, hoping to seize one, very special, tiny particle of opportunity that survives its creation to germinate a star.

With opportunities constantly being born and dying all around us, the first challenge we have is to put ourselves in a position to observe the opportunities. The next, hardest challenge is to determine whether the opportunities we observe are fleeting or real. Making that call is the essence of entrepreneurship.

Unfortunately, the call is never clear. If all it takes to see the "bird opportunity" is a short walk and a set of binoculars, then most people will do it. In fact, many people will pursue entrepreneurship at this level sometime in their career. But, when there is nothing to be seen, these same people will go home. The entrepreneur, on the other hand, will climb into the trees looking for nests. They will study mating habits, count eggs, and predict population explosions. They will prepare capture methods, study market demand, and hire sales teams for the bird surge that may or may not appear.

It's nothing like the entrepreneurship reality TV shows where an inventor gets in front of a panel to pitch a product and some guru makes a decision that the product is good or bad. In the real world, things are much more incremental: An idea creates a concept; the concept conceives a prototype; the prototype leads to a product; the product succeeds or fails in the marketplace. Along the way there are usually many mini-successes and also many failures, some of which can be overcome, and some of which may be fatal. There are no flashing signs. There are no gurus.

In all of this, timing is very important. If you are developing software, the creation-annihilation process can occur relatively quickly—in a matter of months—allowing for many quick changes of direction to achieve success. But if you are developing new hardware, the success-failure-correction process will take longer, sometimes even years. If you are developing new materials or chemistries, the process can take decades. This makes software development very attractive to entrepreneurs and investors alike, while hardware development and especially new chemistries (unless they are medical) tend to be unattractive. It can be very confusing to the new entrepreneur who is mentored to develop a "lean startup" and to "fail fast" while constantly responding to the "voice of the customer". These are great concepts, but they mean very different things, depending on the natural cadence of the opportunity at hand.

On the other end of the innovation spectrum there are the opportunities never seized. Some great invention is made, but the right entrepreneur is not available to grasp it and take it forward. This invention then sits on the shelf and never sees the light of day, never makes an impact on our lives, time passes it by, and it no longer holds any value. This happens much, much more than you might believe. Creation and annihilation occur in our best research centers constantly, but to those on the outside, looking for the next big opportunity, they observe a vacuum. I see this as perhaps *the* major challenge for many of our university technology centers, where conservative technology management and intellectual property practices tend to favor annihilation rather than promote creation.

As I faced my choice to join MCNC or move to Buffalo, it became clear that my personal success or failure did not rely on making just one decision, but was likely going to be determined by a series of future decisions. Aside from that, my choice wasn't *just* MCNC or Buffalo. Even though I was strapped for cash and without a job, I could look for additional opportunities to add to the mix. Even in my job hunt, I was in an endless field of creation-annihilation events and it was up to me to choose one—*the* one—that would become a real success.

How on earth do you do that?

One of the things I had going for me is that I was not at all shy about reaching out to smart people who I thought might be able to help me with my decision. Two of the most memorable conversations I had about joining MCNC were with a former professor of mine at UNC Steven Robinson, and with a local venture capitalist Bob West.

I met Bob in a bar in Raleigh and asked him what he thought about me joining MCNC.

"It's a pretty crazy place", he said. "MCNC is a state-funded organization with amazing technologies, but they have a terrible reputation for getting those technologies commercialized."

I was shocked at his bluntness, but I learned over time that all venture capitalists are pretty blunt in their assessments. Right or wrong, you always know where a VC stands.

"They seem to be on the cutting edge of everything," I countered. "I met some of the management and they are very motivated."

"Sure", Bob said. "The folks at MCNC have their hearts in the right place, and they have developed an incredible technology platform, but when it comes to commercialization, they have no idea what they are doing."

"What's worse," he continued with authority, "is that MCNC has a pretty lousy reputation with the investment community, because their deal terms are just not workable. So, even when people try to do deals, they don't get done. Nobody has time for endless negotiations with crazy terms, so serious investors stay away. Then, there is the North Carolina legislature: They fund MCNC and they call the shots. This creates a huge political aspect to MCNC's work. If you go there, I think it's going to be very difficult for you to get things done."

This feedback was quite sobering. Shelby and all the people at MCNC seemed so supportive. I didn't really understand what Bob meant by "deal terms", but I presumed MCNC was driving a hard bargain. What could be so bad about that? Little did I know that the frustration Bob was expressing was almost universal. Creating entrepreneurial deals with organizations like MCNC and, notably, many universities, is so frustrating that few serious investors do it.

But, at that time, I had no idea. Naively, I focused on the upside.

"Did you know the Legislature signed off on an agreement that pretty much gives all commercialization rights to the management team at MCNC?" I didn't mention that the agreement phased out state funding over the next three years.

"Hmmm, that makes it interesting. But, I'll tell you, if you go there and don't pull off a homerun, your career is toast."

Wow. Getting to know Bob, and Ben Lynch before him, I was starting to learn that people in the entrepreneurial community were much more direct than my non-confrontational peers in the research world. Bob's feedback was sobering to put it mildly, but I wasn't ready to give up yet.

I next turned to my professor, Steven Robinson at UNC and asked him his advice on becoming the business development manager at MCNC. He had a very different view, and his words touched my soul.

"Has anyone done commercial development at MCNC before?" he asked.

That was an interesting question. "Not that I know," I responded. "I haven't seen any. It looks pretty much like all they have done up until now is technology development with funding from government grants and the State."

"So, it seems there is a vacuum, then?"

"Yes…," I replied hesitantly, not sure where this was going.

"Great! You're the kind of guy that fills a vacuum. It's perfect for you. I'm sure you will be successful!"

Steven was an inspiring guy who lived and breathed the study of entrepreneurship. I trusted his judgement, even though I did not fully understand it. He apparently knew me much better than I knew myself, or maybe he was just trying to express enthusiasm for his student, I'm not sure. In any case, while I did not fully appreciate what he was talking about at that time, I will never forget those words. At MCNC, I would be filling a vacuum. The concept fascinated me, for reasons Steven could not have known.

The decision was wrenching. In Buffalo, there was a well-defined role in an established company with clear guidance from an experienced CEO. At MCNC there were *a lot* of unknowns. Although some efforts to "commercialize" technology were happening at MCNC, I had not observed any clarity or consensus on it. There was no defined process, nor an established path to success. As far as I could tell there *were* no successes. At least I hadn't been pointed to any in my interviews. No one had done it before. The complete lack of a precedent fascinated me.

And without knowing it, Steven had used language that appealed to me in ways he could not have imagined. *Vacuum.* Immediately I envisioned an environment that *appeared* empty but had a multitude of opportunities springing up all the time. The word vacuum seemed to fit MCNC when it came to commercializing their technology. Shelby had told me that MCNC was doing about $40 million worth of funded research annually, yet *nothing* was reaching the marketplace! There had to be a lot of creation and annihilation going on leading to all this nothingness. Steven was right: All that was needed was the right person to capture some of that opportunity! He inspired me to go bird hunting. In the end, I chose MCNC and later discovered both Steven and Bob were one-hundred percent right in their assessments.

Years later I ran into Steven at an award event at UNC, where I thanked him for his prescient motivation. I tried to explain how his choice of words had inspired me, but I'm not sure I explained it very well. He nodded enthusiastically and smiled as I talked, shook my hand and gave me a friendly pat on the shoulder, congratulating me on my achievements. But it was clear that my attempts to explain his unique motivation for me fell flat and he may well have thought I was a bit odd. Even so, it was a great pleasure to express my gratitude directly to Steven for his impact on my career, something I was not able to do with all of my mentors.

At MCNC I discovered a unique model of entrepreneurship that I have practiced my entire career. At that time, I did not have the luxury of not generating an income. Ours was a one-income family with two children and another on the way. My wife and I decided early in our marriage to manage our household with a division of labor. She focused on the kids and the family, while I focused on generating revenue. This allowed each of us to work to our strengths and, at least for us, reduced stress at home. The downside to this arrangement was that we were entirely dependent on my income and had only very modest rainy-day savings.

Our division of labor meant my personal situation was just about the worst for pursuing a career chasing high risk ventures! Entrepreneurship requires months and even years of surviving on very little money; I had no leeway to do that. I'd spent my vagabond days getting a PhD and, of all things, riding horses in Europe. Now, with a family and a mortgage, those days were over.

My problem was that I needed income *and* I wanted to be an entrepreneur. MCNC was the perfect solution: I had both—a paying job where I could take entrepreneurial risk while mitigating my own financial risk. This model worked so well I have been doing it at other research organizations ever since.

While I described MCNC as a vacuum when it came to commercialization, I quickly discovered this simple description was dead wrong. What I, and others, had observed to be "nothingness" was truly a churning cauldron of opportunity. The real problem was that these opportunities were never seeing the light of day. Technology development programs were considered research projects and researchers were not thinking of them from a market perspective. In the few cases where MCNC might consider a commercial application, researchers were mostly left to their own devices to determine the best way forward. In most circumstances, commercial interests were considered a barrier to research progress or at best, tolerated as long as the research priorities were not impacted.

Beyond a general lack of interest for engagement outside the laboratory, I found another major impediment to commercialization was the researcher mindset. Researchers are used to swimming against the tide; they are used to creating value by doing those things that are considered not to be possible. Good researchers ignore what everyone else says and persevere based on their own knowledge, intuition, and analysis. Good researchers are pioneers who forge into unchartered territory. They have a mindset that ignores the market.

Unfortunately, while the radical, stubborn, and creative mindset of the researcher is critical for radical innovation, it's often terrible for commercial activity. No one is going to invent the next technology revolution by following the crowd; however, for commercialization, finding and then following the crowd—and ideally being the first to do so—is exactly what you need to do!

I cannot begin to list the number of times that I sat with research teams who were able to accurately predict how the world would change with new technology advancements. At MCNC there were teams working on a multitude of such projects: e-commerce before the term existed, electronics packaging that ultimately enabled Bluetooth communications, radio frequency tracking that drives much of our logistics today, tiny machines to revolutionize healthcare and communications, and internet security before the world wide web existed. Each of these teams worked on technologies that were pretty much unheard of at the time, but which ultimately would have a huge impact on our world. In spite of this, very few teams were considering commercial impact and none of them were developing products. I couldn't wait to help out.

That doesn't mean things were perfect. In joining MCNC I had to take a pay cut—something that was very hard to swallow at the time. I must have been one of the very few MBA students whose income actually went down after graduation! But, on the upside, I was at MCNC to commercialize technology and start new companies: my dream job.

Shelby Clarke was also very persuasive. When I returned to MCNC for final interviews he once again brought out the agreement that had been signed by the North Carolina legislature and assured me there was a path to gain equity in a company of my choosing.

"This agreement will allow us to form companies out of our technologies. We can do anything we want!" he exclaimed. "If you are successful at this job, you can leave MCNC and become part of any company you create. That's a promise!"

He wouldn't put it in writing, but we agreed: If I formed a company and wanted to become part of it, I would get "executive level" equity compensation. I had no idea what that really meant, but I trusted Shelby and we shook hands on it. I joined MCNC as the Manager of Business Development and got to work.

# Planning to Lead

It's quite possible to succeed in life through luck and happenstance alone; but, for most of us, it's much better to have a plan.

Turbulence in life occurs not because of the things we see, but because of the things we don't. These things creep up and surprise us in the worst possible way, often at the worst possible time. Things may look like smooth sailing, when seemingly out of the blue, failure is imminent, usually coupled with a slap-in-the-face realization that, but for our overconfidence, it should all have been obvious. Believe it or not, entrepreneurs live for this.

On the other hand, if you are going to fly into a storm, there is no need to just hope for the best and rely on luck. Like any great warrior you prepare for battle. Consequently, one of the first things I did after I joined MCNC was to work with the executive team to develop a strategic plan.

When I joined MCNC, I thought I had a pretty good handle on the turbulence I was going to face or, at the very least, had the tools to handle whatever came my way. Why would I have taken the job otherwise? Surprisingly, previous experiences had not yet taught me that overconfidence is usually a sign of imminent disaster.

Part of my confidence came from the fact that I didn't come into MCNC completely cold because I already knew Vera Cohen, the rock star technology manager who led the micro electro mechanical systems (MEMS) technology group. And from her I already knew a fair bit about MEMS, enough to feel it might be the "next big thing."

At my former company, Kobe Steel, I had hired Vera, a giant in the field, to help us understand MEMS technology. *Science* magazine (one of our most credible research publications) called Vera the "Queen of MEMS" and she was every bit of that in this rapidly growing, new technology arena. She also had a huge persona. Standing over six feet tall in her customary cowboy boots, she filled every room with the force of her personality. *Science* captured her perfectly. She was a dedicated MEMS evangelist who lived and breathed the technology and I could not help but be inspired.

MEMS were tiny mechanical devices and machines that operated on a scale smaller than the thickness of a human hair. They were being built using the same basic technology fueling the microelectronics revolution in computers, televisions, and cellphones. But MEMS were not just about electrons, they were real machines that could move fluids, lift levers, and rotate platforms at a scale that was unobservable to the human eye. The scale and wonder of the technology were shown in famous videos and images (famous, at least, to us geeks) that were published by Sandia National Laboratories showing various MEMS micromotors dwarfed by spider mites. A spider mite is tiny—approximately the size of a period on this page—but some of the motors were so small, the mite towered over the devices, like a real-life Godzilla. If that's hard to believe, you might still be able to find videos and images by searching "Sandia video and image gallery."

My research group at Kobe Steel worked on diamond coatings and I had desperately tried to find a commercial application for this technology. Diamond coatings were what brought me to do post-doctoral studies at North Carolina State University (NCSU). When I first read about thin-film diamond technology in scientific papers back in Canada, I quickly became convinced that this technology would change the world. While most people think of diamond only in the context of jewelry, it actually has many other possible uses. Diamond is super hard, chemically inert, and non-stick (better than Teflon). It also conducts heat better than copper and has amazing electronic and optical properties. And now, people had invented methods to produce diamond coatings!

Back in Canada, as I read about diamond coatings, I imagined them to be almost like paint, with a thousand applications: non-stick frying pans, ships' hulls coated with diamond, and new electronic and optical devices. From afar, the possibilities seemed endless. I was enthralled, but little did I consider that it would be the things that did not appear in the papers that would come back to shatter my dreams. After all, the scientists writing these papers were only human, and in their publications they tended to accentuate the positives, and downplay the negatives. Consequently, as I began to work with diamond coatings after I joined NCSU, reality proved to be very different: Diamond technology was very expensive; the material could only be produced in very unique, high temperature conditions; and it was very difficult to get the material quality needed for commercial success. While we were doing a lot of great research on diamond coatings at NCSU, I figured that a large company like Kobe Steel would be much better positioned to pursue products and commercial success, and so I moved from NCSU to Kobe Steel.

Kobe Steel had invested a great deal of money into diamond coatings technology and my main role at the company was to find commercial applications. When we began to investigate whether there was a commercial opportunity for diamond technology in MEMS, Vera came highly recommended and I hired her to help us understand the space. She did a great job educating us on the status of the MEMS industry and the role of MEMS applications in the medical field where I thought diamond—being chemically inert and entirely made up of carbon—might have some use.

I learned the MEMS industry was already making a big impact on our lives. Products based on MEMS included accelerometers (used to trigger the airbags in cars), pressure sensors (used throughout industry to monitor critical processes), and inkjet nozzles (that are still the heart of inkjet printers today). I also discovered that medical applications appeared to be a dead-end for diamond. Like many other applications I looked at, there was no doubt that diamond had exceptionally good properties for use in medical devices; however, there were always other materials that were perhaps not quite as good as diamond, but were much cheaper, easier to apply, and better suited for commercial application. While it seems straightforward now, what I learned with diamond technology was an epiphany to me at the time—being technically superior does not equate to being commercially superior! Stuck in my research, working diligently on creating the "next big thing," I had always assumed that one led directly to the other.

After I joined MCNC, I discovered Vera's MEMS group was considered to be a crown jewel in the organization and that she had personally built the group from scratch. She had started with a tiny, internal, "get something started" investment in 1993 to where her group was generating almost $3 million in revenue in 1996, primarily in government grants with some commercial work.

The good news at MCNC was that, unlike my experience at Kobe Steel, where we were solely focused on one area of research, MEMS technology was one of many technology projects being developed at MCNC. But there was a downside to this too. Amazingly, there was so much going on, that no single person knew everything that was going on! There also did not appear to be any guiding principles for choosing what to work on, other than being competitive for government solicitations. This put MCNC on the cutting edge of a whole host of technologies, ranging from networking to semiconductor development, but it also resulted in a lack of focus within the organization. *And* as far as I could tell, while there was a strong desire at MCNC to be entrepreneurial and to commercialize technology, there was no plan in place to do so.

As I got to know the organization, I began to understand Shelby's enthusiasm in hiring a PhD with an MBA. Above all else, we needed a plan.

If your situation is stable, with tomorrow looking pretty much the same as today, then you might believe that plans of the past will carry you forward into the future. A lot of people do this to their detriment— ask CEOs of companies like Blockbuster Video, Kodak, Sears, or the many other venerable companies that dominated their time and then crashed and burned because they were not prepared for changes in their industry.

For me personally, I've always had an entrenched fear in my gut that says tomorrow will not look at all like today—no matter how smoothly things seem to be going. Perhaps this is my genetic make-up, or perhaps it is the result of the constant change in my early childhood, as my parents moved their household many times before finally settling in Canada. In any case, this little bit of paranoia causes me to assume that chaos is always just around the corner. Of course, to find opportunity, I am also *seeking* out chaos, so, perhaps ending up in turbulence is a self-fulfilling prophecy for me.

What I have found is: In a turbulent world, strategic planning is key. The more uncertain the environment, the more important it is to identify the right goal and to create a clear roadmap to get there. Goal setting requires a deep understanding of your situation to separate those things that matter from those that don't. This is the foundation of leadership—being able to look at a sea of distraction and pick out the few things that matter for building a successful future. This is also the cornerstone of entrepreneurship.

Unfortunately, we are mostly trained from our earliest experiences to avoid uncertainty as much as possible. Our education is about following rules, developing a fixed career path, joining an established organization, having kids, planning for retirement, and fading happily into the sunset. In this scenario we learn at best to plan a series of tactical steps in the face of a prescribed set of goals. But innovation happens in chaos. Unmet and even unknown needs drive invention, just like those hidden matter/anti-matter collisions drive creation. For the most part, we are not prepared to plan in the face of uncertainty. Certainly no one ever prepared me for it. How many science or engineering programs teach strategic planning? None of mine did. I had four science degrees at the age of thirty and was never offered a course on strategy.

Disciplined analysis is the bedrock of good planning. The most important thing I learned earning my MBA was that strategic planning first and foremost is about using good analytical frameworks to evaluate a situation. Think of an analytical framework like a scaffolding being erected around a crumbling building. No matter what shape the building is in, the scaffolding gives you a safe and well-defined external structure to work from as you create something functional underneath. We use analytical frameworks to create scaffolding around chaos, allowing us to analyze the chaos without getting distracted by all the moving parts. A good analysis leads us to ask the right questions and set the right goals: Failure at this stage, means failure in everything else that follows.

Shelby pulled the executive team together periodically to review my progress and provide feedback, which was very helpful. However, when it came down to actually writing the plan I was pretty much on my own. As we moved from fun brainstorming sessions, to interviews and finally deliverables, it became clear that I was quite fortunate to be reporting directly to the president of the organization. The management team's excitement to develop a strategic plan quickly wore off. Without Shelby's enthusiasm to back me up, my efforts would never have gotten very far. As it was, it took me almost three months to complete the strategic plan.

Leadership is about just three things: identifying the right path forward (strategy), effectively communicating the path to others, and executing the path. Great leaders do these three things flawlessly. In this context, publishing a 20-page strategy document had nothing at all to do with leadership, and I'm not sure anyone at MCNC ever read the final plan. Of course, this was entirely my fault—the plan was so detailed and overdone it begged not be read. On the other hand, the process of creating the plan was a gift, because it put me in a position where I could start to provide leadership. I have since concluded that strategic planning is first and foremost a personal journey. It is not about creating a document that others will breathlessly consume. Although that is certainly a desirable outcome. It's more about creating confidence in your own mind about the right path forward. Once you achieve this confidence; you are then positioned to guide others to take key actions needed for success. You are then also uniquely positioned to make the tough decisions that will undoubtedly come your way.

One of the most important analyses I carried out at MCNC was a "marketing audit." The marketing audit is an analytical framework based on a series of questions that review a company's marketing environment, its strategic posture, its planning procedures, and marketing mix, often referred to as the "4 Ps"—product, price, place, and promotion.

The market audit showed that there was no real consensus within MCNC around many of the questions I asked, including questions like: What markets does the organization serve? What are the organization's objectives? And what are the main product offerings of the organization? At MCNC, as in many other research organizations, these topics were not top of mind and there was little consensus. People had different perspectives and answered these questions very differently, even at the executive level. This misalignment caused problems within the organization as key people with strong convictions pulled the organization in different directions based on what they personally considered to be important.

Organizationally there was a great deal of misalignment around technology commercialization at MCNC, primarily because this wasn't the market managers and leaders at MCNC served. They served the government grant agencies and successful people (like Vera) advanced in their careers understanding what it took to win highly competitive multi-million-dollar grants from these agencies. They also spent time with their peers at other technology institutions discussing revolutionary concepts and cutting-edge needs in the aerospace, military, and health care sectors. They *knew* where the world was heading—which was great for writing grants—they just didn't know exactly when the world would get there or what *specific* needs industry would have when it did.

Nor did they have time to care! To get an idea of *specific* industry needs would require a deep understanding of commercial customers and their most pressing problems. Managers and researchers at MCNC simply did not have time to listen carefully to people who were not their primary customers. Their primary bread and butter lay with the grant-making agencies and the wise decision was to spend time with them.

When I asked managers and leaders about commercial opportunities for their technology, the response was muted at best. While there was constant organizational interaction with program managers at government agencies like NSF and DARPA, the same could not be said for industry. As Bob West had already observed, there was even a bit of bad feeling between MCNC and industry. Past interactions had not gone well for either side.

As I thought about it, I realized that research managers were expressing exactly what I already knew to be true for salespeople: No research manager could afford to spend time on unproductive, non-revenue generating ideas, just like salespeople couldn't afford to identify customers for products that weren't ready to sell. This left a huge hole at MCNC where no one was taking the time to identify emerging industry needs for our technologies. Evidently, there was a well-established vacuum here and, as Steven Robinson predicted, I was well-suited to fill it.

On the research end, my analysis highlighted just how complex MCNC was with many pockets of research that required expert knowledge to fully understand. Executives and managers knew the "business" of the organization, but they rarely delved deeply into the technology—they simply did not have the time to do so and it became clear this was just an unavoidable part of the research process.

Research is so volatile, and progress is so transient, it is difficult to track in the short term. A researcher may collect data for a year that looks useless and then finally, one day, have a new insight that shows the work was in fact a technical breakthrough. And the opposite also happens. This is why Nobel prizes in science are generally not granted until many years after the work is carried out; it takes years to figure out that some new discovery revolutionized science. While the researchers themselves will have a detailed understanding of every nuance of development in the lab, managers in research organizations are often disconnected from the day-to-day workings and tend to only have a high-level view of what is happening, especially if it is a big organization. To really understand what is going on in a lab, you have to sit down directly with the researchers themselves and listen to them just as carefully as you would to the customer.

As I diligently pursued the development of a strategic plan, it became evident that MCNC actually had two vacuums that needed to be addressed: Not only was no one identifying specific industry needs, but the organization also lacked a comprehensive, organizational understanding of its own technical capabilities. Both of these would be critical barriers to success if MCNC was serious about commercializing its technology.

I had learned many types of analyses in my MBA classes and there is no question that I went overboard in applying my learning to MCNC. I still have a copy of the strategic plan I developed; I use it today as an example of both what to do, and what not to do. I call my MCNC plan the "kitchen sink" strategic plan, because when I wrote it, I used every strategic analysis methodology I knew: Five Forces analysis, core competence mapping, SWOT matrices, qualifiers and order winners, critical success factors, and so on. Each one of these in of themselves offered a powerful scaffolding to help me assess the uncertainty that reigned at MCNC. The fact that I employed all of them was undoubtedly overkill; the final document was a tome; the table of contents alone was two pages. However, the upside was that my varied analytical approaches allowed me to address the second vacuum by giving me a deep and multi-faceted view of MCNC and its technical capabilities in a relatively short period of time.

Not only did I develop a deep understanding of MCNC's comprehensive technical capabilities, I also gained a very good understanding of its operational and even cultural limitations. I knew where the organization was strong and where it was weak; this knowledge would be critically important later on as I was making decisions about which opportunities to pursue. Now, I just had to fill the other vacuum: Identifying emerging industry needs that we could address with our amazing technical capabilities. I had to go out and talk to customers! The path forward was as clear as anything had ever been in my life and it exhilarated me.

# The One that Got Away

Nowhere was the gap between current technology development and emerging market demand more evident than in MCNC's networking services group. I vividly remember a conversation with one of the group's managers. As part of the market audit, I asked him to define what products or services they offered their customers.

"We don't have any products here," he said. "We manage the network for the local universities and occasionally do a bit of consulting. We're just a service organization."

Later, I sat down with one of the software programmers in his division. It was an eye-opening discussion; one I also remember very well, even to this day. She was an accomplished woman, relatively young, and with a laid-back approach to things. She enjoyed her work at MCNC, she told me, because of the freedom it offered and the cutting-edge nature and variability of the work.

"I could write software anywhere, but at MCNC I get to work on the bleeding edge of what's going on."

That piqued my interest. "What kinds of things? Can you give me an example?"

"Well, about four years ago the United States Patent & Trademark Office asked us to put their patent database online. At that time websites were all still static. You know, if you wanted to change anything on a website, you had to go in and change pixels on the screen. Well, we changed that! We were one of the first groups in the world to connect a database to a website making it dynamic and searchable online!"

Proudly, she pulled up the website and showed me how it was done. Even today, if you do a search online for "USPTO Quick Search" you will find the database little changed from the one we looked at that day. By current standards the tool is still useable, but very clunky. In 1997, it was amazing and when MCNC started its work in 1993, it had never been done before.

Given my background in materials science, chemistry, and semiconductors, I'd never thought much about creating websites or programming online searches. Still I didn't have to be a software genius to be impressed. "That's amazing!" I told her. "It seems like there is a lot we could do with this capability for other customers."

"Yeah, we do some consulting work. The system we developed for the USPTO is hardware independent and can be used with any database. So, we have great flexibility and can easily create all sorts of functionality with this if someone is interested," she said. As was the case with many of my discussions with technical staff at MCNC, I didn't totally follow everything she was saying, but I could not miss that they could "easily create all sorts of functionality." It was music to my ears.

Then she glanced around somewhat slyly. It appeared she did not want to be overheard. "We have time on our hands, so we also do some stuff on our own," she told me triumphantly, with a big smile.

"Stuff? What kind of stuff?"

"Well, we've developed an amazing search engine, and we keep improving it. Although, I guess it's passé now that Yahoo is out there."

I took her analysis of the passé state of search engines at face value, but this conversation was in 1997; Google was founded in 1998.

"But we've also developed a cataloging capability!" she brightened up.

"Catalog?" I asked dumbly. "What do you mean by that?"

"Yeah, well, you know, if you have a bunch of stuff and you want to be able to list it on the internet and make it searchable—we have a module that does that. It's a bit boring, but as companies start listing more and more of their products on the web, I think it might be useful. We've also used it to create auctioning, but that's already been done too. There is this startup on the west coast called eBay that has cornered that application."

To have a sense of what MCNC was sitting on in terms on innovations, at the same time, right down the road from us, a young man named Michael Brader Araje was developing OpenSite Technologies, a software platform designed to help companies easily create auctions or "dynamic pricing" for their product catalog. OpenSite sold to Siebel Systems in 2000 for $542 million. And that was just *one* application that the software engineer mentioned that day!

"We can also create surveys—no one is doing that!" I could tell that she was working hard to help me find something—anything—that might have commercial value and also had not been "done before."

"Surveys? Explain that to me."

"Well, with our platform you can easily create a survey online. Think of all the trouble you go to when you want to survey a group of people. You have to develop the survey, print it, send it out, wait for people to return it, and convert all those surveys into electronic data. With our platform, we can create a survey online in a few minutes, e-mail the link to people, and they fill it out online. It's a much better way of doing it—we've actually used it ourselves and it works really well!"

SurveyMonkey was founded in 1999, and Qualtrics, another survey provider in 2002, five years after our conversation. Most recently Qualtrics was valued at $2.5 billion.

My conversation with the programmer was not finished, and the best was yet to come. Given that MCNC was on the cutting edge of what would become e-commerce, there were many other projects that the software team was working on: Some driven by government and commercial contracts, but much of it driven by the programmers' personal interests as they worked to apply the capabilities they developed in creative ways. I was almost overwhelmed with the potential she described, but I will never forget the very end of our conversation. In closing, I asked her which of her projects was the most interesting.

"Oh, that's easy. Bell South recently funded a project for us to demonstrate that we can move a credit card number securely over the network. You know, we do a lot of work with the National Security Agency, so we have a great deal of experience in encryption and network security. And we did it! We were able to demonstrate that, with the right protocols and proper encryption, we could maintain secure communications during the credit card information transfer process."

"Wow. That sounds really impressive," I exclaimed. NSA, encryption, internet security, credit cards being used to securely buy products on the internet; I was blown away. MCNC's depth of capability seemed unending.

"Yeah, it sounds impressive, but you know it's never going to happen. Who in their right mind would ever allow their credit card number to be transferred over the internet?" She laughed at the idea and we both agreed that it was crazy.

While I did not know anything about networking or software or e-commerce, I did not need to be an expert to figure out there was something here. I was struck by the dichotomy of what I heard at the executive level—"we do a bit of consulting"—to what I was hearing at the developer level—"we have the world in our hands!" It's a lesson that I have never forgotten: If you want to commercialize cutting edge technology, you have to get into the weeds and work at the grassroots level, both with customers and the technologists.

I will also never forget the picture of the future the software developer painted for me that day. Yes, she was wrong on some of the specifics, and she was particularly pessimistic about innovations that had been "done before," but she clearly understood where the world was going and predicted the direction very accurately.

*Great technologists are very often directionally correct and specifically wrong.* They are so embedded in a new, emerging technical trend, they can accurately describe the wave that is coming towards us and where it is heading. Can they predict specifically when and where that wave will break? No, that is for others to figure out. We need to learn to listen very carefully when very smart people paint the outlines of a picture of the world that we, and even they, do not yet fully understand.

I also learned that what looks like chaos and even craziness may actually be a bunch of bright, flashing signs pointing in the direction of undreamed success. We just have to heed them.

I returned to Shelby Clarke as excited as I could be. "I've got it Shelby! We have the tiger by the tail in our network services group!"

"Well, go for it!" Coining what became an oft repeated phrase, he chanted "Let's-go-Jes-ko!" with a big smile. The "J" in my name is pronounced as a "Y", and he pronounced the "k" as a "g", so this was a catchy rhyme.

I loved working for Shelby. He was always positive and encouraging.

I quickly formed a team within MCNC's networking division to begin looking for an e-commerce product. Since the technical team assured me everything else had already been "done," we decided to start with the survey application which, to our knowledge, was completely new. We called the effort "Preserve."

Fully convinced that we were on the brink of the wave of the future, I reached out to some connections I had in the entrepreneurial community. The response was positive and surprisingly immediate—especially for me, someone who had never done anything like this before. Within a few weeks I was meeting with the lead investor at Alex Brown, a boutique investment banking company. We met in Houston for an after-dinner drink—that alone caused my head to spin. Who flies to Houston to talk business over scotch?

A week later the firm sent an executive to take a look at what we had. Our visitor ignored my excitement around e-commerce but was quite enthused about the building that housed our networking group.

"We can take this public for a minimum of $150 million," he told me as we walked around the MCNC grounds.

"Public? The whole building?" I asked incredulously. This was quickly spiraling well beyond my pay grade.

"Yeah. For sure. This is where things are at right now. Internet services are big!"

"What about the software development?"

"Forget about the software. It's all about internet service providers—ISP's they're called!"

In those early days as I began to fully understand and communicate the value propositions that existed in the networking division, people within MCNC got pretty excited too. Managers who had previously claimed that not much was going on in the division were suddenly very interested. I've seen this happen many times since. As my efforts to find new opportunities exposed potentially lucrative pathways where people previously thought there were none, perspectives changed, and not always for the better. As interest from others grew, so did my problems. Product design meetings with developers turned into navel-gazing meetings with managers. The more interesting it got, the higher the level of management attending our meetings got. Politics entered the process.

"The universities will never allow this to be commercialized," I was told. "This whole division was created by the State to serve the universities…"

I thought about that signed agreement cutting MCNC loose, but kept this to myself.

That summer, when I returned from a week's vacation, I discovered MCNC management had hired a five-person startup team in my absence to take over commercialization for the networking group. These new folks were networking specialists with more commercialization experience than I had; they had already successfully failed in at least one previous startup. I could claim no such pedigree. They were also much more visionary than I was. They advised MCNC to forget building a simple survey product, and instead prepare to invest millions (we did not have) in voice over internet protocol (VOIP) and gaming networks. According to them, real entrepreneurship was high risk-high reward and MCNC had to either play the game or forget about it. I was aghast and although I was asked to stay on to be part of the new direction, it was clear that I had no choice other than to walk away. I called my contacts at Alex Brown and told them the bad news.

Yes, turbulence is not for the faint-hearted.

I could have been distraught, but I wasn't. I was deeply frustrated that things had gone south so quickly—Bob West's words echoed loudly in my mind—but through my planning work, I also understood that e-commerce wasn't the only opportunity available at MCNC. My strategic plan had identified nine promising opportunities, of which I believed five had real potential for company-building. These were the e-commerce opportunity, Vera's MEMS work, an electronics packaging capability, a radio frequency tagging concept, and a capability called "fluxless soldering." While e-commerce had been my favorite and had risen to the top very quickly, the other opportunities were equally promising. As I began looking for my next venture, I was determined to do a much better job picking my team.

My ouster from Proserve taught me an important lesson: My failure was that I had no trusted champion in the networking group. When management jumped in, the programmers retreated to their computers, wanting nothing to do with this change in direction. Management also offered the most senior member of the group a promotion to join the new startup team. The carefully orchestrated takeover left me dangling, out in the cold.

Nowadays, the very first test I have for a prospective deal is whether I can build a close relationship with the technical lead or leaders. For me personally, a great relationship with the technology team is a protective barrier when others come into mess things up, something that, believe it or not, happens more often than you might think. If I can't build a strong bond with the team, then no matter how good the technology looks, I walk away. New innovations are like tiny seedlings emerging from the earth—they can be crushed in the blink of an eye. The founding team has to be tightly knit because things *will* go south, and when they do, the team has to hold together.

For Proserve this clearly was not the case. The destruction had been laughably easy. It was a successful coup that had been engineered behind my back, presumably with Shelby Clarke's blessing. I begged Shelby not to do it. I even built a financial model for their plan that showed the economic risk to be outrageous, but it was to no avail. Shelby had bought into the idea that a "real" entrepreneurial effort had to have super-high risk and there was nothing I could do to change his mind.

It was a disaster. While the risks were dutifully backed by MCNC with money it did not have, the promised rewards were not forthcoming. As the entire effort imploded, the startup team was fired and Shelby resigned, much to my dismay. Shelby broke a cardinal rule of risk taking by venturing into unchartered waters without analysis, without a plan, and without the requisite experience to handle the storm that came his way.

Turbulence—bet on it.

If you don't prepare for it, then you are very likely fooling yourself and may be in for a very ugly surprise. That's what happened to the e-commerce project at MCNC and that's what ultimately led to Shelby's resignation. The programmers and developers withdrew to their projects, swearing off entrepreneurship forever. And, most unfortunately, nothing came of the great promise that existed for e-commerce technology at MCNC. While the potential for inconceivable riches swirled all around us, the end result was... nothing.

I look back at MCNC's e-commerce opportunity as the Great One that got away. Not so much for me (as I had many other seedlings to tend to), but for the network services group. They missed out on the opportunity of a lifetime. It was also a huge loss to North Carolina having poured $250 million into MCNC, inadvertently creating a goldmine at the very beginning of what was to become the e-commerce gold rush and getting nothing in return.

As outlandish as it had seemed to some people, if we had just followed Alex Brown's advice and taken that group (and the building) public as an ISP for $150 million, this would have solved MCNC's cash problems well within Shelby's three-year time period. And It would have created a significant economic engine for the State in its own right. Alternatively, properly nurturing MCNC's e-commerce innovation could have spurred North Carolina's economy for many, many years to come. Look at Silicon Valley. Instead, it all withered on the vine, never to see the light of day, the magnitude of what was lost forever unknown.

Ironically, the networking services group is the only remnant of MCNC today. It continues as a successful, nonprofit networking group, seeded with funds from subsequent successes that we created elsewhere. The group is still accessible at mcnc.org: a tiny, tiny organization when you consider what could have been.

Creation. Annihilation. Vacuum. For my inaugural effort, the end result in this case was very much what Bob West predicted.

# The North Star

The Proserve incident was a mistake I was determined never to make again. I vowed that my primary criterion for a new technology venture would be a strong technical founder who would accept my guidance in business and marketing as I would accept theirs in technology. When things go bump—and with startups it's not a question of if things will go bump, it's a question of when—I want a team or, at the very least, a person, that I can rely on. I want to be working with someone who is indispensable to the technology development, who sees me as a partner, and who has my back as we work through the inevitable challenges.

Unfortunately, as hard as it is to find that perfect, new innovation, it's just as hard to find that kind of person or group of people. I did not really think about it at the time, but statistically this was going to make my job that much harder. I not only had to find a great technology, but I also had to find a great team to go with it.

Having learned this seminal lesson, I turned to Vera Cohen and her MEMS technology. Vera was not only a rock star in her field, she was a fierce defender of her turf and a leader who wanted to take her efforts at MCNC to a whole new level. As the head of MEMS, she was more than willing to delegate commercial developments to me without giving up her leadership position. From my perspective, I didn't care who was in charge, as long as I wasn't going to be blindsided as I had been with the e-commerce deal. Ours was a good match. I couldn't see a similar e-commerce debacle happening under Vera's watch.

Another important lesson I had already learned from my own research activities and my work at Kobe Steel was to expect the unexpected about what the technology was and what people thought it could do. This was, in part, because the research was in constant flux, but also because team members had different perceptions of the technology. On top of this, the outside world more often than not gave unexpected feedback as well. A case in point was going to Alex Brown with an e-commerce pitch and being told that we should take the network services division public as an ISP.

My final takeaway was deal making was much more about dealing with people than technology. And people will do strange things, especially when money is on the table. As my experience with e-commerce had proven, the most congenial of environments can rapidly become hot-beds of intrigue as research is transformed into something of financial value. As a result, every time I followed a simple thread at MCNC it led me into a rat's nest of changing technology, changing customer perceptions, and changing people. It was all a little crazy—Bob West's first words about MCNC were ringing more and more true.

Within this chaos I learned personal discipline is key: discipline in planning, discipline in execution, and discipline in walking away. As an entrepreneur you have to establish your own true North and constantly monitor your path to make sure you are on the right path. The path has to be your own, because there are many compelling and competing influences to pull you in other directions: technology influences, customer influences, and people influences all conspiring to lead you astray.

This is why strategy development is such an important personal journey for the entrepreneur and it doesn't really matter if anyone else reads your strategic plan. The plan charts the path you believe in and that's what matters. Of course, having set a path, you still need to make constant, rapid corrections or you can easily end up in a terrible place. And don't forget to check your plan because it will remain a great reference point as you try and fail, and try and fail again. A lot of people don't like to talk about failure, but unfortunately, it's an integral part of success.

We often hear of entrepreneurs who persevered time and again and eventually became incredibly successful, but we don't hear about the many that failed. Charles Goodyear believed that rubber could change the world but struggled for many years to make it functional in real products. Eventually, he accidentally discovered the process of vulcanization which makes rubber durable, only to find that his innovation had already been patented by someone else. Goodyear, known today because a tire company founded 40 years after his death bears his name, struggled financially and died penniless. I have seen blind perseverance lead many would-be entrepreneurs astray and in the extreme it can easily ruin a life.

In some ways, entrepreneurs have to be very much like researchers in the laboratory, who follow the "scientific method" as the basis for research and discovery. The scientific method consists of hypothesizing a thesis statement and then gathering data to either support or disprove the hypothesis. If, over time, data consistently support the hypothesis, and no data are found to disprove it, then the hypothesis can be said to be true.

Developing methods—to gather data, record data, and figure out what the data means—is the lifeblood of the scientific researcher. Entrepreneurs face a very similar situation when they hypothesize there is a market need for a new product or service. If the entrepreneur is disciplined, they define the product or service and then carry out market research—data collection—to determine if the perceived need exists.

The difference between the researcher and entrepreneur is primarily time pressure: Scientific researchers are usually shielded from time pressure to ensure their diligence is not compromised. Entrepreneurs, on the other hand, are racing against time, facing competition and funding constraints that threaten their existence from all sides.

Market research can be done through surveys, focus groups, pilot studies, and expert interviews, and it can be very sophisticated and expensive. A significant limitation of the market research approach for new innovations is that it assumes the person being surveyed fully understands the product or service. Unfortunately, with new innovation, this is not always the case. Imagine Goodyear trying to explain the value of rubber to people, especially before he discovered vulcanization? Innovation, by definition, is about doing something that has not been done before. Performing market research on something that no one knows anything about is a daunting task.

There is an almost magical solution to this dilemma: customers. The willingness of a customer to pay for the innovation rather than talk about its value is what separates a customer from any other market research. As an entrepreneur, it's very rewarding to have people support your ideas and pat you on the back for your innovative concepts, it's quite another feeling—the best in my opinion—when a customer pays you to deliver your innovation to them.

Paying customers are the North Star to entrepreneurs. There is nothing more valuable than a clear, shining signal like the sale of your product to tell you that you are on the right path. Entrepreneurship is so messy that any kind of clarity should be treated with reverence. Sales is to market research what sprint racing is to figure skating. The first is a timed event with a photo finish; the second is judged by humans.

Have you ever watched figure skating, or some other judged sporting event, and thought: "I like the second-place finisher much better. How are they so sure that other person won?" Market research is like figure skating, a judgement call, whereas making a sale is like winning the race—you either close the deal or you don't and there is no debate over the outcome. In contrast to entrepreneurs, most academic researchers working on the next big thing tend to prefer the ambiguity of judgment calls over the finality of a not getting a purchase order.

On top of that, few scientists are good salespeople. To be fair to Goodyear, he did try to sell his innovation to customers, including the U.S. Postal Service; however, rubber without vulcanization is pretty messy and he did not get far. Making the sale is the pivotal test of entrepreneurship: Can you get someone to buy what you are selling? Unfortunately, the earlier the stage of a technology, the harder it is to make a sale. The technology may not be ready to be put into a customer's hands, or you may have something so new that the customer simply does not understand it, or, quite often, it's just too expensive.

The other, very human, aspect to the sales process is that it invariably leads to rejection. A lot of rejection. This may be okay to an individual who has little at stake in the outcome, but what about the scientist who might have spent years or even decades developing the technology? For this person, it's not just a rejection of the technology, it's a rejection of a long-term investment, sometimes even a lifetime of work. And of course paying customers can be a huge pain. They demand results for their money and if you are selling early-stage innovation, it is very rare that they want exactly what you can deliver. They want changes, quite often changes that are very hard or even impossible to make.

My first experience with this paradox was at Kobe Steel with the diamond thin films. In searching for a commercial avenue for our work and exploring a host of possible applications ranging from diamond transistors and thermistors to diamond coatings for medical applications, I hypothesized that medical devices and implants would benefit from our biocompatible supermaterial. To determine if my premise was correct, I canvassed local medical companies—there were many local to us—and presented our technical capabilities. Not one of them wanted diamond thin films.

While this was certainly disconcerting, I found three companies that were interested in a related technology: a material called diamond-like carbon. Diamond-like carbon had many of the properties of diamond, but, unlike diamond, it could be deposited at low temperatures on plastic. For medical applications, this appeared to be where the need was.

Two companies wanted to take advantage of the slippery properties of diamond-like carbon as a solid lubricant for medication inhalers. Inhalers had plastic moving parts, which were lubricated with oil, but they tended to be kept for long periods without use, until there was a need—often an urgent need. If the oil had dried out, then the inhaler could get stuck at the worst possible time. As a solid lubricant, diamond-like carbon would never dry out. I would have never known about this application had I not ventured out of my laboratory to talk to potential customers.

Another company had a very different application. They wanted to use diamond-like carbon as a coating to make plastic impermeable to air. It turns out that air goes through plastic like a sieve, but a very thin coating of diamond-like carbon had the potential to stop air from getting through. In this regard, coating plastic with diamond-like carbon had the potential to create plastic products just as good as glass but much cheaper, safer, and easier to manufacture.

The medical device company I talked to was very excited about diamond-like carbon and our potential to produce it.

"Do you think you can make diamond-like carbon? Or do you guys only work with diamond films?" they asked me. At the time, I didn't fully know what diamond-like carbon was, but I took comfort that it had the word "diamond" in it. And I believed in our team of scientists at Kobe Steel; we had so many experts I figured we could make diamond-like carbon happen one way or another.

"Sure, we can do that!" I said, expressing perhaps more confidence than I should have. "But, you know, we've invested a great deal in our equipment. Also, it will take some effort on our part to make it work for you, and that can't come for free."

There it was: a not so subtle demand to get paid. I sensed their excitement, but I also needed to test just how serious these guys were. I also had the inhaler application. Those guys seemed interested too. Maybe that application was better. Who was to judge? I couldn't, so I needed to know if these guys were just talking, or if they were in fact willing to pay for what they wanted.

"Okay. How much do you need to get started?" they asked.

Whoa! That really threw me. While I had been fishing for an order, I hadn't actually expected to get this close to one. My palms turned sweaty as I suddenly felt I had caught something that I couldn't possibly reel in.

"Uh… um… well, you see, Kobe Steel is a big company," I stuttered as I desperately tried to think of a big number that wasn't too big. "I… I've never seen them start a project for anything less than $50,000," I finally finished off, grimacing inwardly at the rejection I expected to come my way.

Of course, I'd never seen our research group at Kobe Steel do anything for any amount of money. We were a cost center funded by the corporate research and development group; we had an annual budget and we *spent* money; we did not sell things. We had no means to even take a purchase order!

"$50K?" the gentleman I was facing pondered, "Hmm… that seems reasonable, I guess… Let me check with our management and we'll get back to you."

The next week I got a check for $50,000 in the mail, with instructions to "get started."

It was truly unbelievable and nothing close to that has happened to me since. Customers don't just send you big checks without nauseatingly detailed contracts to go with them. But, you see, the company had a very pressing challenge. They were selling billions of glass test tubes every year for all sorts of applications including blood testing. These test tubes were prepared with different additives to ensure the collected blood was properly maintained and prepared for whatever test was to be done. The test tubes were all sealed and evacuated to ensure the additives did not spoil over time. To achieve this, the tubes were made of glass since glass ensured that no air could get in and that the vacuum would hold for long periods as the tubes sat on the shelf, waiting to be used.

Asian competitors had recently come into the market with plastic test tubes. These were much cheaper and also much safer since there was no risk of breakage. The drawback on the plastic test tubes was that their shelf life was not very good. Air permeated through the plastic relatively quickly and then the test tubes needed to be replaced. If someone could develop a plastic tube that was impermeable to air, this would be a paradigm shift in the industry. Of course, I knew none of this when I began my visits to local medical companies.

The company I was talking to was by far the leader in the field, but they were worried. To remain ahead of the competition, they had been working with a local university and had successfully demonstrated that diamond-like carbon on plastic worked. The coating made the plastic impermeable to air. They were now looking for a trusted manufacturer for this technology and, as Kobe Steel was an established manufacturing company, they were willing to invest to start the relationship—hence the $50,000 to "get started."

I was beyond excited, but quickly found that my excitement was not at all contagious. My scientific colleagues at Kobe Steel were far from pleased.

"*Diamond*, Jesko! We produce *diamond*! Where do you get off promising someone diamond-like carbon?" they looked at me like I had grown two heads.

"Oh, come on, guys!" I said, very surprised at the resistance. "This is diamond-like carbon. It can't be that different!"

"But we're not experts at that! You should know better!"

One of the scientists in the group took to calling me *Ferengi*, expressing what was likely a broader sense of displeasure within the technology team at Kobe Steel. I was never a fan of Star Trek, so it took me a while to figure out the Ferengi were money-obsessed swindlers in the show—and that's probably the nicest way to describe them! This attitude surprised me then, but it certainly doesn't surprise me any longer. I have found that scientists can get pretty peeved when you pull customers into their world. Tending to avoid direct confrontation, they will find unique ways to express their unhappiness! Ferengi, indeed.

While pretty peeved myself at the unexpected resistance, I couldn't totally fault my colleagues at Kobe Steel. The fact that we weren't experts in diamond-like carbon was certainly true: We were known to be the leaders in thin film diamond materials, not diamond-like carbon. And there certainly were other scientific groups who had specialized in diamond-like carbon. But to me, it felt like my team was splitting hairs. We were making pizzas, and now someone was asking us to produce calzones. How hard could it be? We had a bunch of PhDs and engineers, surely they could figure this out.

But it was not to be. Working on something other than diamond was a big controversy that went all the way back to our corporate leaders in Japan. In the end it was decided that we should not proceed. Kobe Steel wanted to be part of the diamond electronics business of the future, and a business that existed right now to coat a few billion test tubes was not going to change anybody's mind.

The whole experience was a crushing blow to me, and it took me many years to see the other side of it. Our leaders in Japan were as convinced as I had initially been that diamond materials—especially electronic diamond materials—would change the world. I had bet my career on it, but they had bet millions of dollars and their leadership on it. To now make a shift into an unknown application with poorly understood technology at the behest of some wide-eyed greenhorn in the United States made no sense to them. It drove me crazy—literally, I had to go see a therapist to help me get over my frustration. By the time I came along with diamond-like carbon on plastic, I had already spent a number of years trying to identify good applications for our diamond thin film technology. Now, everything in my being told me the carbon-like diamond was our best shot. On top of that, I had a *paying* customer! Did that not count for something? But then again, who was I to foretell the future?

Kobe Steel had research groups working on diamond in Japan, the United Kingdom, and the United States. Our main benefactor was a research manager in Japan who liked to say: "The sun will never set on diamond research at Kobe Steel." But sadly, it did. With no commercial products forthcoming, and with a severe financial crisis wrought by an earthquake in Japan, the diamond research group was eventually disbanded, with me being one of the very first to go.

I didn't feel any better when years later, at a Kobe Steel group reunion in the United States, my old boss from Japan pulled me aside to give me an update. "You were right, Jesko," he said to me with a bit of a wistful smile. "You were right about diamond-like carbon!"

"What? What do you mean right?" I had no idea where he was going with this.

"Would you believe it? Last year, Sumitomo commercialized diamond-like carbon for beer bottles!" he told me giving me a kindly pat on the back.

"Beer bottles?" I asked stupidly, trying to figure out how this had anything to do with me.

"Yes, they were able to convert glass beer bottles to plastic by coating the inside of the bottle with diamond-like carbon. It saves a lot of money, and the bottles don't break."

"Oh, good for them…," I replied weakly, some of the old pain briefly returning.

Sumitomo was Kobe Steel's arch enemy in business, so I can imagine this burned for Kobe Steel too, but my old boss was quite philosophical about it.

"Yes, it's a big business for them. I am glad that they were successful, even though we chose not to do it. I thought you would want to know that you were right!"

Creation. Annihilation. It is happening constantly.

While this episode at Kobe Steel caused me a lot of stress and frustration and even some humiliation, it also taught me a huge lesson in the importance of securing a paying customer, even in the earliest stages of technology development. Diamond thin films were such exciting materials that everyone "knew" they would change the world. We could all name dozens of applications where diamond should apply, and there were many corporate partners who were interested in what we were doing. But, when it came down to picking the right path forward out of the many we had at our disposal, it was a pure judgement call and there was no clear winner. Then along came a paying customer. This burning interest—$50,000 worth of interest—came in an area that we had not even considered. It was a bright, shining, glittering North Star that we ignored.

While I had no way of predicting that diamond-like carbon would ultimately be commercialized, I had seen enough at Kobe Steel to learn that customer involvement—paying customer involvement—was a key part of the technology commercialization process. That $50,000 check had turned something that was confusing and constantly being debated into a pathway with instant clarity—at least to me. One day we had ten applications that were under consideration and the next day we had one, clear deliverable. One day we were stumbling in the dark, and the next we had a beacon of light to guide our way. Although we chose to ignore the sign, others did not. As far as I know, diamond-like carbon on plastic was the only application I worked on at Kobe Steel that was commercialized. All the others were annihilated.

Was it a coincidence that this application was the only one that generated a paying customer? I don't think so.

When I joined MCNC I was determined to apply what I had so recently learned. And unlike my group at Kobe Steel where we were not philosophically or operationally set up to sell anything, MCNC was more than happy to take purchase orders. They also had a plethora of technology to sell, so thankfully I didn't have to push one technology as I had at Kobe Steel. Instead, I had an entire menu of capabilities that I could talk to customers about, ranging from networking to electronic devices and even cutting-edge materials. Having this portfolio made my life much easier. On top of all that, I had also learned at Kobe Steel that I *loved* sales. It wasn't just the money it brought to the table, I loved the clarity of it: the focus that a purchase order gives you and the certainty that there is a real need for what you are doing.

I also learned that my fellow researchers almost exclusively did not share my passion for sales. For them, customer intervention, especially in the form of fixed deliverables and timelines, was at best a distraction and at worst a complete hinderance to research. For them, the focus was simply on obtaining the requisite funding, ideally for a period of three to five years, and then being left alone. This mindset may be ideal for fostering a conducive environment for creative research, but it is terrible for actually getting technology into the field where it can be of use to people. Even today, many research institutions who want to commercialize their technology continue to be challenged in the absence of a mindset that requires researchers to work closely with motivated—paying—customers. The problem is particularly acute at some of our most respected research organizations because, quite frankly, the "Ferengi" attitude persists. For them, sales is a four-letter word.

# Customer Call

I bridged the research/sales divide at MCNC by seeking out research group leaders who embraced purchase orders (like Vera) and by focusing on projects where financial pressures encouraged a more mercenary approach. My simple goal was to avoid any Ferengi name-throwers. It's a rule I still abide by to this day: Don't go where you are not wanted; there are plenty of other fish in the sea. I was fortunate that MCNC was an independent nonprofit organization that did not limit which opportunities could be pursued (like at Kobe Steel). With the anticipated loss of state funding, paying customers would be welcome as long as I could find things to sell and research groups willing to deliver.

For me personally, I was happier than a pig in mud. Sales were desperately needed, it was a job no one else wanted to do, and I loved it! Even with this, customer acquisition would be a learning experience for everyone.

Feeling bad about the recent Proserve coup, Shelby was looking to give me productive things to do. The electronics packaging group was trying to form a new company—to be called Unitive Electronics—based on capabilities and intellectual property developed at MCNC for something called "solder bumping," but they were struggling to attract customers and raise venture capital. Shelby thought we would make a great match. Uncharacteristically, he made my assignment very clear.

"Jesko, you need to help these guys. They have great technology and we've even hired a CEO, but someone has to get more customers through the door—and fast!" Once Shelby decided on something, he always wanted it to be done yesterday.

"Work with the team and turn it into a company!" he thundered. "You'll get your equity!"

Shelby put me in touch with the team leader Drew Thompson who, strangely enough, was "in purgatory" (Shelby's words), sequestered in a dark, small office in another building far off the beaten track. Apparently, Drew had committed a serious-enough indiscretion to warrant exile, although I never learned what it was. I headed across campus and got a very chilly reception.

I learned much later that Drew and his team believed I was coming in to steal their emerging company out from under them. They had put years of work into developing the technology and had even written a business plan—which was actually a visionary technology bible—and they saw me as an interloper "business guy" coming to walk away with the prize just as they were on the precipice of success. Scientists are often distrustful of business people, sometimes for good reason. Needless to say, our initial meetings were not love fests—we circled each other like hungry dogs fighting over a scrap of meat. Drew, especially, was brutal in his conversations with me, making it clear that he felt that my contributions were pretty useless.

I had a few things going for me as I prepared to help the Unitive team. First of all, I had no interest in the company. Next to the networking opportunity, I saw MEMS as a much bigger prize, and Vera actually wanted to work with me, whereas the Unitive group clearly did not. I had already learned the importance of working with people who wanted my skills, rather than those needing to be convinced they needed them. I was here to do Shelby's bidding and move on. I also had Shelby's backing, which trumped everyone else's unhappiness with the situation. Finally, Vera vouched for me. She and Drew were good friends, and her support took the edge off his antipathy.

Drew had a PhD in physics from the University of North Carolina and was an expert in electronic packaging. Electronics are constantly getting smaller and more powerful, to the point where we now carry unimaginable computing power in our back pockets. What is not commonly known, is that electronic innovation requires packaging innovation to physically connect these tiny electronic marvels to the outside world. Drew was an expert in electronic circuit packaging. He was part of a team at MCNC that had developed a technology called "solder bumping" that was part of a bigger trend called chip-scale packaging.

Chip-scale packaging was becoming important because electronics were getting smaller and smaller, to the point where conventional packaging technology no longer sufficed. The typical solution at the time was to make very tiny wired connections to the chip—a technology called "wire bonding"—using robotic systems called wire bonders. These systems were very fast and cheap but with limitations.

To understand the challenge, imagine you are traveling in your car and want to charge your phone. That works fine if you are travelling by yourself, but it gets tricky if you are a family of six all battling for the one cigarette lighter socket at the front of the car. This is exactly the scenario that electronics designers were facing. Electronics were getting more and more crowded and engineers were running out of room to make electrical connections to the powerful circuits they were designing. Solder bumping solved this problem by distributing tiny bits of solder—solder bumps—over the surface of the electronic chip, positioning the bumps wherever an electrical connection was needed. It would be the same if you distributed an electrical power connection to every seat in the car—voila, family strife ended!

These new chips, with their electronic circuits and fields of solder bumps were then flipped over—that's why it's also called "flip chip" technology—and attached directly to the package with each solder bump ensuring both electrical connection and mechanical integrity. This new electronics packaging approach eventually enabled the products we love today like Bluetooth earpieces, ultra-powerful smartphones, tablets, and smart watches. In 1997, Drew and his team were easily ten years ahead of their time.

MCNC had built its solder-bumping capability in anticipation of this new trend, but wire bonding was so cheap in comparison it created a barrier. At that time, MCNC could put solder bumps on a four-inch wafer of electronics for around $1200. A single wire bond, in contrast, cost less than half a penny! The cost of a single processed wafer at MCNC would buy 240,000 wire bonds!

Needless to say, MCNC was not making a lot of solder bumping sales outside of some relatively small contracts and grants for military applications. Fighter jets needed really small electronics packages and cost was not an object, but the volume of work did not support the solder bumping group and it was bleeding cash.

Drew was a world-expert in electronic packaging technology and, as such, was on the cutting edge of what was going on in "flip chip" packaging. He was also an eloquent speaker and an evangelist for solder bumping for flip chip electronics. Like Vera, he had built a team and successfully raised funding through government grants to support new technology development. At the same time, Drew was also quite rough around the edges, being frequently blunt to the point of rudeness. An odd couple, we hit the road together in search of customers.

One of our first meetings was with IBM in Fishkill, New York. Through Drew's connections in the industry, we had managed to secure a meeting with a manager of new product development at the facility. We met in a small room in an ancient building and Drew stood up to give his pitch. While Drew could be terrible at times one-on-one, when he gave a pitch like this, he was a star. The manager enthusiastically embraced the solder-bumping approach.

"This is the wave of the future!" he raved once Drew was done with his presentation. "I can't wait to see it in our new products!"

Drew was clearly pleased with the reception. He proudly sat down at the end of the table whereas the manager and I sat across from each other. Now it was my turn.

"I'm glad you like our technology!" I enthused in return. "How do you see IBM using solder bumping?"

"Oh, packages are definitely getting smaller, this solves a lot of problems for us! I can't wait until its available!" he gushed.

"Well, actually it *is* available! We can start working with you right now! Do you have a budget available to work with us?"

"Budget? What…?" the manager's enthusiasm dialed down a notch.

Glancing over at Drew, I noticed his look of pride had suddenly disappeared. He had gone quiet, shrinking down somewhat in his chair. His brow was furrowed, as he attempted to communicate something to me silently, with quivering eyebrows, though I had no idea what it was.

I continued, unabashed.

"Yes, well, we all agree that this technology is important to your future. I was just wondering, given how important it is, whether you would fund a development program with us. You know… pay us so that you can design this technology into your next generation of products."

"Development… ah, well, actually, budgets for this year are fixed… um…"

At this point our conversation was interrupted by a loud hiss of air. Looking over at Drew, it was evident that he had just released the height adjustment on his chair, sinking down sharply, perhaps to put more of the table between himself and this uncomfortable conversation.

"What about next year?" I asked, undeterred. "Can we talk about budget for next year?"

"Well, maybe. I … How much are you talking about?" the manager asked.

Finally! We were talking money.

"Oh, I think an initial program might run eighty to ninety thousand. Just to get started…" It had worked for me once before, so why not try again?

"Eighty thousand dollars!" the manger exclaimed, "Wire bonding costs almost nothing!"

"Yes, but this is development. Eventually, solder bumping will be cheaper than wire bonding. I think you would want a program to make sure that you're competitive going forward. Texas Instruments is doing it."

Before the manager could respond, we heard a final, loud creak from Drew's direction. Drew is a pretty big guy, but by now he had slid down in his chair to the point were only his head and neck appeared above the table. He couldn't go any further without falling to the floor. He studiously avoided eye contact and stared silently at the table's edge, which at this point was just inches from the front of his nose.

Between Drew's disappearing act and my insistence for a funded program, the manager was getting a little flustered. Clearly, he was looking for a way out.

"Well, maybe next year's budget. Yes, I could see something next year. Maybe..."

Maybe... The kiss of death in sales. "Yes" is, of course, the best possible outcome when you are selling. But "no" is actually not bad when you are establishing if there is a real need for your new technology. "No" clearly establishes that the prospective customer is not interested. They are either the wrong customer or you have the wrong product—this frees you to move on to other, more productive endeavors.

"Maybe" is worse than "no," much worse! Now you have to decide whether to spend more time on this prospect or to cut your losses. The worst-case scenario is that you spend a lot of time and money trying to convert that "maybe" into "yes" with no success. This happens more often than you might expect, and it happens most often when you are desperate to land a certain customer. It can cost millions! Over the years I have learned to put "maybe" in the "no" category. It saves a lot of heartache.

As we walked out of the building, Drew was vacillating between being impressed and being appalled.

"I can't believe you asked for money," he whispered forcefully, glancing furtively over his shoulder to make sure we weren't being followed by someone with a "no solicitations" sign. "That guy is a friend of mine! I see him at technical meetings! And eighty to ninety thousand! That took some balls. But damn, that was embarrassing!"

"What was with the disappearing act?" I countered, trying to gain the upper hand.

"Are you kidding? If I could've dug a hole in the floor and crawled in, I would have! That was the worst meeting I've ever been in!"

In spite of our differences, Drew and I learned to get along. We had many customer meetings together with him pitching, and me asking for an order.

Years later, much to my surprise, Drew would tell me that these sessions had a big impact on his life. He moved on from technical management to technical sales and, including Unitive, went on to be an integral part of three startups that ultimately sold for close to $1 billion. Years later I even hired him to help *me* with marketing.

In addition to the experience I gained working sales for Unitive, I was lucky enough to gain experience raising venture capital for the first time thanks to Shelby. As the designated point person for investors, I worked closely with Dr. Gabriel Tanner and MST Capital Partners of Switzerland, negotiating their lead investment in the Unitive venture. They were interested in financing a new flip chip startup and Unitive looked like a good prospect for them.

Negotiating MST's initial investment, I had no idea, really, what I was doing, but I was certainly not alone in this regard. One of the reasons deals did not get done at MCNC was because nobody knew how to do them! It was exactly as Bob West said. Perhaps the only difference between me and the others at MCNC, was that I sought outside help wherever I could. I had a wonderful mentor, Arthur Lemieux, who was instrumental in guiding me in my first efforts to raise money.

In the case of Unitive, while obviously inexperienced, I was at least professional, and Gabriel Tanner was quite patient, so we were eventually able to structure a deal that both MCNC and MST accepted. It was a tremendous privilege to be able to learn these things *on the job* under the guidance of such wonderful people.

Together with other partners, MST eventually funded Unitive to the tune of about $17 million and it became the first independent commercial venture to emerge out of my portfolio of activities at MCNC.

Unitive struggled initially, but the business took off with the adoption of Bluetooth technology in the early 2000s. Bluetooth devices needed high density packaging and suddenly cost and "newness" were no longer overwhelming barriers. Those tiny, Bluetooth wireless earpieces for smartphones simply could not be manufactured using conventional electronic packaging and they were in very high demand. Consumers wanted these new devices and were willing to pay exorbitant prices for pieces of electronics not much larger than a peanut. Suddenly growth was staggering. Unitive was acquired by Amkor Technology in 2004 and remains part of that company's huge electronic packaging business today.

# Technology Overload

Even as solder bumping became my most pressing assignment, it was not my only one. As much as Shelby wanted me to support the solder bumping group, he was most excited about another MCNC innovation: an electromechanical microrelay.

A relay is a simple device that opens and closes an electrical circuit. A light switch is an example of the most fundamental kind of relay. However, a light switch requires human touch to open and close the electrical circuit that controls the light. An electromechanical relay, on the other hand, does not require human intervention. It responds to a small electrical signal to open or close another, larger electrical circuit. Relays have many applications including powering up the lights of your car, controlling the compressor in your refrigerator, switching exhaust fans on and off, and much more. A great example is the "ludicrous mode" that enables the Tesla Model S to accelerate faster than most super cars. Why? Because it has a very innovative relay that allows a huge amount of current to be transferred from its batteries to its motors. Relays are used everywhere, and in 1997 the global market for relays was well over $1 billion.

Shelby wanted a technical team at MCNC to build a microrelay that would be thousands of times smaller than any other relay on the market. Even before I joined MCNC Shelby had been working with one of his managers to identify products and services that could replace the State subsidy. They had focused on solder bumping (Unitive) and the microrelay. The difference: Solder bumping was an established technology at MCNC, while the microrelay was just an idea on paper.

Beyond the technical challenges of developing a microrelay, the financial challenge seemed even more daunting. Shelby had studiously avoided delving into the financial details, sticking to the idea that MCNC could simply replace the annual $6 million subsidy with revenue from new products or services. He thought $6 million was a tough challenge, but not an impossible one. From the beginning, I did not see it that way. The $6 million subsidy was pure profit and I estimated that MCNC required $30-$60 million in new revenue in order to replace the $6 million subsidy/profit that was being lost. This was obviously a much, much bigger hill to climb than Shelby was letting on. It meant doubling or tripling MCNC's revenues in three years! This was a tall order, under the best of circumstances, and these were not the best of circumstances. In 1997, the solder bumping capability was ahead of its time and lacked immediate customers, and the microrelay was a just picture on a piece of paper. Nor did we have customers lining up to buy either product.

All of this did not seem to bother Shelby in the least. He was excited about the new products we could build.

"We call it 'Cricket'," he said, proudly, showing me a diagram of something that looked like a sardine can with the lid rolled back. Apparently the curled up "lid" was electrostatically powered to straighten out and curl back up on command.

"When you apply an electric current, that piece there rolls forward. And when you remove the current, it rolls back. You know, like a tiny carpet. We were originally thinking about putting a little hole under it so that the rolling and unrolling closes and opens an airway—the idea was to make a microvalve. But we found this article on microrelays, and think that's a much better application."

Shelby waved a printout at me from a website called Electronic Buyers' News. I glanced at the title: "MEMS the Word," written by Bryn Hammel.

"You need to read this, Jesko. According to this article, microrelays are where we need to be! And, if we put down two electrical contacts, then, when the carpet rolls forward it will touch both of them and close an electrical circuit. We can make a microrelay!"

Whew. Despite Shelby making it sound easy, it sounded pretty complex to me. I needed to see one of these microrelays to understand what he was getting at.

"That's an interesting approach, Shelby!" I responded, trying to hide my confusion under enthusiasm. "I'd love to see one of these switches in action."

"Ah, well... We haven't demonstrated an actual switch yet... But we've been able to demonstrate the rolling and unrolling. We call it 'Zipper!' We have a patent on it, and we think it can be used for a lot of applications."

Cricket. Zipper. Rather than having things cleared up, I was quickly getting more confused. Of course, this was not unusual. Most innovations are very hard to figure out initially, because they almost always deal with things never seen before. It didn't help at all that Shelby was showing me half-baked diagrams and talking about miniature rolling carpets that could make microvalves one day and microrelays the next.

I looked at the diagram in Shelby's hands and rubbed the back of my neck uncomfortably. While I hadn't been at MCNC very long, I had already learned to expect these kinds of discussions, and further, that the gap between passion and execution was often huge. Grand visions were crafted overnight, documented in vague terms, implemented very quickly, and often forgotten when things did not pan out. This approach was great—and even required—in a creative, innovation environment, allowing the organization to stay on the cutting edge of technology evolution. It fostered rapid, breakthrough inventions and inspired funding agencies to favor MCNC's grant applications. It lost its luster, however, as we turned towards commercialization.

There was no doubt that Zipper was a cool technology. Who could have imagined a micro-scale, automated rolling carpet? Paint it red and you could arrange a black-tie gala for a flea circus! But could we go from this diagram to $60 million in microrelay sales in three years? This seemed a stretch under even the best of circumstances.

I knew this was not the moment for doubt, so I focused on expressing cautious optimism.

"Okay, I'll look into it, Shelby. I'll go talk to Vera and see what it would take to build one of these."

"Oh, no, this is not out of Vera's group. This is out of the electronics group."

"You mean the solder bumping group?"

"No… No. We have another group that works on all electronics *except* bumping."

"And they are doing MEMS?" I asked, feeling a bit dizzy.

MCNC had what is called an "eat-what-you-kill" environment, where managers—called principle investigators (or PIs)—had to constantly find funding to keep their groups afloat. Funds were scarce, so any idea that could be marketed to grant-making agencies was pursued. This fostered free-for-all innovation but also caused ideas to be horded, generating all sorts of confusion as to who was doing what.

"Yeah, it's a bit confusing…" Shelby acknowledged. "Well, this Zipper idea was a project they got funded for microfluidics, not electronics, and the electronics team ended up building some prototypes to demonstrate that the curling and uncurling works. And it works really well!"

In a heartbeat we had gone from talking about microvalves, to discussing microrelays, and now microfluidics. Confusing? You bet. But not uncommon in technology innovation environments. I felt like I was looking at a tangled ball of yarn, trying to figure out if there was anything of value in there. I knew that if I wanted to be successful, I would have to find a way to undo some of the knots.

Conceptually, microfluidics—the idea that you could perhaps build entire chemical factories on the surface of a microchip and fit them into something the size of a key fob—was a new concept that was just taking off. In these factories, tiny pipelines would carry fluids or gasses from one process to the next to create nano-scale chemical reactions for precision chemistry or analytical applications. There was a lot of interest in micro-scale technologies that could pump fluids or switch them from one micropipe to another or control them in any fashion. Two decades later the company Theranos would be valued at $9 billion based on this kind of vision—and then go bankrupt in disgrace when it couldn't deliver. Here MCNC was at the very start of microfluidics and the Zipper-powered microvalve fit into this class of potential solutions. Listening to Shelby, I could easily imagine the Zipper-microvalve idea gaining enough interest to get funded, but I still had my doubts about commercializing a Zipper-based the microrelay.

"And they have a project to demonstrate a microrelay too?" I asked hopefully.

"Naw, but read the article," Shelby responded, handing me the printout. "Microfluidics is going to take forever to commercialize, but there are all these companies that want microrelays right now! Let's-go-Jes-ko!"

Looking back, I think Shelby missed his calling and should have been in sales. He was a scholar, professor, manager, academic leader—but his real skill was that he could sell ice to Inuits when he got excited about an idea. I took the printout and headed off.

It was clear from the article and additional research, that Shelby was definitely right about one thing: There was a lot of immediate industry interest in microrelays. Companies like Alcatel, AMP, Ericsson, and Siemens were publicly expressing confidence that this was an important technology direction for their businesses. In her article, Bryn Hammel quoted various program managers at major companies who had microrelay development programs. The message was clear: Microrelays were nascent and very promising. I felt bad about my initial misgivings. Shelby was right, this seemed like the kind of commercial opportunity that MCNC was destined for.

Having established that, on paper at least, the microrelay sector was an interesting arena, I needed to establish the *real* appetite for microrelay technology. If I'd learned anything from my diamond-thin-films experience, it was that everyone loves a new baby. New technology, like a new baby, attracts all sorts of admirers. They want to look at it, coo and cuddle it, tickle it under the chin, make it laugh, and maybe even hold it for a while. But that doesn't mean they want to take it home to change its diapers, or, heaven forbid, pay for college.

The microrelay definitely fit into the "new baby" category, but I wasn't sure it was also a real business opportunity. To find out I knew I had to get in front of some of the folks at AMP and Siemens and the other companies. My problem was that I was far from being a relay industry expert and I had no connections that could help. My only option was to make a cold call; the question was to whom?

It used to be that I found it impossible to make calls to strangers. It was even worse if I needed something from them. By the time I arrived at MCNC I had already learned that if I wanted to be an entrepreneur, I had to be prepared to make cold calls—lots of them! Even so, making these calls still gave me heart palpitations, and I tended to avoid them until there was no other option.

To make things easy for myself, my very first call was to Bryn Hammel. She knew way more about microrelays than I did, and nervous as I was, I thought this was a good place to start. Bryn was (and still is) a great writer and had thoroughly researched her article. This made it easy for me to compliment her on her work and to let her know how helpful her article had been to me. It was immediately apparent there was no need to be nervous, Bryn was the nicest and most helpful person I could have turned to.

We discussed a lot of the background material that had not made it into the article. And she confirmed there was a real interest in MEMS microrelays. The problem, she explained, was that no one had yet demonstrated a working MEMS microrelay. "A lot of the MEMS relay programs appear to be in research," she told me. "If you have a microrelay solution, I can tell you there is demand for it! And your MEMS group is so highly respected, I'm sure you would get interest from the companies I interviewed."

Of course, we didn't have anything near a microrelay solution either...

While Bryn had named companies and project leaders in her article, I didn't have phone numbers where I could reach them. "Would you share some of your contact information with me?" I asked hopefully. I felt I already knew the answer to this question, but I had long ago learned that if you don't ask, you don't get.

Bryn laughed at my naivety. "You know I can't share that information with you," she responded as predicted. But then added, "What I will do is contact some of the people I interviewed and ask them if they would like to talk to you. If they express interest, I'll put them in touch."

I'm not sure why Bryn was so helpful, other than perhaps, she was as excited about MEMS technology as everyone else. Having done her research and having uncovered a compelling new technology trend, perhaps she wanted to see it succeed. Whatever the case, she kicked off my business development career in MEMS. Within weeks I had a list of premium contacts in leading companies who were interested in microrelays! Names, contact information, a direct line to key decision makers, essentially pure gold in sales.

But what the heck was I going to sell? I had a picture of a sardine can, and a story about a miniature rolling carpet. If I had learned anything from Bryn it was that there were lots of people out there with pictures, but none with real solutions. At MCNC, we were in the same boat. On the other hand, Bryn had confirmed that our MEMS group, especially Vera, "The Queen of MEMS," was highly respected within the industry. Yet the Zipper wasn't even their technology!

As I worked to gather names and contacts, I also met with the inventor of the Zipper.

"Shelby wants me to do what?" he asked looking very bewildered.

Perhaps I should have been surprised that the key player in this new product direction was uninformed, but by now, I knew to expect the unexpected at MCNC.

"He wants a microrelay. Here," I explained patiently, as I pulled out the rapidly deteriorating picture of the sardine can and pointed to what looked like a drain in the middle of the structure. "Instead of making a hole for fluid for a microvalve, Shelby thinks you could put in two electrical traces and close a switch when the metal flap rolls forward."

"What is that?" the inventor asked, looking at the picture with a frown.

"What? That... This?" I asked, waving the picture, flustered by the unexpected turn in our conversation. "This is the Zipper!"

"Nah. It doesn't—I didn't draw that. I dunno. Maybe it's an early version from a brainstorming session."

"But... the Zipper is real, right? I mean, you've made it work, right? That's what I've been told!"

"Oh, yeah, sure we have. It was a program I got funded that ended a few months ago. We showed that we could make the metal curl and uncurl using electrostatic forces. But it sure doesn't look like that!"

Okay. Who cared what it looked like? I felt somewhat relieved. At least there was a Zipper. "So, can you make a switch? Like Shelby suggested? Just use the metal flap to connect and disconnect two electrical traces?" I waved my arms around trying to act like a switch to make my point.

"Yeah, I guess. Maybe…," he responded, trying to ignore my animated gyrations. "It sure would make a great research project."

"Research project?" My arms stopped in mid-motion. Shelby's three-year clock ticked loudly in the back of my mind.

"Yeah. We've just shown that the curling part works. But making it into an electrical switch is a whole new thing. That might take a couple of years. And, it has to be funded, you know? Is Shelby paying for this? I can't do a thing without funding."

"Funding. Years…?"

"Yeah, I need at least $50 K to get started. My boss won't let us start a project for less."

Damn. This was not going at all as I had intended or even hoped. I'd come to see if the Zipper would make a viable microrelay design and here I was being sold on a multi-year research project. And $50,000? Where did he get that number from? It seemed like he was reading my playbook. I felt a bit weak in the knees.

I was also learning an important lesson: Everyone has their own pressures. MCNC was a service organization that kept pretty good track of how people spent their time. One of the most critical metrics was the "percent sold" metric. This measured how much of your time was spent on money generating projects. The target for percent sold was over 75% for MCNC's research staff. If a scientist or engineer had an important skillset, they were generally oversold, and were therefore reluctant to do more work, since extra work did not lead to any personal benefit for them. If a person was undersold, then they wanted work, but not without a fund code, since this was the only way to get their percentage up.

The inventor I was talking to was in the second category, his funding had run out, and he was making it clear that he couldn't or wouldn't lift a finger without new funding in place. On the other hand, if I could get him some funding, he was also making it clear that he would be more than happy to carry out research on the microrelay. But, in this case, "research" was definitely not what I wanted. I wanted a prototype that I could put in front of a customer. And fast! What could I do? I left him with a "maybe!"

My next step was to meet with Vera to try to understand the politics of the situation. I was being asked to work on a MEMS device outside of the MEMS group. How would that play out with Vera? When it came to MEMS technology, it was clear that Vera and her team were the 800-pound gorilla, not just at MCNC but throughout the emerging MEMS industry. Why was Shelby pointing me towards a one-man team with little resources? I'd already learned that Vera spoke her mind unequivocally, and blunt feedback was what I wanted. As usual, Vera did not disappoint. She was no-nonsense and to the point, and, in retrospect, entirely accurate.

"I don't care what you do, Jesko," she said. "But the Zipper is new technology being developed by people with limited experience in MEMS. I think the chances of it working for a relay application are close to non-existent."

Vera went on to explain that through their work with the Navy, her team had yet to solve a big problem: At the small scale of MEMS devices, when surfaces came into contact, they tended to stick. Electrostatic devices were a particular problem because they weren't able to generate the forces needed to overcome this "stiction."

The Zipper was electrostatic.

As I listened to Vera, I sighed inwardly. In the back of my mind I was thinking of the list of prospects that I owed phone calls to. Perhaps the cart had gotten ahead of the horse. I thanked my lucky stars that this crazy Cricket-Zipper-micro-carpet project was only a minor one in my portfolio.

"You should talk to Matt Steel," Vera continued patiently, pulling me out of my negative reverie. "He's one of my most experienced engineers. We have already put a great deal of thought into all kinds of actuating mechanisms and switches. I'm pretty sure that he'll be able to help you—or at least make sure you don't do something stupid."

Ah, Vera. Always happy to speak her mind!

Desperately hoping for clarity, I took Vera's advice. I sought out Matt Steel and found him to be just as capable as Vera said. In fact, he turned out to be one of the best engineers I ever worked with. Matt wasn't just an engineer; he was an entrepreneur.

What makes a great entrepreneurial engineer? First and foremost, they have to be great engineers. I have never worked on an innovation that did not need to be changed in some way to become a commercial success. My experience with diamond films *versus* diamond-like carbon was the norm: New innovations rarely, if ever, fit a customer's needs perfectly. Quite often they don't fit them at all! Great engineers find ways to mold new innovations to the needs of the customer. I soon discovered that Matt was one of these great engineers.

The other characteristic that made Matt special: He was also exceptional with customers. I have had the fortune to work with many excellent engineers who are great at solving problems, but do not have the listening and communications skills needed to build a rapport with the customer. Building good rapport, with a back and forth exchange of ideas and information, is often critical if new innovations are to be moved into commercial applications. Matt Steel had *all* these skills.

Finally, Matt had previously worked in the commercial sector for IBM. He had experience dealing with real-world problems and was much more attuned than most to the importance of developing product requirements, establishing delivery timelines, and meeting deadlines.

With all of that, Matt quickly became my go-to resource for any commercial projects for Vera's team. He could advise on engineering solutions, meet with customers to discuss engineering requirements, and provide realistic development plans for delivery.

In our first meeting on the microrelay, Matt schooled me on some of the technical subtleties of MEMS structures and how these subtleties might affect the construction and operation of a MEMS electrical switch.

"MEMS devices suffer from stiction," he explained. "Stiction is static friction that occurs when any two surfaces touch. There are capillary forces, van der Waals forces, and even natural electrostatic forces that cause surfaces to stick to each other. It's not such a big deal for large structures, but these forces act like glue for tiny structures in MEMS. When parts touch in MEMS, you need pretty large forces to pull them apart, otherwise they are stuck forever.

"The other issue you have with relays, in particular, is that when you close the contacts together, electricity flows and you get something called microwelding as metal from one contact is transferred to the other by the electrical current that passes between them. Even if the Zipper is able to overcome stiction, I don't think there is any way it can overcome micro-welds."

Wow. I couldn't believe that the dream to build a microrelay could be so easily shattered. On the other hand, I was learning yet another important lesson: It's one thing to read a few articles about a hot, new market demand, to dream up a product, and to put ideas on a piece of paper; it's quite another to come up with a *real* solution. I was discovering that the gap between dream and reality was huge. It was like seeing an oasis in the distance and suddenly discovering that Mount Everest was in your way.

Matt saw my disappointment and tried to mollify me. "But, don't give up, Jesko. If there is a need for microrelays, then there may be other ways to make this work. Give me some time and I'll get back to you."

I later found out that Matt was in fact quite motivated to make this work. He explained to me that the primary revenue for the MEMS team at MCNC was service work. As such, they did design and consulting work for both government and industry customers. At conferences they often saw their designs in other people's product presentations. He and the rest of the MEMS team were hungry to do something of their own. It did not take much to convince Matt that the microrelay had great potential as a first product for the MEMS group.

We reconvened a few days later and it was clear that Matt had done his homework. He had read a number of papers on microrelays and was now well-versed in the technology. He had also done calculations on the forces that would be needed to properly close the metal contacts and to break microwelds should they occur. He explained about the importance of making a "wiping" contact to ensure the metals connected together properly when the switch was closed.

The level of detail was amazing, and I was thoroughly impressed. How had he become such an expert in just a few days? I was more than thankful that I suddenly had this level of expertise at my disposal. I was also thankful for his flexibility; he seemed to have no problem at all jumping into the unknown.

"As I see it," Matt said. "You have three options to drive this relay. There is electrostatic actuation and that just won't work. Whether you use the Zipper or some other electrostatic solution, you just won't get the force you need to create a reliable switch. Another option is electromagnetic—that's how conventional relays are switched. But creating an electromagnetic switch on a microscale has not been demonstrated, so we would be starting from scratch if we tried to do that."

I was starting to look worried again, but Matt grinned, having saved the best until last.

"There is another solution and it might be perfect for this application. It's called a thermal actuator. It was invented by one of our engineers and it generates huge forces on a microscale. We even have a patent on it!"

He showed me a drawing that looked very much like the skeleton of a fish, minus the head, with the tips of the spines buried in two fixed blocks on either side, so that the entire "skeleton" floated between the blocks.

"We can run an electrical current from one anchor block to the other going through the spines. When we do that the spines heat up and expand. Given they are fixed at their tips to the two anchors they have no choice but to bend forward as they expand. When they bend, the bar at the center—the spine of the "fish"—moves like a battering ram. It's very powerful."

"Can you turn this into a microrelay?"

"Sure, all we need to do is use the tip of the battering ram to close an electrical circuit, and we have a relay."

"Fantastic! How long would it take to build one of these?"

"Already designed." As usual, he was way ahead of me. "It will take us a few weeks to get the production masks and then another few weeks to make the first prototypes with nickel electroplating."

"How much will it cost?"

"Cost? Nothing! I'll do it in beakers in my office and we have a grant from the Navy that funds exactly this kind of work. We'll charge it to that."

Wow. No wonder this team was considered to be a crown jewel at MCNC!

My final challenge was to go back to inform Shelby about our change in plans. The good news was that the microrelay with the thermal actuator seemed to be a good idea. I had a list of prospects, and initial market research indicated there was a significant need and a large market opportunity. With the thermal actuator, the microrelay appeared technically feasible and we could move fast to demonstrate that, one way or another. The bad news was that 'Cricket' was dead. Shelby was very bullish about Cricket, but it was clear to me that the Zipper technology was not going to cut it. It was not just that the electrostatic technology was not suited for microrelays, it was also clear that the one-man team behind the Zipper was not operationally suited to tackling this problem—at least not within the timeframe that Shelby had in mind.

I convened a meeting with Shelby, Vera, other executives, and Matt Steel to discuss the change in direction using Matt's compelling technical arguments. It was a slam dunk and we got approval to proceed on the spot. Shelby was not one to dither.

I walked out of the meeting elated, but more than anything else relieved. It was clear when I met with the Zipper innovator that he was a very capable engineer who had come up with a compelling invention. But, when it came to actual execution, there was no comparison to Matt and Vera and the rest of the MEMS team. They stood head and shoulders above anybody else when it came to delivering practical solutions.

Unless, of course, they chose not to. It was well known that Vera had no problem shutting something down if she thought it was impractical. But that was okay too. I liked the clarity that she and her team offered. I didn't want an impractical dream or a research project. I wanted a working product that I could hand to customers for evaluation. I was more than happy to be working with a team that had the same perspective. And it was clear Vera supported Matt's version of the microrelay.

In the meantime, Matt worked miracles and was already fabricating first prototypes in his office of all places. He had not been joking. It was a crazy setup: There was a beaker of clear liquid on his shelf with what looked like two paddles dipped into it, wires were attached to the tops of the paddles using alligator clips, and the wires led to a power supply. Apparently, when the power supply light was "on" microrelays were being produced!

"What the heck is this?' I asked the first time I saw it.

"That's our microrelay production!" Matt laughed as I frowned. "Don't look so worried, Jesko. The solution in the beaker has nickel dissolved in it. The wiring and the power supply allow me to electroplate the nickel. I'm using a special masking process that allows me to selectively electroplate nickel microrelays. I'm proving the concept here because I can do it a lot quicker than trying to do it in the fabrication facility."

"So, you can make working relays, right here in your office?" I asked, astounded.

"Yup. And once I prove things here, I can move right to the production floor. It's a pretty simple process."

It was fast, and it was free! We were working with first prototypes almost overnight. I was ecstatic. We had what looked like a compelling market opportunity. We had a patented, unique technology. I was working with a world-class team, and they clearly had the ability to execute. With this progress, I finally felt confident that I had everything I needed to pursue my very first venture. What I didn't fully appreciate is that I was missing the most important piece of the puzzle: a (real) customer.

# Mining for Prospects

Customers are tricky.

It's no secret that focusing on customer needs is the key to success in building any business. As entrepreneurship has become an increasingly important part of the U.S. educational curriculum, this aspect has become a mainstay of the courses students take, and the federal government even awards grants for business students/budding entrepreneurs to go out and talk to customers. Sometimes the advice goes a bit overboard. "Make one hundred phone calls to prospective customers and find that crucial need and then fill it!"

Then you're a millionaire.

But, if understanding customer needs were easy, if all it took was one hundred phone calls, then everyone would be a millionaire. It turns out that customers are tricky, but they are not tricky on purpose. It's important to understand, when it comes to new products, and especially new technology, the people across the table from you are often just as confused as you are. As a result, they may honestly express a need that they don't really have, or they may have a need that they cannot express!

The bottom line is that no one can predict the future, not even your customer. If you rely on them to do so, you may be disappointed.

Henry Ford predicted in 1940 that the next big thing would by flying automobiles. In the 1950s, the idea of a flying car was all the rage, and I am sure if you asked people about it at the time, they probably considered a flying car to be a fantastic idea—especially during rush hour. But the flying car never happened. Why? Because, there is a huge gap between dreaming and doing. While a flying car is, in concept, a wonderful solution to all our travel problems; in practice, it's a terrible idea for all sorts of reasons.

Matching the technology needed for a practical car to the technology needed for a safe plane turned out to be much harder than first thought. Doing it at a reasonable cost was even harder! A "cheap" plane costs around $300,000, never mind the expense of upkeep. Would you pay that for daily transportation? Probably not. At that price, the idea of driving to the airport in an S-Class Mercedes and then letting professionals do the flying becomes very attractive: You'd be driving a world-class luxury car, flying in the safest possible manner, and saving a lot of money doing it. Never mind that you're also avoiding the nightmare scenario of bringing road rage to the skies!

So, the flying car is not so much a need as an aspiration. Today, almost 80 years after Ford first made his proclamation, companies like Uber and Google are once again talking about flying cars. Lucky for them, they have a lot of money to spend on this crazy idea. And, who knows? Maybe someone will actually make it work. Nevertheless, aspirational needs are great for dreamers and rich people, but they are terrible sinkholes for entrepreneurs who, at the end of the day, need to make a living. We are looking for *real* needs.

The flipside of the aspirational need is the unknown need. In some cases, this is a need that is on the tip of the customer's tongue; the customer knows it's there but cannot articulate it. In other cases, a need may be hidden until the customer is shown a potential solution.

The American public never knew they had a need for fast food, until they were introduced to McDonald's by Ray Kroc in the 1950s. Ray did not invent the fast food concept—it was pioneered by the McDonald brothers—but he brought the concept to the masses through franchising and other clever business models. Before he did that, people were quite happy with sleepy drive-in restaurants. Of course, once people learned about the low-cost, fast food being offered by McDonald's, every town in America wanted one. Customer's first needed to see the innovation to love it.

Imagine, before the time of Ray Kroc and McDonald's, sending out a group of students to survey a hundred consumers on their receptivity to fast food. I think such a survey would have caused some serious confusion as respondents tried to answer questions about something they had never experienced. Imagine even trying to explain fast food to someone who has, for their entire life, eaten in a sit-down, cook-to-order restaurant.

"Hi, we have a new food concept where we will serve you your food three minutes after you order."

"Three minutes! How do you cook food in three minutes?"

"Well, it's not any food, we just serve hamburgers and fries. And they're cooked before you even get there. See, we have a system—"

"I don't like warmed-over hamburgers very much. I like food straight from the kitchen! And what do you mean 'system?' Is that healthy?"

I have had many conversations just like this. It is very hard to truly understand the value of an innovation by just talking about it. This is especially true if the new solution is somehow considered inferior or has less features than the "ideal" solution that is already in the customer's mind. If all you've ever experienced is sit-down dinners, getting something perceived to be cheap with less choice and a less comfortable environment may not be appealing.

To gain acceptance of new innovations, you have to show, and you have to sell. That's exactly what the McDonald brothers did. They innovated and built a restaurant that served hamburgers and fries almost as soon as they were ordered. Customers were leery at first but loved it once they tried it. Customers had to see and experience fast-food hamburgers to understand the concept and want it.

Technology customers are exactly the same: If they have never seen an innovation, or if they have seen it but don't understand it, then it's hard for them to express a need for it.

I see entrepreneurship—or at least technology entrepreneurship—in terms of two containers. One container holds technical innovations, both existing and future. The other container holds all manner of customer needs: real, aspirational, and unknown. Aspirational needs are red herrings, to be ignored. Real needs are wonderful, but often either already fulfilled or unfillable. Unknown needs are diamonds in the rough.

The entrepreneur may focus on one container or another for a time, but in the end, both of them have to be teeming. The entrepreneur's job is to fill both of these containers. Other than filling these two containers, the simple goal is to bend the container of innovations toward the container of needs to make them somehow overlap. This is where entrepreneurial magic happens. Think of it as a Venn diagram: Commercial success occurs wherever the two containers intersect. It's a very simple picture that is incredibly difficult to execute. In my case, I had a teeming cauldron of innovation at MCNC, with the electromechanical microrelay front and center; Now, I required a basket of customer needs.

With Matt busy working on prototypes, I turned my attention to finding customers. As word got out that we might have a new technical solution for a microrelay, people were more than happy to speak with me. Everyone loves a new baby, and our microrelay was the newest and cutest.

The microrelay prospect list that I had developed with Bryn Hammel consisted of a host of large corporations: Tyco, AMP, Siemens, Alcatel, and Ericsson among others. Some of these companies had existing relay businesses and were pursuing microrelay technology for competitive reasons. Others were relay users and wanted to evaluate this new technology for their applications. As I began discussions with these groups, I found out very quickly that I was not prepared.

I knew enough to create a script for my calls, to be sure to ask the right questions and be consistent with the various people I talked to. My script had more than twenty questions, and I found out almost immediately that no one had time for that. The discussions were stilted and boring. While the questions were important to me, they did not do anything for the people I was talking to, and I don't think I ever made it through the entire script. To remedy this, I adjusted my script to focus on the four areas most of my prospects were willing to talk about. These included a description of our technology, a description of the prospect and how they fit into the relay industry, a discussion of how the microrelay might match with their current or potential needs, and target pricing and volumes.

I quickly learned that my technology presentation was amateur at best. I had gotten quite excited about our thermal actuator and my initial presentation focused entirely on this underlying technology. "How cool is this?" I wanted the world to know all about the relative force of thermal actuation over other options.

This approach might have worked well at a scientific conference, but it was of limited interest to my audience of relay professionals. For the most part, they didn't care if our device was electrostatically or thermally actuated, as long as it met or exceeded industry standards. They wanted to know that the microrelay met performance requirements, that it was proven durable, and that it was safe under all conditions. They wanted to see all the information they were used to seeing. This included "spec sheets" and "application notes" and documentation with performance comparisons. In many ways it was like talking about a fast food dinner with people who had never seen fast food before! My prospects wanted a menu and I didn't have one. I had no idea where to even start with these kinds of requests, but thankfully, I had Matt to turn to.

Once I explained the communication barriers to Matt, he did his homework to learn how traditional relays were presented to the world. Almost overnight he was able to create specification sheets for our relay that looked very much like those of traditional relays. Early on, there were many specifications that we did not yet know, so we just left these blank. Surprisingly, our audience didn't care too much if there were areas where we did not yet have data. Their greatest concern was seeing information in a format that was familiar to them so that they could understand what the heck we were talking about. We needed to present fast food in a way that the sit-down customer understood it. Anything else led to confusion and reduced our credibility in the eyes of the customer.

In working with Matt, I was fortunate in that he produced working microrelays relatively quickly. The ability to deliver is what separates great entrepreneurial teams from others. The beaker in Matt's office might have looked like a high school science experiment, but it did the job, right when we needed it. With my eye closely watching Shelby's three-year countdown clock, one of my goals was to get samples into the hands of customers as fast as I could. I figured customers could evaluate the microrelays, and if our devices worked for their application, we could start talking business.

As we began delivering sample devices, however, we immediately encountered our next challenge: Customers were taking delivery of our devices and breaking them!

They didn't break them on purpose, of course, they just expected these devices to work like any other relay. Traditional relays were bulky devices, about the size of a couple of sugar cubes. We, on the other hand, could easily fit four relays into a package that was about the size of a dime. Product engineers didn't know how to deal with switches they could not see, and they didn't know how to test them without damaging them. In response, Matt created professional application notes for the handling and testing of our devices that became an essential part of our communications with product engineers.

Overall, I was amazed by how much our success hinged on effective communications. I had assumed that our technology would simply sell itself, but soon found out that this was far from the case. Our technology pitch opened many doors with corporate technology scouts who were motivated to identify new products for their company. Once we were through the door, however, we were put into the hands of the engineering teams who were more hardnosed. Worse, their perspective was often colored by their own biases. As such, we needed to make sure we were speaking the language our audience understood and that we were presenting a compelling value proposition that made economic sense.

None of this was easy. We learned and iterated pretty much every day, honing our pitch, and improving our product to the point where the technology professionals got what they expected.

That being said, there were some companies—mostly those in the business of manufacturing and selling relays—that would listen all day to our technical presentations. For the most part, these companies were concerned about the competitive threat of our device. Accordingly, they laid out the red carpet for us. They would invite us to their facilities, grant us large audiences with their best technical talent, and suck us dry of every last technical detail we were willing to part with.

On the one hand these companies were very seductive prospects because they represented a "silver bullet" for our commercialization effort. If they liked our technology, they could commercialize it for us—or so we thought! On the other hand, these were very dangerous prospects, because they could simply use the information we were providing to build their competitive capability. Even under the best of circumstances, if these "maybe" customers were just window shopping, they were still taking up time and resources that would have been better spent on real prospects.

Whether you are trying to sell an established product on a sales call, or trying to develop new products with prospective customers, differentiating between real prospects and window shoppers is critical to any entrepreneurial success. At the end of the day, an entrepreneur has to make a living, and nobody can afford to spend time with those who will never buy.

As I'd learned at Kobe Steel, asking for an order was a pretty effective filter for differentiating between serious potential customers and everyone else. Unfortunately for us, big orders from our microrelay customers were a nonstarter. The mechanical relay industry was a mature, even declining industry. Nobody had $50,000 to bandy about for pie-in-the-sky development programs. In fact, the norm in this industry was for innovators to *give* stuff away! When companies developed a new relay product, they sampled the product for free to prospective customers for evaluation.

I hated it. It was perhaps the first sign that we were targeting the wrong business.

Another problem we ran into was our inability to articulate a compelling reason to buy our devices. The main advantage we had over traditional electromechanical relays was size. Our devices were so tiny you couldn't even see them! Compare that to those obnoxious, bulky relays that other companies were selling! We also pitched that our relays could be integrated together and combined with electronic circuits to create more functionality—something you could never do with the discrete devices that were currently available.

But, much to our chagrin, "integration for more functionality" was not something that our prospective customers thought a lot about. The relay industry was about 100 years old and some of the engineers we talked to seemed close to that. These product engineers cut their teeth on innovative relay technology many decades before we showed up. They were not college kids trying to change the world. They wanted relays that met performance requirements at the lowest price point. Their applications were in automobiles, industrial machinery, and bulky communications equipment, none of which had a significant size constraint. They wanted price, price, price and made it clear that the price needed to be constantly dropping. In meeting after meeting I was getting the same message. I was starting to feel like I was trying to sell sand in the Sahara.

As is often the case our breakthrough came from an unexpected direction. It's another reason that one hundred phone calls won't suffice: Technology commercialization is so difficult because success often lies in the unknown.

This, of course, begs the question: If it's unknown, how on earth do you get there? Persistence and luck are probably the best answer, with the caveat that, with persistence, you often create your own luck. This is probably why a lot of people do not become entrepreneurs. For most people, a path that appears to depend largely on persistence and luck may seem quite unattractive. Of course, an argument can be made that *any* success depends on persistence and luck. It's just that with entrepreneurship these elements are front and center, whereas when you become an analyst at a bank it does not feel that way.

In this case, my luck was that my wife Monika was a librarian.

# Striking Gold

When we lived in Canada, my wife worked for the public library system and became friends with Jill Carney, a colleague who was similar in age, marital status, and who was also raising kids. But what they had most in common was that, unbeknownst to each other, they both independently moved to Raleigh from Canada at almost exactly the same time.

When Monika found out that Jill was living in Raleigh, it was natural for our families to meet. I wasn't keen on such social events, being much happier at home or in the office on the weekends, but I had long since learned to take visits like this in stride and do my best to be social for my family's sake. I put on my "visit with distant friends" game face and braved the ten-minute drive to what I expected to be a pretty boring afternoon.

Jill and Brad Carney lived in a very grand brick house with an immaculately landscaped backyard in an elegant subdivision in North Raleigh. I felt I had done well in coming to the United States, but the Carney's appeared to have done even better. "So, what do you do for a living, Brad?" I asked casually, as men are wont to do when the other guy obviously has a leg up in life.

"I'm a manager at Nortel Networks."

"Nortel? You mean, like, Northern Telecom?"

"Yes, we're a telecommunications equipment company. We used to be Northern Telecom, you know, out of Canada? But we just rebranded the company Nortel."

Of course, I knew all about Nortel. I had even considered a job with Northern Telecom when I finished my PhD, before I took the post-doctoral position at NCSU. Northern Telecom changed its name to Nortel Networks when networking became all the rage in the 1990s. My MBA classes at UNC took place in a Nortel building, located right in the center of Research Triangle Park. It just came totally out of the blue that Brad worked for them, although it shouldn't have come as a surprise, really, because Nortel was expanding rapidly in our region and a lot of Canadians were making the trip south.

The fact that Brad worked for Nortel was good. Very, very good. The afternoon was suddenly looking much more interesting than I could have dreamed.

"Yeah, I know Nortel. I just didn't realize you worked for them."

"Oh, for sure. That's why we moved down from Canada. Nortel is growing like crazy down here. We're now the largest employer in the Triangle!"

I knew that too. You see, while I didn't have any reason to believe that Nortel would be interested in microrelays, they were one of the highest-flying technology companies in the world, and I was convinced—again, without evidence, but with a lot of bravado—they would need some kind of MEMS device in their future. Why? Because Vera and her group had made the case to me that there was a big future for MEMS in telecommunications; and with Nortel we had one of the largest telecommunications equipment companies in the world right in our back yard! Introducing MCNC MEMS to Nortel was one of my goals, but I had no way in. Try as I might, I had not been able to find anyone senior enough in the organization to get me an audience with anyone that mattered. It was like that day, that I walked into MCNC to get a job and bumped into Shelby Clarke right there in the lobby. I doubt I would have gotten that job if I had just left my resume at the front desk. Getting face-to-face with a decision maker who has a pressing need for what you are selling is key. At Nortel, I had not gotten anywhere close to that. Until maybe now…

"And what are you doing down here?" Brad asked me the magical question.

Normally, I would provide some bland answer: I work in technology, blah, blah, blah. But this was different, *way* different. I had a *manager* from Nortel in front of me, and I could pitch MEMS to him! And, so I did. I explained to Brad how cool MEMS technology was and how it was going to change the world of telecommunications. I let him know that Nortel's arch-rival, Lucent, already had a big effort going on in the area. I let him know that we were the best. For me, this social occasion had turned into an opportunity to sell, and I was loving it.

I know. I know. Here we were socializing, and I was about to interject a blatantly partisan business request into the conversation. I just couldn't let the opportunity slip by and so went for the close. "Do you know anyone at Nortel that might be interested in our technology, Brad?"

"To be honest, product development is way far removed from what I do. I'm on the business side."

I struggled to stay positive, although inwardly I grimaced. I had done this so many times and failed to make any headway with Nortel. It was an impenetrable fortress, and yet Canadian. You'd think they would make it easier for me!

Maybe he saw my crestfallen face, maybe he just wanted to help a fellow Canadian, maybe he was just a heck of a nice guy (and he definitely was that); I could see Brad was working hard to help me in some way.

"You know, I think the best shot might be a few weeks from now. We have a big strategy meeting down here and we'll have all the senior tech guys from Ottawa participating. We might be able to set up a meeting afterwards."

Monika eventually dragged me away, but not before I got Brad's personal commitment to get the all-important meeting set up.

And Brad was true to his word. One afternoon, a few weeks later, a large group of engineers from Nortel filed into the massive boardroom at MCNC. I soon learned to love the Nortel engineer: Smart, disciplined, with a measure-twice-cut-once mentality, they were also congenial and a pleasure to work with. On this day, their leader was a man by the name of Gregory Hansen. He was clearly the boss in the room. All the engineers deferred to him and his business card carried the impressive title of "Director of Electronic Circuit Development." It appeared that Brad had delivered beyond my wildest dreams. On our side, I brought in the best of our engineering team and, of course, Vera Cohen, who would be the star of the show.

Vera had an amazing ability to talk about MEMS for hours *and* keep everyone on the edge of their seat the whole time. That's what she did that day. You can't see MEMS devices with the naked eye, but she had videos showing micro-springs that held micro-lenses; tiny structures that moved in real time like elegant, floating manatees; mirrors that flipped up and down upon electronic command; and micro-motors driving laser positioning systems with unimaginable accuracy. Her presentations were always amazing, but that day she delivered a tour-de-force that I will never forget.

Fortunately, Gregory Hansen felt the same way. When Vera was done, he didn't pause. He stood up, and exclaimed: "This is amazing! I have no idea how Nortel is going to use this technology, but I am convinced that this will be part of the future of our company!"

If Brad had been in the room, I would have hugged him.

A lively discussion ensued in which it quickly became apparent that, while Vera had done a great job inspiring everyone, the breadth of her presentation had left the Nortel team overwhelmed. As we went from technology options to real needs it was hard for the Nortel team to articulate how anything they had seen could help solve the real problems they were facing. It was almost like Vera had shown them an alternate universe that was astonishing and exciting yet had no relevance to the planet they were living on. They clearly had the sense that MEMS might enable a whole new world of functionality, but they could not pinpoint exactly how it might help them with their product designs.

As I listened, it was clear the engineers were inspired. There was a palpable energy in the room and even a sense of adventure, if we could just figure out how to use this stuff to make a better electronic circuit! But the gap between inspiration and reality was too large. Energy began to dissipate, and the Nortel engineers were left scratching their heads.

I have since learned that this inspiration-reality gap is very common for new technologies and it is perhaps one of the greatest and most frustrating hurdles a new technology faces. I also believe that, in the early stages, it is the single, largest barrier to commercialization. We can all enjoy watching *Star Trek* in the evening, but we don't go to work the next day trying to figure out how to implement a teleportation device. It's the same with prospective customers: They see a new technology and envision incredible new functionality for their business but, in the end, reality sucks all the energy out of these fanciful ideas. You end up with that awful "maybe."

The only way to get past this is to sell. And to sell, you have to get specific—to propose something that the customer must say either "yes" or "no" to. Fortunately, on that day I had just the thing. "What about a microrelay?" I asked, boldly.

On the one hand, I was desperate not to let all this excitement just fade away into nothing. On the other hand, I knew I had to put something specific on the table that Gregory and his team could accept or reject. I had one shot and I had to do it before they left that room. Rejection was a risk I was more than willing to take.

"What's a microrelay?" Gregory asked in return.

Matt didn't need much encouragement to talk about his baby. He got up and gave a brief presentation on the microrelay. Unlike Vera's inspirational talk, Matt's was pretty cut and dry: Here's what a microrelay looks like; here's how it works; here are the specifications…

I looked hopefully over at Gregory. What would it be? Acceptance or rejection? The rubber was about to meet the road. Scary on one hand, adrenalin inducing on the other.

"I didn't know this existed, but I think this is what we have been looking for," Gregory exclaimed almost in wonder.

These were magical, magical words to me.

While we knew that Nortel was a telecommunications company, we didn't really know what Nortel's business was. In a sense, we were just as ignorant about Nortel's business as they were about our technology. Without our meeting that day, we would have always been two ships passing in the night.

Instead, we learned that one of Nortel's major product lines was office telephone systems. In fact, they were a leader in this space. Their products were landline systems that managed phone calls into and out of offices. Nowadays there are many suppliers of such systems, but at the time Nortel dominated this segment. Gregory's team was responsible for a product called a linecard, which is essentially the brains of the phone. If you pick up a handset from a landline, there is a click and humming sound as the line opens up for you to make or receive a call. This function is controlled by the linecard and the click that you hear is actually a relay opening up the line. As we learned that day, each linecard had between three and five relays and Nortel was selling 10 million linecards a year.

"These linecards used to be manufactured on circuit boards," Gregory explained. "The electronics and the relays were soldered to the board and the whole board was maybe four inches by six inches in size—all packed with electronics. Our team has taken all the electronics and shrunk them into one integrated chip that has all the functionality of the linecard and is no bigger than an inch on all sides.

Unfortunately, we have not been able to shrink the relays. Now they dominate our boards and our cost! We have this cheap electronic chip with these huge and relatively costly relays still sitting on a board all around it. It has been frustrating for our designers and we'd love small relays that can be manufactured right onto the electronic chip itself. This would be truly amazing. It looks like maybe your technology has the potential to do it!"

Integration, functionality, small size. It was music to my ears, but was there a business here?

Like any developing technology, estimating the actual cost of the relay—and the profit on a customer's price point—was difficult, if not impossible at this stage of development. Right now, in Matt's crazy beaker setup, each relay was costing us hundreds of dollars to produce. We could estimate what the relay would cost in production, but the answer was highly dependent on the final design, which would ultimately depend on the customer requirements, which, of course, no-one yet knew.

The cost particularly depended on the relay's final size, how many we could produce in one "batch," how long each batch took, and the materials used. Using best-case and worst-case scenarios for these parameters, I was able to estimate that the cost would range anywhere from six cents in the best case to 40 cents in the very worst case. "How much do you pay for your relays, right now?" I asked Gregory.

"Yeah, that's another problem. It used to be the relays were a small part of our cost. We'd pay $80 or $90 for all the electronics on the linecard and $10 for the five relays. Now we pay a few dollars for the one electronic chip and we are still paying $10 for the five relays! If we could get that cost down to a dollar a relay, it would have a huge impact on our business. To be honest, as long as you are competitive, cost is not the driver. It would change our world even if we could just integrate them."

Was this too good to be true? They were currently paying $2 a relay and had a thriving business. Gregory was clearly sending a message that the price point was less of a concern than the ability to integrate. So, if we could deliver a much better product at the current price, that would be okay…, at least to start with. I quickly did the math: $2 times three or maybe even five relays times 10 million linecards. It could be a great business for us with a significant level of profit.

Although I never thought I would see it, this one opportunity might just meet Shelby's entire goal of replacing the State legislature subsidy! What's more, at this point, we still had two and a half years to do it. My spirits were rising exponentially. I consider myself to be a cautious optimist, but this seemed like a slam dunk, even to me.

"When can we get started?" I asked Gregory.

# Gathering Clouds

Entrepreneurship is a full contact sport. When you have something of perceived value, there are lots of people out there who want to take it away from you: customers who want it for free, competitors who want to steal it from you, peers who are jealous of you, investors who want to own it, and other investors who want to own you. A boss of mine used to say: "Everyone wants to eat your lunch." Unfortunately, this is true.

Think of entrepreneurship as a sport being played on a field with a ball. The "field" is the market you choose to compete in, the "game" is the business that you choose to build, and the "ball" is your unique offering in the market. Entrepreneurship is a very unique sport in that you as the entrepreneur get to define the game to be played, and you also create the ball to be played with.

The ball might be a more efficient sales channel, it might be a new business model, or it might be a new product or service. But it goes without saying that you can't play without a ball. There are many would-be entrepreneurs out there who aspire to play the sport, but never find a ball. They can only stand on the sidelines and watch others play. For many years I found myself in this position.

Before I went to university, I'd trained as a professional horse rider in Germany and decided that my first ball would be training people and horses for money. I raised $75,000 in cash to start a horse-riding establishment in Canada while earning my PhD. And while I found this effort to be personally very rewarding, I soon found out that keeping horses is very, very expensive, and as a business it was sadly bereft of any financial rewards whatsoever.

Happy and poor works for a while, but it gets old as time wears on, especially as you are considering starting a family. I soon found myself in search of another field, another game, and another ball.

I chose NCSU for my post doc because their thin-film diamond technology group was one of the best in the world. I had become convinced that diamond coatings would be the next big thing; that thin-film diamond was the ball that would allow me to play the sport I was destined to play. Of course, in that regard diamond was also not what I had hoped it would be. As I scrambled to find yet another ball, I discovered a customer that needed diamond-like carbon, but I couldn't get that off the ground either. Next up, my brief effort with Proserve also ended poorly.

It seemed to me that in each case I was using all my talent and energy only to end up with no ball to play with. Again, and again I found myself on the sidelines while other "real" entrepreneurs received recognition and accolades. My point is, you must have a ball to play this sport, and it is very, very hard to find one. Great business people and even iconic companies fail at this all the time. As I moved from one project to another, one customer to another, one grand vision to another, I was certainly proving that I was good at failing too.

I didn't know it at the time, but my failure rate was normal. In my career, I have succeeded in finding a successful ball every five years or so. Given that I'm looking for opportunity all the time, this success rate includes a lot of failure. Playing the game does not mean you will succeed: As in particle physics, entrepreneurship is statistically much more predisposed to annihilation than creation.

When your entire career is dedicated to finding a breakout ball, a meeting like the one we had that day with Nortel was beyond exhilarating.

A ball! A ball! A ball! *That* feeling, *that* kind of meeting, is what every entrepreneur lives for. It's what makes entrepreneurship so uniquely exciting, such that you are often blinded by the sheer force of the moment. You should be saying to yourself: "Be careful, things may not be exactly what they seem." Instead, you throw caution to the wind and get ready to slay dragons to protect that shiny, new ball that you think you have. And in the moment, you can't know. You might be a knight in shining armor, getting ready to conquer armies and save the world. Or you may simply be a quixotic figure, preparing to do battle with windmills.

Walking out of that conference room, everyone was doing mental high-fives, beyond excited about this opportunity to finally develop a compelling product for a very significant customer. More than just a product, we all had a sense that this was our ticket. We had finally found a customer with a need—a *real* need—that fit directly with what we could deliver! Going forward, the formula seemed simple: Make the microrelay work, deliver a product, and maybe even spin it into a company as Shelby had encouraged us to do. Do that and we had a shot at riches! We had finally found our chance to create something where there had been nothing.

While I doubt that Gregory's team was quite as euphoric as we were, I am sure they were truly excited at the prospect of integrating relays into their linecards. This approach would significantly increase functionality, create a new path for cost reduction, and make Nortel even more competitive. That's what these engineers and managers lived for.

And on paper, this was no pipe dream. There was an excellent precedent for what we were trying to do. One of the most well-established MEMS devices on the market was the accelerometer: A device which was (and still is), used to trigger airbags in cars. This device consists of a very simple mechanical structure that looks like a tiny springboard hanging over an empty swimming pool, all of it so small that it cannot be seen with the human eye. Around the springboard is a bunch of electronic circuitry that monitors tiny changes in the springboard's position.

The tiny MEMS springboard moves back and forth with the acceleration and deceleration of the car, and its movement can be measured very precisely. If the movement of the springboard is too much—because the car is decelerating too suddenly—then the sensor knows the car must be crashing and it triggers the airbag to save your life. Today, accelerometers have moved well beyond cars. They are everywhere, monitoring your every move: They measure how many steps you take; they monitor the movement of your phone; they are in your gaming consoles; tablets, cameras and so on.

We envisioned the microrelay having similar possibilities. We imagined a tiny switch, surrounded by electronics, to create all sorts of new functionality. The need expressed by Nortel was our very first indication that we were on the right path. Their application was particularly compelling because it fit our vision exactly. We wanted to build a mechanical switch into an electronic circuit to create new functionality that had never been realized before.

Of course, whenever you experience highs, there are also lows, and these lows are as uniquely negative as the highs are positive. The highs and lows experienced in entrepreneurial activity are a characteristic—I would even say a feature—of this sport. Experienced entrepreneurs learn to become somewhat inured to the extremes, but it is very easy to be blinded when you finally, finally get a ball in your hands. And it is only human to feel wretched when you get gut-punched by something that snatches it back out of your hands.

This is exactly where I found myself on that fateful day in 1998, flying back to Raleigh from the ice storm in Ottawa. What had started so promising in that first meeting with Nortel had ended in complete and utter failure less than a year later. It had failed gradually, like a slow-motion train wreck, always leaving us with just enough hope to keep our dream of success and riches alive. This is not at all uncommon for entrepreneurs: Once we have a cherished ball, we steadfastly hold on to it under all circumstances. If we succeed, our stubbornness is glorified as perseverance—an essential quality for any entrepreneur. If we fail, it's disparaged as craziness, that we held on to our dream too long, ignoring all signs of impending doom.

Our meeting with Nortel—*the* meeting—had been so perfect. We walked out of there with our new ball affixed with glue to our fingers, fully convinced that we were on the road to success. Matt and his crew went off to build the perfect microrelay for Nortel. Even more importantly, we had direct access to a true champion for our technology: Gregory Hansen. When I met him in that first meeting, I had not fully grasped Gregory's stature within the Nortel organization. I soon found out that he managed a team of over 1000 engineers! As such, he was a very busy man, but always gracious in his interactions with us. And true to his word, he put us in touch with the engineers at Nortel responsible for relays and greased the skids for a full evaluation of our devices.

In spite of this, I quickly learned having the boss as a champion was not a magic ticket for us to circumvent normal corporate bureaucracy. It's easy to believe when you have the boss on your side that things will be easy. Far from it. Gregory's approval was simply an invitation to come into the corporate fold. Once in, we had to follow procedures and protocol like anyone else.

Soon after our meeting, I phoned Gregory with the goal of organizing our collaboration to build the next generation linecard. I looked forward to expanding our friendship and doing great things together. With great anticipation, I called his direct number only to find myself immediately on the phone with his personal secretary. I introduced myself and quickly got down to business.

"We met with Mr. Hansen the other day, and I would like a follow-up call with him. Is he available?"

"Follow-up call? Can you give me your name again? What company?" The secretary was brusque.

"Yeah. Jesko von Windheim. MCNC. In North Carolina? We met with Mr. Hansen and a group of his engineers last week and we're developing a microrelay for them. But I need to confirm some things—"

"Oh, I'm sorry, yes. Well, Mr. Hansen is very busy. I don't see anything on his agenda for you. I'm not sure what to say, but I will definitely have to discuss this with him first. And you are doing what? What did you call it?" A firmness was creeping into the secretary's voice that I did not like at all.

I worked hard to remain polite. "A microrelay. We discussed it with Mr. Hansen last week when he was in Raleigh."

"In Raleigh? I personally organized every aspect Mr. Hansen's agenda last week! Mr.… ah… Sir. I certainly know that there were no meetings about a… a… micro. There were no meetings at your organization. If you are trying to sell something—"

"Oh, no. No! I'm sorry." It finally dawned on me what was happening. "I understand now! No, no. NO! I'm not selling! Honestly. This meeting was added at the last minute here in North Carolina by my friend Brad Carney. So, this probably wasn't on your agenda. It was a *special* meeting. Don't worry about it, I'm positive Mr. Hansen will want to talk to me."

"Brad? Look, Sir. I'm very sorry, but I must speak with Mr. Hansen first. He is extremely busy, and he is certainly not available at this moment. I will discuss this with him and get back to you."

"Get back to me? Okay, can we talk this afternoon?"

She was very professional, but at this point I may have heard a snort on the other end of the line. Very sweetly, she addressed me like a child: "I'm afraid you don't understand. Mr. Hansen is travelling in Asia right now. I won't see him until next week at the earliest. I'll call you after I meet with him. Thank you."

Click.

In spite of our run-in, the secretary was true to her word. She called me back two weeks later to schedule a call with Gregory. He certainly was very busy, so it took another week before he could get on the phone with me. All in all, it had been more than four weeks since we first met at MCNC. Given my desire to do things overnight, it was excruciating.

Gregory, however, was as gracious as ever. He continued to express enthusiasm for the microrelay.

"We just need to get it evaluated, Jesko. We have a really strong relay team here, and I'm going to put you in touch with them so that they can do a complete technical evaluation. I've already let them know about your technology. In the meantime, I will remain your contact on the business side."

I thought it was a good step forward. I put Matt Steel directly in contact with Nortel's team of relay engineers and gladly took on the "business" role with Gregory Hansen. What I hadn't counted on was the time that everything would take.

Quite often people will tell you—or, at least, have told me—that inserting a new technology into an established market is an optimal pathway for commercializing new innovations. The reasoning behind this is pretty straight forward: You sell your product to an established customer (e.g., Nortel), who has an established product and sales channel (linecards for office telephones), and you have an immediate volume of business (50 million relays at $2 apiece). Presumably you simply displace incumbent, old technology and ride into the sunset on the coattails of your customer's established profits.

It's seductive reasoning but not nearly as easy as it sounds, because the other characteristic of an established business is that all the risk has been squeezed out of it. Not only is your customer already making money, but everyone is sleeping well at night doing it. There is no turbulence! For this reason, no matter how "innovative" an established business professes to be, when engineers and managers and executives come up against the reality of the risk in a new technology, they balk. Who wants turbulence if there is an option for a smooth flight path? They can do this by simply saying "no," or they might give you a "maybe" like the manager at IBM in Fishkill, or they can slow-roll technology evaluation—testing your product for years to squeeze out all possible risk before considering its introduction.

Given this, from Nortel's perspective there was no motivation to move quickly on the microrelay. They had an established business with an established product, and they were leaders in the marketplace. Sure, they would like to see improvements, but, at the end of the day, if improvements didn't happen, there was no obvious downside. On the other hand, adopting a new technology could have disastrous consequences. Measure twice, cut once—that approach made a lot of sense in an industry where, when people picked up the phone, they expected a dial tone under all circumstances.

Each test cycle we did with the Nortel team took excruciating months. We would send samples; they would agree to test; we would wait a month or so with no results; I would phone Gregory Hansen—or more accurately his secretary—to see if he could prod the relay engineers; we would wait another month; and then maybe get a result. Results were good, but improvements were needed. As so often happens, our ball was imperfect, and we would need to make changes. Consequently, there would be some design and fabrication on our side which would take a month or more before we could start the cycle again.

In the meantime, in the back of my mind, Shelby's doomsday clock was winding down inexorably towards our 3-year deadline.

Desperate for other commercial applications for the microrelay, I found one at a startup (the polar opposite from Nortel) called Simpler Networks in

Canada who had heard of us through engineers at Nortel. This startup was trying to do something no one had ever done before: to replace the public telephone exchange's physical patch panel with a fully-automated electrical cross-connect switch.

You've probably driven past patch-panel buildings—also called central office buildings—before without realizing what they are. Usually ugly, windowless, brick buildings in the middle of nowhere, these buildings house all the interconnections that are needed to connect landline telephones to the public telephone system. In the early days of telecommunications, a human operator was needed to make physical connections between two telephones, as you may have seen in old movies. Operators would sit in front of a large patch panel and physically move connections on a switchboard in order to connect one caller to another. The operator was soon replaced by automated switching systems of which the linecard was an important piece. The linecard automatically connected a phone call to a central switch, which then automatically routed the call to wherever it was supposed to go, and human operators were no longer needed.

Improved, automated switching, mostly using relay technology, was central to this revolution in communications. But the patch panel in the central office, the system that physically connected your land line phone into the larger network, was never automated. Simpler Networks wanted to change that by building the mother of all switches called an electrical cross-connect switch. Their initial product was to be a switch matrix with 200 inputs that could be automatically switched to any one of 200 outputs. In order to realize this in one system, they would need $200 \times 200 = 40,000$ independent relays! And this was only the start; they envisioned even bigger cross-connect switches in the future.

This relatively humble product was a non-starter using conventional relay technology. Not only were conventional relays too large—a 200-port switch matrix would be the size of a washing machine—the idea of servicing individual relays in these systems was a nightmare. Simpler Network's new, expressed need seemed like everything we could have hoped for: small size, integration, and unprecedented functionality. It was the perfect storm for our microrelay technology, and it was attracting interest in other companies beyond Simpler Networks.

While we had been excited about Nortel's need for 50 million relays, the volume requirements for electrical cross-connect switches was in another stratosphere. Forecasts from Simpler Networks and others projected a need exceeding 30,000 *systems* per year. Even the simplest systems needed 40,000 relays! We were looking at a need for *billions* of microrelays. Nortel had looked great, but now it seemed like we had hit the motherload.

But of course, it wouldn't be that easy. If it had been, someone would already have done it. On the one hand, the volume this opportunity represented was amazing. It was just the kind of opportunity that would not only drive a high growth business but would also attract mainstream venture capital. On the downside, the price that these relays could support was terrible! We were being told that the price had to be less than seven cents per relay! My very rosiest estimate for the cost of manufacturing was six cents. This was not the kind of business anyone would be interested in. Dejected, I told Matt about our conundrum.

"Well… there might be some things we can do on cost," he told me with a furrowed brow. "I can think of more efficient designs. That would allow us to pack more devices into each production run."

"How much more efficient?"

"So far we have been focusing on making the relays work. I think, when we optimize the design, we'll be able to make them about half the size they are now. So, if that works, you would get about twice as many relays out of a production run."

"That would be huge! I could cut all my cost estimates in half!"

"Okay. Okay. Don't get too excited, Jesko. I'm just guessing at this point. Who knows? The more efficient design may not work. I mean, be careful. We haven't even proven our current design for Nortel and now we're already talking about making major changes to hit this crazy price point."

I knew Matt was right. To come up with an economic scenario that would make things work out, we were starting to make some very rosy assumptions. It was frustrating because the need seemed clear and compelling, and there was a good chance we had a solution. But—and it was a solid but—the solution might never be cheap enough. In this situation the proclivity to fool yourself intensifies greatly. You have your ball and you are desperate to not let it go. You know how rare it is to even be here. You want so much for your innovation to intersect with a need that you are willing to lie, even to yourself, especially when there is a clock ticking and you are running out of options.

"Of course, we can do it! I'll let Simpler Networks know we think we can do it," I exclaimed.

"I guess. It's your call," Matt replied.

The other problem we had with the cross-connect switch was that, in this case *all* the prospective customers were startups, quite often not much more sophisticated about telecommunications applications than we were. Even worse, they were mostly underfunded. There were no $50,000 checks from them to get started. In many cases they needed us to prove our technology would work in order for *them* to be able to go out and raise funds. It was the worst possible place. We were facing design risk, cost risk, financing risk, and even our customers were risks! Moving forward with these opportunities had all the potential to turn into a nightmare.

Nortel's linecard application, in contrast, was much less exciting, but also more realistic. While there appeared to be an equal level of design risk, the price point was heavenly compared to the cross-connect application. And Nortel was a huge company that would have no problem funding development, *if* they wanted to. Unfortunately, when it came to relays, Nortel was just as stingy as the rest of the industry. They wanted to evaluate free samples before making any commitments.

In the end, we pursued both applications. We couldn't afford not to. With the clock ticking and MCNC running out of cash, it was clear that, like Unitive before us, we would need to raise capital and venture out on our own if we wanted to succeed. In this scenario, while Nortel represented a blue-chip product opportunity, their product alone was not enough to generate investor interest. The cross-connect switch, on the other hand, had compelling volumes and an exciting story from multiple potential customers, even if they were mostly startups themselves. To raise the money that our venture needed, it was clear that we needed both.

With that in mind we started building a business case anchored by the relatively stable Nortel application in the short term to be fueled by explosive growth of the high-risk electrical cross-connect switch in the long term. It was a business case sleight of hand supported by carefully targeted marketing message. Although we had much more confidence in the Nortel application, we also knew that investors would not be inspired by a vision of replacing relays in linecards. With internet communications expanding day-by-day and voice over internet protocol (VOIP) on the horizon, an argument could be made that the Nortel relay was a dying business. The cross-connect, on the other hand, was incredibly risky, but exciting and was sure to attract investors, if pitched properly.

This kind of contradiction is not uncommon if you are an entrepreneur. You are pitching one thing to attract investors (super high volumes for cross-connect switches) and in reality, doing another (relays for linecards), meanwhile praying that it all works out in the end. Selling a deal always requires some smoke and mirrors. To some extent, investors expect it, but at the end of the day, any pitch made to investors has to be consistent with reality; you can't cross the line to pitch something you know is untrue or highly unlikely.

We were lucky in that, independent of the cross-connect growth story we were pushing, the Nortel application was a solid business-building opportunity, even if investors were not inspired by it. I believed the Nortel application was the best opportunity we had, and I was all in, which made things all the more painful when the wheels started coming off.

# Into the Storm

How do the wheels come off in a venture? Often in multiple ways. It was the end of 1997 and with $2 million already cut from our budget, many of the technical groups at MCNC were starting to feel the pressure from the State subsidy curtailment. At the same time, Shelby's short circuiting of good risk management practices in support of the networking group's full court press into gaming networks began to show signs of impending doom. Preserve would have been an incremental, low-cost step towards commercial activity for the networking group. In contrast, the gaming network was becoming an increasingly high-cost, all-or-nothing adventure into the unknown. Things got eerily quiet in the fishbowl.

Then our relays started blowing up. Literally. We got failed samples back from Nortel that were nothing more than black carbon and shattered bits of metal. Matt, generally as cool as Steve McQueen, was flustered.

"What the F…? What the heck did these guys do to our relays?" he demanded, rhetorically. He was in my office showing me the remnants of what had once been fully functional devices. Even with the naked eye you could see that things were not as they should be. Although you could not see individual structures, our devices were usually shiny and regular in appearance. These were not. They were black and pitted, looking more like scraps of charcoal than the beautiful devices we sent Nortel.

Under microscope they looked even worse. It looked like someone had carried out miniature trench warfare on their surfaces: There were explosive pits and dangling streams of metal that had previously been part of the elegant fishbone structure. Among the ruins were globules of metal, signifying extreme temperatures where nickel had melted and re-solidified.

"You're kidding me," I said in wonderment. "What the heck did they do? Take a hammer to them?"

"A hammer wouldn't do this. This looks more like a blowtorch."

"Hmmm, a blowtorch test? Have you talked to the Nortel engineers?"

"Not yet. But I'm scheduled to talk to them tomorrow."

"Okay, this has to be some kind of mistake. Let me know as soon as you hear from them."

When Matt returned to my office the next day, his look of concern spoke volumes. By now, we'd gone through a number of evaluation tests with Nortel, and I'd never seen Matt express this level of concern. Certainly, things had not been perfect, especially in the beginning. But whenever we had problems, Matt solved them. He improved the device design, fabricated new relays, and sent them back with good results. He worked magic in the early days, in those beakers in his office. He could make anything work.

"It's called a lightning strike spec," he told me, soberly.

"What the heck is a lighting-strike spec?"

"It's not good. It's an electrical jolt of 15,000 volts for 10 milli-seconds. That simulates a lightning strike."

"Why on earth …?"

"Well. It seems that Nortel has concerns about their customers dying while they are on the phone. Apparently, that would not be good for business." Matt's rare black humor was not inspiring me to feel any better.

"Actually, it makes a lot of sense," he continued, more seriously. "When you pick up a phone in the middle of a thunderstorm, Nortel doesn't want you to be fried if lightning strikes nearby. This test makes sure that the relay can withstand a lightning strike to the phone line, so the caller stays safe, no matter what."

"Wow. Okay. I sure wish they had done this test first instead of all the other stuff they had us do. So, what do we need to do to fix it?" I was confident that Matt could figure out how to pass this test. He'd always done it before.

"Let me look at it," Matt said as he left my office.

I was worried about this new revelation, but also confident. I had the best MEMS engineering team in the world on my side. We had already passed a bunch of tests. What was one more? I knew our team could do it!

But I was wrong, Matt returned to my office two days later with a look of resignation on his face. Defeat. My heart dropped like a stone.

Matt saw my look of concern and didn't try to sugar coat it. "Yeah. It's bad. I tried to figure out how to design around the spec, so I got a hold of a relay that is currently approved for the linecard and I pulled it apart."

"Pulled it apart?"

"Yeah, you know, I took the cover off to see how its built. Damn, I can't believe I didn't think of doing that before."

"Cover? What the heck do you mean? What's so important about taking a damn relay apart?" I was on the edge of my seat and I couldn't believe that Matt, who was usually so succinct, was dragging this out.

"Well, I discovered how they design those relays to withstand the lightning strike spec and it's terrible news for us. You know why those relays are so damn big?"

"No. Of course not, Matt! I'm no relay engineer! Get to the damn point!"

"Okay. Okay. 15,000 volts for 10 ms is a heck of a lot of energy, even if it is only happening over a very short period of time. The way they design those relays to handle the energy is they make them bigger! They actually hang huge hunks of metal on them for the sole purpose of absorbing energy."

"Absorbing energy?" I was lost.

"Yeah. A piece of metal can absorb energy, just like a bathtub can fill up with water. The bigger the tub, the more water it can hold. The bigger the hunk of metal, the more energy it can hold. Well, it turns out that the linecard relays have hunks of metal that are just large enough to absorb 15,000 volts for 10 ms. That's why those relays are so damn big!"

"Is there anything we can do? Can't you design around it?"

"No, that's the problem. It's just plain physics. And, in this case, physical laws are against us. With our relays, we're actually doing the exact opposite of what needs to be done to pass this spec. We're making our devices smaller and that's why we see such spectacular destruction. There is just no way our tiny devices can pass the lightning strike spec."

It was the worst possible news. But I still had fight left in me. "Okay, but that's only one stupid spec! We passed all the other ones. What's that? Nine out of ten? Isn't that good enough?"

In spite of the situation, Matt managed a laugh. "No! Of course not. This isn't like a test in school where 90 percent gets you an 'A'. We have to pass them all. 100 percent. And this is *the* most critical spec. I talked to their engineers. We didn't just fail. Our devices were *vaporized*. We achieved a level of failure that has never been seen before! This kills it."

I was shocked. Shocked by the result and shocked by the abruptness of it all. My blood boiled at the thought of it: Engineers were always such bloody sticklers! And half the time it was just a huge navel-gazing exercise. This couldn't be right. I wouldn't—couldn't—take "no" for an answer. Nortel was too important. There had to be some way around this.

Screw it up in engineering, fix it in marketing. I prepared for battle.

"I'm gonna talk to Gregory Hansen. We'll find a way to fix this. Maybe *they* can design around it on their linecard. There has to be some way."

Matt shrugged his shoulders and didn't try to dissuade me. He had respect for my ability to sell. If I wanted to try to convince Nortel to buy relays that would fry their customers, he was not going to stand in my way.

I got on the phone immediately and, of course, reached Gregory's secretary. And of course, he was busy and it would be difficult to schedule a call. Wasn't it Thanksgiving in the States? And then there was Christmas. Blah, blah, blah. It would be very difficult to schedule a phone call. But I was having none of it.

"No. No. No phone call. I'm flying up." I told her. "I need to meet with Gregory, and I'm coming to Ottawa to do it."

"Meeting? Well, I'm not sure, I..."

"Talk to Gregory. Tell him I have to meet with him. I'll fly up any time he wants. You can pick the date."

She was dubious, but she did talk to Gregory. And he responded as I would have expected. Always gracious and polite, he couldn't turn me down if I was going to make the effort to fly all the way up to Ottawa. It was late November, and his secretary and I finally agreed on a date that worked with Gregory's schedule: the second week of January.

I was on pins and needles for a month and a half as I waited to fix this thing. In the meantime, it was becoming abundantly clear that Shelby's clock was ticking faster than ever. Shelby's meetings with the MCNC Board of Directors increased in frequency as he attempted to address a cash crunch that had become steadily magnified by his ill-fated, high-risk investment into gaming networks within the networks services group. The rewards had not materialized, and the risk was coming home to roost. Yes, it was just a month and a half, but it seemed like a lifetime.

It's hard to describe the feeling of a deal gone bad.

To understand, you have to start with the elation of that first meeting in the MCNC boardroom, then consider the central nature of the relay in all of our plans to raise money and build a business, then layer on the level of effort and time and commitment that we had put into it, and finally top that all off with the sudden and crushing finality of our epic failure on the lightning strike spec.

We had walked out of the MCNC boardroom convinced we finally had a ball and could play the startup game. We felt invincible. All our dreams seemed within our grasp, wealth and fulfillment were just around the corner. Now, the dream, which had so recently felt like certainty, was crushed. Our lifeline to an independent business, outside of MCNC, was gone. With the larger cash crunch at MCNC, it appeared that even our jobs were in jeopardy. Under these conditions, many would-be entrepreneurs will make bad decisions. You've probably read about situations like this in media and wondered: "How on earth was that person so stupid?"

Desperate times require desperate measures, and desperate measures can push you off the cliff. Theranos is one example, but there are many more.

For six weeks, as the pressure built at MCNC and our plans for a relay business lay in tatters, I felt like a caged animal being prepared for slaughter. It was clear to me that I had one shot left—to meet with Gregory Hansen and convince him to buy our relays. I'd find some way to make this work. I had to.

I am not sure what drives persistence in a person. Stubbornness mixed with a bit of arrogance, perhaps. For myself, all I know is that I get into situations where I simply cannot convince myself to stop. It becomes physically impossible for me to give up my pursuit. Of course, there are times where my rational mind tells me it's time to quit and walk away, like I did with the Preserve project. But then there are other times, when the idea of walking away just cannot penetrate my skull. That's what happened to me with the diamond-like-carbon project at Kobe Steel. All my peers went in one direction and I went in another, and I couldn't bring myself to make a change, even though it negatively impacted my health and my career at the time.

The microrelay was like that too. I couldn't stop myself from pursuing this deal. I would have walked into hell on bare feet to try to save it. As it was, I didn't have to walk into hell, but I did fly into one of the most devastating ice storms to ever hit North America.

The storm started with a quiet drizzle on January 4, 1998, and by January 8 it had wreaked havoc across a large swath of Ontario through Quebec up into Nova Scotia. In all, the 'Great Ice Storm' dropped almost three inches (seven cm) of freezing rain in Ottawa creating ice sheets of epic proportions. Five million people lost power, 35 people died, transmission line towers—those huge metal structures that carry electrical power lines across our nation—pancaked under the weight of the ice.

In the middle of it all, I got a call from Gregory's secretary. "Oh, you can't come up here. Everything's shut down. You wouldn't believe the ice, eh?'

But what I couldn't believe is what I was hearing. I hadn't paid any attention to the weather in Canada—it was very nice in North Carolina—so this was news to me. It was like God's hand was reaching down and trying to stop this deal from happening, but I wasn't having it. I could already foresee the next meeting being set at Easter. Fitting, perhaps, for a deal I was trying to raise from the dead, but too far away by a long shot.

"Do you have power?" I demanded.

"Oh, yes we do. You see, we're a manufacturing site. So, we have our own generators. We are the only facility up and running in the whole region!"

"Well, I'm coming up then!"

"Oh, really! You shouldn't do that! It's just not safe! I'm not even sure hotels are open. *Nothing* is open!"

But it turned out that the Westin Hotel in Ottawa had generators too. Moreover, planes were flying and, most importantly, landing. "I'm coming up," I told her on a second call.

It was a lonely flight. Not many people were rushing up to the ice kingdom. The Westin Hotel was eerie too. The generators were working, but everything seemed half lit. Outside, things were surreal. I remember the ice and most of all a haziness that hung over everything. It wasn't raining anymore, but there was a light blanketing fog. And other than the Westin Hotel and the Nortel facility, once I reached it, there were no lights, no cars, no people. I was a very lonely salesman on a distant planet.

The surreal nature of the outside world contrasted sharply with the normalcy in the Nortel facility. Here, people were going about their business without any acknowledgement at all of mother nature's ferocious assault on the region. Nortel was proudly and smoothly powering forward, all cylinders firing as they should be.

Somewhat to my surprise, Gregory received me himself. Though I'd had my doubts at times, I found out quickly that he was indeed an influential figure in the organization. Many of the people in the facility reported to him and he had unfettered access to the executive suite. Even more to my surprise, he had set aside the day to host me. He personally guided me around, showing me the facility, meeting with the engineers, and even setting up a meeting with one of the top executives in the company. He was amazing and the impression he made that day has endured.

For all his kindness, it was also clear that my desperate attempt to turn our relay project around was a non-starter. The engineers I met with were as crystal clear as Matt had been, except that they spoke with brutal authority. They were the decision makers after all. The meeting with the Nortel executive was completely unexpected and fascinating, as we spent twenty minutes in private, discussing the explosion that was happening in telecommunications. Then I toured the manufacturing facility, topped off by the gift of a hand-held, Nortel-branded ice-scraper. It was icy outside after all.

Closure came in the form of a friendly handshake and suggestion that I might find a better reception for our technology in the photonics group, coupled with a name—Jake Wilson—and a phone number, with a clear message not to come back this way again. A true "Dear John" letter, but delivered in person by Gregory Hansen. I cringed inwardly at the first-class brush-off. He was pawning me off on a group in "photonics"—what the heck was that?

I had to hand it to Gregory: He was one smooth operator. I'd gone up, ready to do battle, *determined* to win the relay business, and I had been killed with kindness. A year's effort, significant time and money invested into a linecard relay, a job on the rocks, a dream shattered, and I had an ice scraper and a handshake to show for it. I felt like I had just been dumped by a girlfriend, in the nicest possible way.

I guess I should have seen the humor in it, but all I felt was sick. Sick, sick, sick. I had "failure" written in huge letters on my forehead. Bob West's words again came back to haunt me. I had a throbbing headache. To top it all off, my flight back to Raleigh had me in a stupid, lurching plane, shaking my head back and forth like an idiot.

You see, it wasn't just the trip to Ottawa and the failed microrelay that were bothering me on that flight home. It wasn't just bitter recriminations. To me this was much more than just another failed venture. The fact was: I was frightened. I was working ten to eighteen hours a day and *failing*! It was a terrible, terrible feeling. If this had been a sport, I just left everything on the field and still came away with a big fat zero. And it wasn't just that my hard work had failed me. Whatever talents I had; they had failed me too. I had nothing left to give. And now what? It's not like I had some sort of Plan B for life.

On top of all that, things at MCNC were deteriorating at a breakneck speed. Shelby's decision to invest significant sums in the network gaming platform was causing huge cracks to form in the foundation of the organization. Although I was not privy to day-to-day executive activities, I saw enough to know that our fishbowl was transforming into a pressure cooker made of glass. This environment of fear put strain on everybody, spawning unpredictable behavior, and an every-person-for-themselves attitude. Turbulence did not even begin to describe what I was experiencing at MCNC.

Even worse, it now seemed that failure was becoming a pattern for me. I had come to the United States to pursue diamond thin-film technology, but that failed. I had championed diamond-like carbon for plastics, but that failed. I pursued e-commerce at MCNC, but that failed. I led the charge on microrelays with the help of the best engineering team in the world, but that failed. I had ignored the sage advice of Bob West. I had turned down Buffalo. I was getting a master's class in the downside of risk taking. Why the *heck* could I not be normal? My friends all had real jobs and were doing *great*! They lived in fancy houses and drove fancy cars and went on fancy vacations.

They played the corporate game and simply shrugged off the crap that rolled downhill. Why on earth could I not be like that?

As we came in for our landing at Raleigh-Durham, my head throbbed miserably and I still felt like smashing it onto the bulkhead in front of me.

To this day, I remember arriving home.

In contrast to Ottawa, it was a warm, sunny afternoon in Raleigh. My very pregnant wife was outside when I pulled up. I felt depressed, very much like the time I lost my job with Kobe Steel. I was thinking the worst. Nothing like a third child on the way and no job, I grumbled to myself as I parked. I got out of the car and tiredly retrieved my luggage, my body language oozing misery and dejection and self-pity. With nothing much to say, I simply showed off my hard-won prize: the Nortel ice scraper. The irony of it all was grating.

"That's it," I whined. "This is the sum total of my achievement with Nortel."

Monika knew how important this was to me—to us. We were now almost a family of five and my job was hanging by a thread. She'd lived through my past frustrations and had a good sense of how this failed effort with Nortel was affecting me. On the other hand, Monika was and continues to be blessed with a unique ability to simply ignore unpleasantness.

Also, her perspective was different than mine. She had no aspirations to conquer the world and she was pretty happy with what we had already achieved. We'd come a long way from a basement apartment in Rockwood, Canada, with a mattress on the floor and with twisted, whitewashed plywood imitating kitchen cabinetry. We had a used Honda Accord with power steering and *air conditioning*—a big step up from the Ford Escort we had driven to North Carolina from Canada. We had a nice house in Raleigh that was almost big enough for a family of five…

She looked from the grimace on my face to the ice scraper in my hand and back again. Then she burst out laughing. She laughed loud and hard. It's a guffaw that I hate. It's so stupid, it doesn't even sound real! How could she do this to me in my hour of need?

I tried hard to remain grim, to hang on to my self-pity, to hang it around my shoulders like a safety blanket, but I couldn't do it. Soon I was laughing too. You win some, you lose some, and if you can't see some humor in it, you'll go crazy. Thank God for Monika's attitude.

I still have that ice scraper and it has always held a prominent place in my home. I have never used it to scrape ice.

# Pivot

The term "pivot" has a special meaning for the startup community. We don't say: "We failed and now we are desperately trying to do something else." We say: "We pivoted."

This use was probably coined by some Silicon Valley guru entrepreneur who was raising a new round of funding and knew very well that his venture capital buddies needed to hear something better than failure and desperation. Communication is everything in life. In contrast to the terminal, ugly nature of the word failure, the word pivot conjures grace and intent. It's like a ballerina performing a perfect pirouette after decades of training. Startups pivot all the time. It's pretty much expected: "Yeah, we were building a flying car, but we've pivoted to an app that counts calories in ten languages."

Doesn't that sound impressive? It implies so much. The flying car sounded pretty cool, but *pivoting* to the app suggests that this new direction is even better! It also gives the impression that the change in direction was brilliantly conceived and flawlessly executed. Yes, if nothing else, good entrepreneurs are masters at selling a grand vision for the future, and the simple word pivot is part of that sell.

Well, we pivoted with MEMS, but it was neither brilliantly conceived, nor flawlessly executed. Our pivot into photonics was thrust upon us by a market that screamed for a solution that we held in our hands but could not comprehend. You see, it's one thing to see a need; it's quite another to understand it and respond effectively. Fortunately for us, we were dragged into photonics by some very insistent customers who forced us to wake up. We did so in the nick of time.

Our pivot highlighted how great technology teams can be directionally right and specifically wrong. The MCNC software engineer who first taught me about e-commerce in the network services group was probably the best example of this phenomenon that I have ever encountered. But our MEMS team was not far behind. Early on, when we first sat down to discuss potential applications of MEMS technology, the engineering team correctly identified telecommunications as the area with the greatest potential for MEMS commercialization. Within telecommunications they identified optical communications (which they referred to it as "electro-optics") and electrical communications (which included wired and wireless applications). It was between these two that we veered very slightly off path.

"Electro-optics is a tiny market with esoteric applications," the team assured me. "It's not worth going after. MEMS need high volumes to be cost effective and electrical communications are huge, especially wireless communications. That's going to take over the world."

They were correct on every count, except for their assessment of the electro-optics opportunity. Electro-optics was not even the correct term for it: We were talking about optical communications and its underlying technology more commonly referred to as photonics. Not that we knew the terminology. Our engineers were perfectly right in the sense that photonics had indeed been a sleepy little cottage industry. But even as we met to discuss our strategy, the photonics market was exploding, and it was exploding so fast that no one on our team—and most certainly not me—was aware of it.

It is frighteningly easy to miss the real target when you are working on a revolutionary, new technology. It's like a moon-shot: If your angle is just a little bit off, you might have a spectacular launch and flight, but will miss landing on the moon. With our microrelay, we were diligently working on the next generation bottle rocket as the optical communications space shuttle was launching next door. We had no idea. Regrettably, when you hear the noise, and feel the rumble of the rocket engines it's often too late. Imagine running outside to look to the sky only to see a plume of smoke. In a heartbeat, the opportunity has come and gone. The shuttle, which you can no longer see, has taken a lucky few into space, and everyone else is standing with both feet firmly planted on the ground wondering what could have been. That was almost us.

In our case, we made a tiny miscalculation when we approached the telecommunications market. We had the team, we had the technology, and we had unique capability to design and deliver MEMS devices. We just pointed all of that capability in the wrong direction . Simply put, as we worked on the microrelay in our beakers, we were blissfully unaware that a tsunami was building in an ocean of opportunity called optical communications.

The photonics wave started forming in the 1980s when a new technology called wavelength division multiplexing—referred to by its acronym WDM—was developed in the laboratory. At the time the world was starting the move from communications based on electrical signals, using copper cables, to communications based on light, using optical fibers.

Optical fibers are thin strands of glass, less than half a millimeter thick that can be stretched for miles and miles. A major breakthrough occurred when Corning, one of our most venerated U.S. companies, invented fibers that were pure enough to successfully pass light over these long distances with only small losses. This innovation opened the door for using light signals, instead of electrical signals for communications. The great thing about optical communications is that you can communicate much more information, at a much faster rate, on a single strand of fiber than you can with electrical signals on a single strand of copper.

To understand the power of optical communications, a good analogy might be a roadway carrying cars and people into a city. Imagine a one-lane road in California running from Santa Barbara down the coast into Los Angeles. It's a single lane where the cars can only travel at 30 miles an hour. The distance is about 90 miles, so on this imaginary road only a relatively few people will get in and out of Los Angeles every day. Given the large number of people who want to make the trip, there will be a huge traffic jam.

Now, imagine you can magically transform this road into a high-speed rail line with a bullet train that can instantaneously reach speeds of 300 miles an hour. In this new scenario, a lot more people are going to make it in and out of Los Angeles.

That's what happened when we went from copper to optical fiber, except the speed of the data stream wasn't 300 miles per hour, it was the speed of light which is 670,600,000 miles per hour! The value of transmitting information more quickly and efficiently was so high that telecommunications companies were highly motivated to transition from electrical cables to optical fibers, especially for long-distance communications. Those that didn't make this shift, were left behind.

Optical fiber communications were great, but WDM was the real innovation and smart engineers were just getting started. By the mid-1990s, WDM technology started to really take off in commercial applications by taking advantage of the fact that light comes in different colors. Anyone who has seen an optical prism or a rainbow knows that white light can split into myriad colors ranging from violet, through blue and green, then yellow, orange and red, with many more shades in between. The WDM innovation initially took two colors out of that rainbow—each color representing an independent stream of ultra-fast communications—and combined (multiplexed) them onto one fiber. The two data streams could zip along the fiber at the speed of light, and then be split apart again (de-multiplexed) at the far end. It was like suddenly being able to run *two* high-speed bullet trains on one track! The value creation was unprecedented. With only a few changes of equipment at either end of the fiber, that fiber was now worth twice as much. The telecommunications industry went crazy.

In this environment, companies that were building WDM equipment, like Nortel and Lucent and startups like Juniper Networks and Ciena, were doing very well, indeed. A measure of this could be found in the Nasdaq composite stock index which tracks the value of the top one hundred technology companies in the United States. Between 1995 and the beginning of 2000, the index went from 1000 to 5000; an increase of 5 times in just five years! Previously it took 15 years (from 1980 to 1995) to increase the value of the index 5 times. In large part, this surge was driven by innovations in communications. There were immense riches to be made and the telecommunications goldrush was on.

The WDM innovations kept coming. Soon we were up to *eight* independent lines of transmission on one fiber and then *sixteen*. Today, using an advanced version of WDM, we can fit up to 160 independent data streams on one fiber! In less than a generation we have moved from a single stream of cars driving into Los Angeles at 30 miles an hour to where we now have 160 bullet trains, all travelling simultaneously on a single track. It's an information ultra-highway that fuels almost everything we do today, putting giga-bytes of information instantaneously at our disposal in the palm of our hand. If you are amazed, like I am, by our ability to stream live events and movies, in high definition, to our smartphones in real time, anywhere around the world, optical fibers and WDM are largely what has made that possible.

The next challenge that engineers faced was how to move information on and off the communications ultra-highway. What if you don't want to go all the way to Los Angeles? What if you want to get off at Ventura or Thousand Oaks or Beverly Hills? Various technologies were developed to do this, but the most important one was the optical switch. The very simplest optical switch was called a $1 \times 2$. In this switch, a tiny mirror could be dropped in front of an optical signal to send it in another direction. An analogy would be shining a flashlight at a wall in front of you, and then putting a mirror in the way at 45 degrees to instead direct the light to a wall beside you. With optical switching technology, the "bullet train" no longer had to go from just one spot to another. It could now be instantaneously re-directed to Ventura or Thousand Oaks or Beverly Hills or anywhere in the world.

For communications visionaries the simple $1 \times 2$ switch was never good enough. Very much like the high capacity, electrical cross-connect switch Simpler Networks wanted for electrical communications, many companies wanted to build optical cross-connect switches for optical communications. Early efforts focused on $4 \times 4$, $8 \times 8$, and $16 \times 16$ switches. Lucent was crowned the king of optical switching when they came out with the LambdaRouter—a 256-port optical switch. But even this was not enough for some companies—they predicted a 4000-port optical switch was needed!

Another very important device needed to make optical communications work was the optical attenuator. While the optical switch was the rock star of its time, garnering all the attention and notoriety, the attenuator was the quiet cousin no one paid mind to. However, the attenuator solved a critical problem for WDM in that light doesn't move along a fiber perfectly, as there are always some losses that cause the light to get less bright.

To understand the problem, imagine shining a light beam through fog. The light won't reach as far as you would like because the signal is diminished considerably by hitting the fog and scattering off in random directions, instead of moving straight ahead to where you want it to go. Most people have experienced this in their car as they drive through fog—not being able to see nearly as far as they would like to and perhaps even being blinded by light that scatters right back at them. The same happens to a light signal as it moves along a fiber. There are imperfections in the fiber—like fog for the car lights—that cause some of the light to scatter away from the true path in the fiber, diminishing the signal as it travels along to its endpoint.

Because of these losses, the optical communications signal cannot go on forever. Every few miles it has to be refreshed—or boosted—so that when it reaches the other side of the country or the world, it's just as pristine as when it started out. The boosting is pretty easy, but the real problem is that different colors lose power differently in the fiber, so some colors arrive at their boosting station without much loss, while others have dimmed considerably. You experience this optical phenomenon every time you use the fog lights in your car. They are yellow for a reason: Yellow light scatters less and reaches further in fog.

The problem for optical communications is that signal boosting does not work very well if some colors on the fiber are dim and some are very bright. When you boost this signal, the dim colors are properly refreshed, but the bright colors get too bright. When that happens, the optical communications signal is compromised. For a human, it's very much like looking directly at the sun: The bright light from the sun washes out everything in the sky and makes it difficult to see anything else.

This is where the optical attenuator comes in. Attenuators work very much like the dimmer switch you might have for your living room lights. Each stream of light—each color—hits its own attenuator; the dim colors may not be attenuated at all, but the brighter ones are dimmed in such a way that all the different streams of communications have exactly the same level of power after they pass through a set of attenuators. Then, all the signals are boosted at once so that they look exactly the same as when they started out a few miles back. Some miles later the entire process happens again, and, of course, it all happens at the speed of light.

This entire process ensures flawless, high band-width communications, no matter where in the world a signal is coming from. Movies, video conferencing, pictures on Facebook, messages on Snapchat, or any other social media have all evolved from these incredible hardware innovations of the 1980s and 90s.

*This* was the space shuttle that was taking off next door as we diligently worked in our labs with Gregory Hansen and his team on a microrelay for linecards for electrical telecommunications. Linecards that would soon be pretty much obsolete as the bulk of communications moved onto the optical telecommunications ultra-highway that we call the internet.

I consider it a blessing I did not know all this as I flew back from Ottawa on that fateful day in January 1998. Otherwise, I'm sure my depression would have been much, much worse. As bad as it was to have failed with the microrelay for the electrical switch, it would have paled in comparison to the thought of having missed the photonics revolution.

Fortunately for all of us, we were saved. And it was Gregory Hansen who saved us: His Dear John letter opened a door and guided me right up to the launch platform.

In my misery on that day in Ottawa I had totally discounted the reception I received: Gregory Hansen's attentiveness, the tour of the facilities, the meeting with the engineers, and the one-on-one meeting with the executive. In my self-absorbed state, I had focused entirely on the rejection of the microrelay and had discounted everything else as Canadian politeness. The brush-off to some unknown person—Jake Wilson—in something called photonics was just fuel on the fire of my misery. And of course, there was that damned ice scraper! It was a dagger in my heart—a hideous symbol of my failure. In the aftermath of that fateful trip, I fixated on that more than anything.

So, when I got a call from an apparent stranger named Jake Wilson a few days after my return to the United States, I was totally unprepared. "Jake who?" I asked stupidly.

"Uh, Jake *Wilson*. You got my name from Greg Hansen?"

"Jake—oh, yeah! Jake *Wilson*! Of course! Of course. How are you?"

"Very good, thank you. We're still digging out from under all this ice, but other than that, all is good!" Jake was very friendly, just like Gregory Hansen had been and pretty much like every Canadian I had ever met.

"Well, I've got a great Nortel ice scraper here, in case you need one." I said, sullen, trying to get a dig in, still licking my wounds from my recent rejection.

Despite my belligerence, I was also somewhat intrigued. In all my dealings with Nortel thus far, no one had ever called me. It was always me calling Gregory, or more accurately me calling his secretary, me asking for updates, me pushing for meetings. And here, out of nowhere, this person had my phone number and was calling *me*. And he was making quite an effort to build rapport.

"Ha, ha," Jake laughed, cheerfully. "The ice scraper! Greg gave you one of those? He's giving those away to everybody! It's a great joke. The ice is three inches thick and he's giving away hand-held ice scrapers!"

"Ha, ha," I responded halfheartedly. Very funny. Maybe Jake wasn't such a nice Canadian after all.

I was also wary. This guy was no engineer. He was too smooth; it sounded like he might be in sales. Was Nortel now trying to sell *me* something? It was not at all unprecedented that I would try to convince a company to buy MEMS and they would come back and try to sell us something, like a piece of equipment they thought we needed. That would add insult to injury and would be worse than any ice scraper.

But Jake had nothing of the sort on his mind.

"I'm the manager for business development for our photonics group. All of our design and manufacturing is in the United Kingdom, but I work out of Ottawa. My job is to work on emerging business opportunities, and we think you can help us."

"You guys want a microrelay?" I asked, dumbfounded. After all that pain…

"No, no. NO." Jake could not have been more emphatic. He definitely did not want a microrelay. "We need optical switches. Do you guys build optical switches?"

Optical switches? I'd never had a single conversation with our engineers about optical switches. Lots and lots of discussion around electrical switches, but never optical. In Vera's presentation I had seen some crazy structures that included pop-up mirrors, some of which even rotated on stages. But these were not our designs. These were crazy devices designed by others and being built in our facilities. In fact, Vera called them "science projects." I also knew for sure that, other than the microrelay, we had no other product development going on in our MEMS group. But I didn't have to be a genius to get a sense that this guy was buying so, I did what any entrepreneur would do: I started selling.

"Optical switch?" I responded, thinking quickly. "Uh, of course, we do! What kind of optical switch do you need?"

"Our first product target is an 8 × 8 switch matrix. That's what we have immediate demand for. Eventually, we need to get to 256 × 256. Can you guys do that?"

At least I knew from working with Simpler Networks what a switch matrix was. I also knew that an 8 × 8 matrix required 64 independent switches, all working flawlessly. Simpler Networks wanted an electrical switch matrix, using microrelays, which by now were our bread and butter. Nortel wanted an optical switch matrix, which was a whole different ball game. And 256 × 256! That would require more than 65,000 independent optical switches!

"Well, uh, sure… but, you know 8 × 8 is definitely state of the art… and we are almost past capacity with work orders." I hedged desperately, reasonably confident that we had nothing to offer. Like any good salesman I was trying to find a way to set expectations ridiculously low, but at the same time not lose the customer. "So, I think lead times would be quite long. But we love you guys at Nortel! So, um, let me talk to my engineers and get back to you."

At this point I had a simple goal and that was to get off the phone. Although this call had come out of the blue, and this conversation was totally unexpected, I knew immediately that Jake was a serious customer. He wanted—no *needed*—switches right now. He had approached us. He was not going to go away, and I just needed to buy time to come up with a good answer.

"Sure. Thanks, Jesko. Can we talk again tomorrow?"

Tomorrow!? I thought back to the months it sometimes took to get Gregory Hansen on the phone. "Yes, of course." I replied.

With that one, simple statement I was pulled into an amazing vortex called "internet time." There is normal time that we are all used to, where you have seconds, minutes, hours, days, months, and years. But in the world of optical communications, everything moved at internet time, faster than life in the "new economy."

In science fiction fantasies, spaceships are put into warp speed at the push of a button. Usually we know this is happening because all the actors get very serious and individual stars in space suddenly turn into streaks of light. If it's done well in the movies, you feel pushed into the back of your seat, and you feel that you are actually travelling at light speed, even though you have not moved at all. That's how it felt for me that day, moving into this strange new paradigm of internet time. One moment I was thinking about the world of MEMS and microrelays. The next I entered at warp speed into the world of optical communications.

After finishing the call with Jake, I immediately hustled down the hall to see Vera.

"Nortel wants optical switches, Vera. Are we doing anything like that? Haven't we built some for the army?"

"Yeah, we've built them, but they designed them. Those are all foundry customers. And they are all just demonstrations. We've shown that our fabrication process can create pop up micro-mirrors and we've even put them on rotating platforms to steer them around. But they are all other people's science projects—none of that is ready for primetime."

Vera was highlighting both the strengths and weakness of our business model. For the most part we used our fabrication equipment to build MEMS chips for other people. This was called a "foundry" business in which we owned the fabrication facility (also called a "fab") that other people used to build their stuff. Other than the microrelay, which was our own product design, we primarily made money building chips for other people.

"Surely, we have something...?" I half-demanded, half-requested. I had to be careful, because Vera didn't respond well to pushy demands, but I was desperate. This was a "$50,000 to get started" situation. I could feel it in my bones.

"I'm not sure we have anything ourselves...but we build a lot of optical stuff for other people. There's OMM and Lucent."

"OMM? Lucent?" I asked stupidly.

"Yeah, OMM—Optical Micromachines. They are building an 8 × 8 with us. And Lucent is building their LambdaRouter switch with us. They've also built smaller switches, 1 × 2s."

"Are you kidding me? We're building the LambdaRouter?"

"No, no. We're not building the router! We just build the beam-steering chip that goes into the router to get the 256 × 256 functionality."

I was ready to faint. The beam steering chip was one of the most famous MEMS chips out there with pictures of it being heavily promoted by the

Lucent team. This was a perfect example of how MCNC had so much technical development going on, it was impossible to keep up with it all. Here I had been working with the team for all this time, but I was ignorant…

"But those aren't our chips, Jesko." Vera reminded me patiently, as if I was a child. "Those are our customers' proprietary designs. Sure, we build them, but they are not ours and we sure as hell can't sell them. OMM and Lucent give us the designs and we just build what they give us. We're just a foundry for MEMS devices."

Vera looked up to see if I was following this elementary class on how we made money. The look on her face was somewhere between humor and aggravation.

"By, the way," she continued, evidently giving me a passing grade. "you also can't tell anyone. We have very serious secrecy agreements that prevent us from telling anyone that we are the ones building those chips. One of the reasons you haven't heard about it before is exactly because of those agreements. It's on a need-to-know basis only."

"Vera! Come on! We can't just stand by scratching our butts! Nortel wants optical switching! And they're serious! What do you want me to do? Tell them to buy from OMM?"

"Hell no! Go talk to Matt."

# Switching On

Vera had been very smart in building her business at MCNC. In the 1980s, North Carolina invested over $100 million in MCNC to build a state-of-the-art semiconductor design and manufacturing facility. At its inception, the facility had the capacity to design and fabricate the most advanced semiconductor chips in the world—it was a technological wonder that exceeded the capabilities of industry leaders like Intel and Texas Instruments. MCNC was the first organization in the world—or close to it—to design and fabricate a 1 cm × 1 cm (10 mm × 10 mm) electronic chip with one million transistors!

The problem was that, while MCNC focused on semiconductor research and development, companies like Intel and Texas Instruments focused on developing products that generated revenue and profits. With their profits, these companies had the wherewithal to invest in new technologies and new manufacturing infrastructure that soon surpassed MCNC. By 1990, one million transistors were a laughable achievement, but there were no new funds available from the State legislature to upgrade MCNC's capabilities. Even if the State had wanted to, it was impossible to compete in the semiconductor industry without a thriving business that could generate cash. New production facilities were costing half a billion dollars or more, and these state-of-the art production plants were now producing chips with hundreds of millions of transistors on a square centimeter.

Around that time, along came Vera, who understood the semiconductor business and also understood that MEMS were emerging as an important new technology. Vera also recognized that MEMS did not need state-of-the art equipment. MEMS needed exactly the $100 million facility that MCNC had in place. And, thanks to the North Carolina legislature, it was all paid for! Consequently, when it came to MEMS fabrication, nobody could compete with Vera and MCNC. Even companies like Lucent—companies that were very successful and profitable—didn't have the capital to compete with the MEMS production capability available at MCNC in what was still an emerging market.

On top of that, Vera went out and solicited grant funding—millions of dollars in government grants—to help support MCNC's transition from semiconductor manufacturing to MEMS manufacturing. In relatively short order, nobody could touch the MEMS capabilities at MCNC. Vera was the Queen of MEMS.

As part of the transition from semiconductors to MEMS, Vera worked with Adam Mueller, a recent graduate in materials science from NCSU, to develop a service called MUMPs—Multi-User MEMS Processes. Adam developed a rule book for using the MCNC facility that was simple to follow, allowing any engineer or scientist to easily design their own MEMS devices for fabrication at MCNC. This rulebook set out all the necessary parameters or "design rules." For scientists and engineers interested in MEMS—and there were a lot of them in this new hotbed of technology—the rulebook was a godsend.

For emerging MEMS designers, who had no place to fabricate their designs, it was like being a chef, without a kitchen or ingredients. Vera and Adam between them provided a state-of-the-art "kitchen" with ingredients, equipment, a set of basic recipes, and a simple, public rulebook that taught the designer how to use it all to cook a great meal at a low, low cost. It allowed the MEMS designer to be a head chef for a day, without having to invest in an entire restaurant to do so! Vera and Adam made it very, very easy to design and build a MEMS device. Budding MEMS designers were ecstatic.

The creation of the opensource MEMS design and fabrication infrastructure was brilliant, but it was the pricing that was truly genius. Not only was the access easy, it was also incredibly cheap. At the time, a typical production run in a facility like MCNC's would cost $125,000 or more. If a MEMS device designer didn't have their own $100 million production facility—and nobody did—then, every time they designed a new MEMS device, they would have to pay that kind of fee to a foundry in order to build it! No engineer or team had that kind of funding. Not Lucent, not Nortel, and certainly not the many startups that were springing up to build MEMS devices for optical communications.

Vera and Adam changed the rules by consolidating 50 customers into one production run. This brought the cost per customer down to $2500. On top of that, Vera went out and got federal funding to help subsidize the effort, at which point customers only had to pay *$400* to have their designs fabricated!

To me, this was entrepreneurship at its very best. The world flocked to Vera's door. She and Adam had no problem at all filling their MUMPs production runs every few months. And, as optical communications and photonics took off, photonics devices were what people built. For $400, any startup, corporate development engineer, or any university researcher could afford to build a MEMS device at MCNC. And, with the published design rules, it was easy!

Internally the whole MUMPS effort fell somewhat under the radar at MCNC. It certainly fell under mine. At $400 per customer the entire effort generated a little less than $100,000 per year whereas Vera's total revenue exceeded $3 million annually. MUMPs was a tiny program and at the time it just seemed unimportant.

In its early days, I'm not sure even Vera recognized MUMPs' importance. She and Adam certainly were proud of what they were doing, and justifiably so, but at the same time, it was just one of numerous programs they had going. Given the nature of MUMPs—almost blindly producing products for others—there really was not much to say about it.

I found it very interesting that, like e-commerce, this gem was somewhat hidden at MCNC. I've since discovered that hidden innovations are in fact not the exception, but rather the rule in laboratory environments. Technical teams almost always underestimate their innovations. Or, perhaps more accurately, they under-report them. It's not that they are trying to hide these things; it's just that these are simply stuff they do every day. Why make a big deal about it? By the same token, those innovations being touted by the organization—like the infamous Zipper—are just as often not the world-changers they are made out to be. It's one of the reasons I strongly believe that, in order to commercialize laboratory innovations, commercial personnel must be deeply integrated into the research platform, very much like I was at MCNC.

Later on, as I began to understand the value of MUMPs better, and as government subsidies went away, we eventually bumped the price up from $400 to just under $5000 per site on a production run. Nobody flinched. In fact, we had many customers who bought multiple sites on each run. It was still cheaper than any other option out there. Every 10 weeks or so, we filled the production run to capacity and customers loved it. How good was this innovation? Today, twenty years later, it's still available. You can find MUMPs online.

In sales we talk about the "sales funnel." As a company, you want to use marketing and promotion to attract as many *credible* customers as possible to the top of your sales funnel. Once these potential customers contact you, then your sales team can filter them down to the point where paying customers come out of the bottom of your funnel. It's a process called *conversion*. With your sales funnel you are converting interested parties into paying customers.

As I woke up to MUMPs and the many customers that were designing devices with us using that service, I could hardly believe what Vera and Adam had achieved. MUMPs wasn't just a technical innovation; it was a marketing and sales innovation. Vera had even designed a short course—that people *paid* handsomely for—which included a "free" first production run! The short course was promoted heavily in the MEMS community and created the top of our sales funnel. Once customers were using MUMPs, they were hooked. It was so easy. Later as customers got serious about commercializing their designs, like Lucent and OMM, we converted them directly to their own $125,000 proprietary production runs. It was marketing genius.

With a bit of homework, I soon learned that a huge proportion of *all* optical MEMS devices were being fabricated by us. I estimated that we were producing as much as 50% of the designs in the market at that time, but our market share could have been even more. The reason we were in the dark is because MUMPS designs were produced blindly by us. These were proprietary designs developed by other technical teams and our engineers were instructed *not* to look at the them. Unless asked, we typically fabricated and shipped MUMPs devices without any idea what they were! On the other hand, the names of our customers were all available to me, so it was easy to do some digging. Based just on publicly available information, I quickly discovered that we were already in the photonics business—we just didn't know it. Microrelay be damned!

OMM was a great example of the type of customer we were serving. OMM ultimately raised $130 million for a business that was based entirely on chips being fabricated on MUMPs. Meanwhile, Lucent was being recognized worldwide for their LambdaRouter. Their system was centered around an amazingly elegant chip design consisting of tiny, circular mirrors, with each mirror designed to swivel in three dimensions, like a spotlight, to switch light from one place to another. Imagine 256 of these miniature mirrors on a circular wafer, four inches in diameter. Each tiny mirror could accept an incoming light signal—a certain color as generated by the WDM multiplexer—and point it to a second mirror on a second wafer, also with 256 mirrors. This 256 × 256 optical switch matrix was the mother of all switches. It could take any incoming "bullet train" and point it anywhere in the world!

This wasn't just an off ramp; this was a train station of epic proportions. The optical communications community went crazy, and we were building that chip on MUMPs.

Lucent published many beautiful pictures of this optical switch and their team was recognized worldwide as a leader in MEMS technology innovation. Even today, a full twenty years later, you can still search for LambdaRouter and see pictures of these beautiful, tiny mirrors, looking very much like miniature, swiveling spotlights. No one knew it at that time—not even us—but, while Lucent was certainly a leading innovator in design, thanks to Vera we were *the* innovators in fabrication and production.

It was crazy. The rocketship wasn't taking off next door. It was taking off right in our living room, and we hardly knew it! Then, even as we began to work directly with customers like Nortel, even as we began to learn about the dynamics of the optical communications market, and even as I began to understand the true value of our MUMPs customer base, there still remained a huge, gaping problem. None of it was ours. Certainly, we were the fabrication kings, but the true value lay in design. The true value lay in the *products* that our customers were creating, not in the services we were providing. It soon became crystal clear that if all we had was a services business model, then we would remain bystanders to the really big show. Perhaps with a front-row seat to an amazing fireworks display, but bystanders, nonetheless.

With a single conversation, Jake Wilson changed all that. He opened the door for us to climb aboard the optical communications gravy train with our own photonics product. Nortel didn't want to design their own MEMS devices and then build them with us. They had no interest in MUMPs. They had seen us deliver a microrelay, and now they wanted us to deliver an optical switch. It was as simple as that. All I needed was a product to sell them, and I had a day to figure it out.

Having finished my conversation with Vera, I raced to Matt's office. Matt had channeled his lightning strike spec depression and was frenetically trying to come up with a solution for a microrelay that defied physics. In spite of his initial pessimism, he was also not one to give up without a fight. In that way, he was very much like me. He was gnawing on the problem like a dog with a bone and was completely unprepared for the ninety-degree turn we were about to make.

While I knew the microrelay had its problems, I was firm believer in the underlying technology. Our thermal actuator has proven itself to be robust and reliable. A testimony to the quality of this invention was how easily we could build functioning relays with it. Working with new technology is often an exercise in futility as you try to apply it to real-world applications. Things fail and fail. The thermal actuator was not like that. Sure, we had failed the lightning strike spec, but that had nothing to do with the actuator itself. It worked, and implementation had been easy. We made fully operational devices in beakers in Matt's office for God's sake! Having pulled myself out of the depths of depression with the demise of the microrelay, I immediately moved to the precipice of irrational exuberance with the idea of a photonic device. I had to imagine, building an optical switch out of the thermal actuator would be easy! That is an entrepreneur for you: At the drop of a hat, it's a brand new, very sunny day.

"Matt, can we use the relay to make an optical switch?" I asked as I entered his office, clenching my fists in anticipation.

"A what? An optical switch? What the heck are you talking about?" Matt asked, flabbergasted. He was used to my erratic requests, as I jumped from one customer demand to another, but this was a new level of mayhem, even for me.

"I just got off the phone with a new group at Nortel and they want optical switches. Can we do it?" I felt like a kid, fidgeting and waiting for an answer from his dad.

"Hmmm," Matt frowned, at least humoring me. He was his usual, thoughtful self, thinking things through to make sure he could give a good answer, but I was impatient.

"Can't we just use the relay? I mean, we move that bar back and forth to open and close an electrical circuit. Just get rid of the electric circuit and put a mirror on the damn bar! We can slide the mirror back and forth at 45° into the optical beam and we'll have a switch!"

"Ha! Now you're a MEMS engineer! What? You want us to attach micromirrors to our relays with tweezers? Don't quit your day job!"

"Matt. This is serious! It's Nortel and they are ready to deal. I can smell it. We've got to come up with something!"

Matt respected my ability to sell as much as I respected his ability to engineer. When I told him that I had a deal available to close, he didn't question me.

"Alright, alright, let me think about it for a few days. I'm sure we can come up with something," he replied.

"Uh… I have a call with the guy tomorrow," I grimaced.

"What? You told me you just got off the phone with him! These guys have slow-rolled everything and now there's a huge rush?"

"Yeah. This is a different group. I'm telling you, it's totally different. They're in a hurry."

"Man… OK. Let me think about it and talk to some of the other guys. Let's talk in the morning."

I felt fidgety and restless the rest of the day. The shift from the abysmal failure of the microrelay to the radiant hope of the optical switch was so abrupt that it was disorienting. I had spoken to Matt with confidence, but after reflection I felt nothing of the sort. After one phone call with a stranger I was already building an entirely new business empire in my mind. An empire made not of microrelays, but of optical switches. It was laughable, I know, but I had no choice. I was a man drowning in an ocean of failure. With my last breath I was reaching for a life preserver, praying it was not an illusion.

When we met the next morning, Matt was upbeat. I was not surprised. "Yeah, I think we can do this! We can't build it like we do the relays, but if we can machine the entire device out of silicon, then I think we can get a pretty good optical switch."

Our MEMS group was unique in the world in that we could carry out any of the major MEMS fabrication processes. We could do a process called LIGA to produce electroplated nickel structures, like we did for the relay. We could also do a process called surface micromachining, which was used for MUMPs. And we could do bulk micromachining, a very new process, in which entire structures were etched very precisely into silicon chips. Bulk micromachining essentially gave you the ability to create thousands of extremely precise sculptures on a miniature scale. It was a perfect approach for creating mirrors with the precision needed for optical communications applications.

"That's great Matt, can we build an $8 \times 8$?"

Matt frowned. "I don't think we can do that with the thermal actuator. I haven't finalized a design yet, but I'm pretty sure we'll run into space limitations with the fishbone structure because of the way the mirrors all need to be aligned. I think the best we could ever do with our actuator is a $2 \times 2$."

"Well, if that's what we can do, then that's good enough." I wasn't going to be picky. Yesterday morning I had nothing and now, a mere 24 hours later, I had an optical switch. On top of that, I had a customer. Sure, they wanted an $8 \times 8$, and all I had was a $2 \times 2$, but I wasn't worth my salt if I couldn't get something started with what I had. Perhaps the life preserver was real! Now it was my job to sell. I picked up the phone and called Jake Wilson.

"Hey, Jake. We can't do an $8 \times 8$, but we can ship a $2 \times 2$ in about eight weeks," I said with a certainty I didn't have. I also knew that I had to make it sound like we did this every day. I also knew Matt would kill me on the delivery time, but I could always fight that battle later.

Sure enough, Matt sitting right beside me, frantically shook his head back and forth, silently imploring me to be less aggressive on delivery. Although we had a lot of experience building relays, we'd obviously never built an optical switch like this.

"And, uh, well…," I hedged, responding to Matt's cease and desist signals in real time. "Maybe twelve weeks. I'd have to check scheduling with our production manager. But don't worry, if you want the 2 × 2, we'll work out a schedule that works for you."

But Jake didn't want it. "It has to be at least an 8 × 8. Actually, what we need is a 16 × 16. But we're willing to start with an 8 × 8," he said.

I grimaced inwardly. While there was a lot of hype out there, including hype from Lucent and OMM, I *knew* that currently *nobody* had a commercially viable MEMS optical switch of any kind. I now knew that because I had so recently been educated that we were building most of the damn things! And if we were not building them, we were getting requests for quotes to build them, and our team knew many of the designs out there were patently unbuildable. So, why not start with something simple, instead of a crazy moon shot?

However, I quickly learned that in the frenetic, hyper-competitive environment that existed in the photonics industry, needs were not driven by reality, but by perception. And when it came to optical switches, size definitely mattered! To this day, I believe the 2 × 2 we had in mind would have been a great product. But with others claiming—*claiming*—to have an 8 × 8, and Lucent promoting the 256 × 256 LambdaRouter, this set the standard that everyone else was measured by. Nortel thought they were behind and needed to catch up. On that day, it certainly was not my place to dissuade them. To add value, we had to play the game.

Nevertheless, it grated all the more that *we* were building many of the competing chips but couldn't talk about it. And most, if not all, of the MEMS optical switches had significant design problems. OMM still had tough engineering issues to figure out, like how to get 64 tiny mirrors to align perfectly, along with other technical problems, which they tended to blame on us, so our engineers were hearing about their concerns regularly. In fact, to my knowledge, OMM never got their device to work at a level where it could be commercialized. After $130 million of investment, the company eventually closed its doors. The story for Lucent was similar, as their fantastical 256 × 256 LambdaRouter ultimately suffered the same fate as OMM's 8 × 8.

But none of this mattered. In sales you don't get very far trying to convince the customer they are wrong. In the telecom boom of the late 1990s, the demand for optical components was in hyper-growth mode, and every new device had to be more magical than the last. WDM had set a strange expectation that all new photonic devices would generate untold riches. Soon the lines between dreams and reality were blurred as corporations, entrepreneurs, and investors grabbed for those riches as fast as they could.

By these standards, Nortel was actually being quite reasonable in asking for an 16 × 16 switch. There were many others who were looking at Lucent's 256-port LambdaRouter and claiming it was old news. For these folks, port count had to exceed 1000! Fortunately, I had long ago learned that customers don't always know what they are talking about, even when they are pounding their fists on the table. You have to measure what they say against your own understanding of reality, or pay the price. It's not uncommon for a customer to ask for something outrageous, and even make you feel stupid because you assume they know their business better than you do. But that is definitely not always the case: Sometimes customers lie. Most often they simply have no idea what they truly need, especially when dealing with new technology that they don't really understand.

It's one thing to get sucked into a vortex of demand; it's quite another if that vortex is not real. To determine what was real and what was not, I knew what I needed to do; I had to test Nortel.

"Jake, we can build you an 8 × 8 and I'm confident we can expand that to a 16 × 16. But you are going to have to prove to me that your interest is real. For us to deliver first prototypes to you is easily going to cost $250,000. Are you guys up for that?"

"I don't think that will be a problem." There wasn't even a flinch. That's when I knew it was real.

"Okay, give us some time to put a proposal together, and we'll get back to you," I said before ending the call.

On the one hand, I was elated—the life preserver was real! Not only was it real, it suddenly looked like an ocean freighter! On the other hand, we didn't have a product! As I looked back, I could see that this was diamond-like carbon all over again. In that case, I had gone out to find a customer for diamond and came back with a pressing need for diamond-like carbon. At MCNC, I went out to sell microrelays for electrical switching and came back with a pressing need for optical switches! The one important difference was that this time, I had a technical team that was highly motivated to back me up.

Having hung up the phone I turned to Matt, who was laughing.

"You're crazy, Jesko," he said, through his laughter. "I can't believe you do what you do."

"C'mon, Matt, this is real! You guys are the best! It's just a damn 8 × 8. Yesterday we had nothing, this morning you were ready to build a 2 × 2. A few more days and you'll have this figured out… Won't you?"

"Alright, Jesko. Give me some time to look at this. Honestly, I've never considered building an optical switch. I thought all these people out there were nuts to try it."

With that, Matt went off to do his magic. As he had done with the microrelay, he did his research and very quickly came up to speed with the optical switching application. He was already well-versed in all the MEMS literature and had the added advantage of being able to draw on our entire team of engineers, who were the world's best at building any kind of MEMS device. More importantly, he wasn't just interested in the technology, he immediately started to think about practical solutions. He wanted something that would work as a product and hopefully overcome the challenges that we were seeing with competing devices.

I met with him again, just a few days later.

"I think I've found a solution. It's just as I originally thought. The only way this will work is to bulk micromachine it out of a single piece of silicon, otherwise you will never get the precision that you need."

The precision needed for an optical switch was insane. The problem was the optical signal bounced around all over the place in the network to get from point A to point B, and in that complicated process you could not afford any losses to the signal. For an optical switch, that means very close to 100% of the light going into the switch also had to come back out. This is very difficult because nothing you build is perfect; everything has its own bit of fog to scatter the light.

When you make a mirror, even a perfect one, a tiny bit of light that hits the mirror is scattered, and that may be all you can afford to lose. If the mirror is not positioned perfectly, then the extra loss from misalignment can easily be too much. Imagine pointing a laser to hit the surface of the moon from Earth, a very slight change in angle here on Earth would cause you to miss the moon entirely. By the same token, a slight mispositioning of a mirror in an optical switch will cause the optical beam to go awry and result in losses that make it useless. This was, in fact, the key problem that was affecting all of our competitors' switches—they all suffered from mispositioning problems. This is why Vera called them "science projects." To the novice these switches looked amazing; to optical engineers, they were far, far away from real product.

"And," Matt continued, "we'll have to use electromagnetic actuation. Our thermal actuators are too large, and micro-electromagnetics are the only way that we can get the density of mirrors that we need for a 16 × 16."

"Electromagnetic?" I didn't like the sound of that. "We've never done that before! Why can't we just use MUMPs and electrostatic actuation like OMM and Lucent?"

"To be honest, Jesko. I have no idea how those guys are gonna get to the specifications they need. I calculated that these mirrors have to be positioned to an accuracy of half a micron! There is no way that MUMPs will get you there—you have to bulk etch it, like I said. I mean, unless those guys know something we don't."

"Half a micron…," I almost whispered. That definitely gave me pause. Half a micron is 500 nm. Whenever you start talking about nanometers of precision, you have a real problem. A typical human hair is 100 microns—that's 100,000 nm! A distance of 500 nm is about 2500 *atoms*. Matt was absolutely right: Silicon bulk micromachining was the only process that could meet the positioning requirement.

Silicon "bulk" micromachining employs chemical solutions to etch structures out of silicon wafers that have been manufactured as a perfect crystal. Because it is a perfect crystal, you can create structures—for example, pyramids or inverse pyramids—which essentially have atomic perfection. This perfection at the atomic level led us to believe this was the best path to achieve the required precision. The only problem was that, although we were leaders in bulk micromachining, we had never done anything with electromagnetic actuation. It seemed to me that this was way outside our wheelhouse. I told Matt this.

"I might have that licked too," Matt said with a smile. "In reviewing the literature, I found a professor at Caltech who has actually demonstrated all the elements of a 16 × 16 switch with electromagnetic actuation."

"Caltech? Out in California?"

"Yeah. California Institute of Technology. Along with MIT, they are one of the best engineering schools in the country."

"And one of their professors has developed the technology we need for a 16 × 16?"

"Yeah. It's bulk micromachined and its electromagnetic and his approach offers the kind of density that's needed to make the switch that Nortel wants. And the professor has already demonstrated an optical switch!"

"So… Okay. But that's a professor at Caltech. That's not us."

"Yeah, I've already talked to him." Matt smiled, clearly holding something back, making me drag it out of him.

"C'mon, Matt!" I felt like a kid trying to hit a piñata. Blindfolded and hitting into empty space, but full of anticipation for all the candy that's out there somewhere.

"Okay, Okay! The good news is that Caltech patented his approach. The even better news is that he doesn't think anyone has licensed it yet."

Technology licensing was not a completely unfamiliar concept to me. I had licensed university technology during my time at Kobe Steel. The problem was it had not been a pleasant experience. It was like arm-wrestling with an octopus. Every time I had one arm pinned down, a slimy new one popped up to take its place. Deals took forever and after I tried it a few times, I swore I would not do it again.

On the other hand, we needed this technology and Caltech had it.

I work with many people who would like to be entrepreneurs. They are often scientists or engineers. The most passionate ones have grand ideas of technologies or products or services that they believe will change the world and simultaneously open a magical lock to fame and riches. I've rarely seen it work that way. Even if you do have a great idea, it's likely that someone else has already thought of it—or something close to it. Competition for wealth creation is as tough as it gets. It's very, very hard to think of something completely new.

Consider poor Charles Goodyear who spent much of his adult life convinced that rubber would change the world. Then with a stroke of luck and genius he was rewarded for his persistence by inventing vulcanization, the key breakthrough required for commercial success. Imagine his excitement, in 1839, when he went off to patent it, and his terrible sadness when he found out he was too late—Thomas Hancock had gotten there first, apparently by just eight weeks!

Of course, Charles didn't have a phone, a car, or a plane, but at the very least he should have gotten on his horse to find Thomas and made an alliance. Perhaps he could have licensed the technology for a product he had in mind. Or perhaps Charles could have gone and worked for Thomas. At least he would not have died penniless. And maybe Charles tried all of these things and failed because Thomas had no interest. The bottom line: If you want to be an entrepreneur, don't get hung up on inventing something yourself. Just figure out how to get the rights you need to move forward.

To me, Matt's willingness to embrace any optical switch solution, no matter who invented it, is what separated him from other engineers. He wasn't just extremely capable, which was a blessing; he wasn't just thorough, which was also a blessing; and he wasn't just responsive, which was a huge blessing. He understood business implications and acted accordingly. He not only searched for and found a technology that might work for our customer; he immediately knew the value of finding a technology that was available for licensing. Matt pointed me in the right direction, and unlike Mr. Goodyear, I was going to get up on my horse and ride!

I was on the phone to the Caltech Technology Transfer Office that afternoon and was immediately connected with the director of licensing Lester Samuelson. Based on my previous licensing experience, I expected the worst. Lester surprised me.

"What do you need?" he asked. That alone surprised me. What do I need? I was used to universities trying to tell me what I needed. In fact, in all my dealings to license technologies from universities, both before and after the time I worked with Lester, the folks at Caltech—including Robin Vass who took over Lester's position—were one of a very few that made things easy for me.

Licensing early-stage technology is a very complex business. An inventor, who patents their idea, gets the exclusive right to use that idea for a set period of time—usually 20 years. If someone else uses the inventor's patented idea, then the inventor can take that person or company to court and in some cases get a lot of money. In this way, a patent holder can block anyone else from using their idea as it is expressed in the patent. Or the inventor can choose to allow others to use the idea for a price through a patent license.

A license can be exclusive, in which case only one person or organization gains the legal right to use the patented technology; or it can be non-exclusive, in which case many people or organizations can gain the legal right to use the patented technology. If you are racing towards a gold rush and someone invents the shovel, you would love to get exclusive rights to that shovel so that you will be the only one selling shovels outside the gold mine. The inventor, on the other hand, might be concerned that you will produce inferior shovels, or that you cannot produce enough shovels to fill the demand. In that case the inventor might grant non-exclusive rights to a group of people who then all compete against each other to sell shovels.

Universities don't typically invent boring things like shovels. They often make more fundamental inventions, like new materials that would improve the shovel, or some gizmo that would entirely replace the shovel. In these cases, there is always more development to be done and the markets are largely unknown—think of our diamond work that morphed into diamond-like carbon, or our relay that morphed into an optical switch.

These unknowns make it very difficult to put a deal together and, unfortunately, universities are their own worst enemy. I once worked with a very prestigious university to try to license a coating technology. A university professor had invented a non-stick coating technology and a well-established venture fund approached me to see if I would help them start a company around it.

The fund was ready to write a check for $1 million and pull other venture capitalists into the deal. Given the solid financial backing and the quality of the scientist involved, it felt like a great opportunity to commercialize the technology.

The university offered an exclusive license to the technology in all fields except medical. In return they wanted the following: All their patenting costs were to be paid by us (that's normal); they needed certain minimum, annual payments (expected for an exclusive license to ensure that we actually commercialize the technology); they wanted a modest equity in the company (workable, but not preferable); and they expected a ten percent royalty on all sales that involved the material.

Ten percent! That seemed high for a non-medial application, so I did some research.

It turns out the coatings industry was not hugely profitable. The average profit margin for non-medical coatings applications was six percent. A license fee is based on the sales price, and it eats directly into your profit. So, if your profit is six percent and your license fee is ten percent then your effective profit is a four percent loss. Not a good business proposition! We didn't know exactly where this technology would end up, but we knew that a ten percent hit on the profit margin would make it a very undesirable business in the long run. So, this request was a non-starter—in reality for this business, the royalty needed to be around one percent or so. The final deal killer was that they also wanted veto power over how we used the technology in the future. Unfortunately, the people we were dealing with had no idea of the business implications of what they were asking for. As I tried to explain the financial and strategic impacts of their demands, they simply assumed it was an effort to negotiate, and so we had to walk away.

Unfortunately, this type of uninformed negotiation is more the norm at universities, than the exception. You are often dealing with well-meaning people who overvalue the brain power of their faculty, the commercial status of their technology, and the quality of their brand.

Long after my time with MCNC, a friend once summed it up in a very clever analogy. He is a venture investor and I was visiting him in his office on the famous Sand Hill Road in Palo Alto, California to pitch him a technology I planned to license from a university. He laughed and shook his head at my foolishness. "It's just not worth your time, dealing with universities, Jesko."

"I know they're a pain, but I can make this work!"

He paused for a while and then suddenly changed the subject as he pointed out the window. "You see that shack out there?"

I was sitting on the windowsill in his office, overlooking the parking lot that ran next to Sand Hill Road. We were just around the corner from Menlo Park, prime real estate for West Coast venture groups. I looked where he was pointing and saw a rusted metal shack that sat to the side of the parking lot.

"See that shack? I'll sell it to you for $2 million."

"What!?" I looked at the rusted-out building, open to the elements and partially leaning to its side. It seemed like you would just tear it down to make space for a few more parking spots. "You're kidding. No way!"

"You see? You just made my case for me. That building and the patch of land it's sitting on was recently assessed at $4 million! So, you just turned down the opportunity to make an instant $2 million. You see? That's what it's like dealing with universities. You can offer them the deal of the lifetime, but they won't know it and instead will think you're trying to gouge them. When you educate them, they think you are negotiating! The other problem is that every interaction takes forever. Who has time for that?"

It was a very clever analogy that I have never forgotten and have found to ring true again and again. Universities tend to shoot themselves in the foot because of their fear that they might miss out on some incremental riches, but in doing so, they close a lot of doors. Many companies and investors choose not to deal with organizations that make unreasonable demands and take forever to respond.

Lester, on the other hand, was not like this at all. His response was immediate, and I was in California two days later, face-to-face, in an office that was bursting with papers and documents. There was hardly a place to sit. We discussed the Caltech optical cross-connect technology that Matt had identified. I told Lester that we wanted to make an optical switch but were still in the early stages of our efforts. He suggested we sign an option agreement since it did not seem we were at the point where we were ready to work out a license.

An option agreement is an agreement to get a license in the future. You work out the basic terms of the license but set a period of time before it kicks in. The option may be free, or it might cost $5–$10,000. This way, the licensee pays nothing, or very little, upfront, but is given some time to carry out product development, get first customers, obtain financing, etc., before having to sign up for a full, and much more expensive, license.

Lester and I agreed on an exclusive, no-cost option for a period of one year. If we converted the option into a license, I agreed to pay all patenting costs with no upfront fees, very modest minimum payments, and a royalty not too exceed two percent. Two percent!

Years later, when I went back to Caltech to license another technology, I asked Robin Vass, who had taken over Lester's position, why Caltech was so easy to work with.

"It's simple. We aim to keep our faculty happy and get technologies out the door. We recognize that there is still a lot of work to be done on anything we patent, so we're happy when someone will put the time and investment into it. And sometimes our faculty themselves want to license their technology—we certainly do not want to be battling them!"

What a great and very rare perspective in the university-tech transfer world. I have not worked with Caltech for a number of years and very much hope that the environment is still the same.

On that day, however, I was just counting my lucky stars that Lester made things so easy. At his core, Lester was a deal maker—focused on key points; ready to cut a deal or not; wanting to move on with life! I signed the option agreement *that afternoon*, slept in the Einstein Suite at the Athenaeum at Caltech—which I recommend to anybody who is fascinated by science—and returned to MCNC a hero. Matt was shocked.

"You mean we now have the exclusive rights to this technology?" he asked, incredulous. In less than a week we had gone from zero to hero on optical switching.

"Well, it's an option for exclusive rights, but as long as we pay the patent costs within a year, it's ours."

"You're kidding."

"Nope. Now all I need is a design from you, so I can sell it to Nortel!"

And that's exactly what we did. Matt came up with a design to build an 16 × 16 optical switch for Nortel using the Caltech technology and I sold the development of the switch for a little under $250,000. As I put the deal together, it reminded me exactly of the diamond-like carbon opportunity. In both cases we were working with a customer need that we previously hadn't known about. In both cases the need was so intense that cost was a secondary concern for the customer. In both cases there was high risk because we were applying our technical capabilities in ways that we had never even imagined. But, with a paying customer and unique engineering capabilities, I felt the risk was well worth taking. And this time I had a team behind me chomping on the bit to make it happen. This was key: having a motivated, powerful, competitive team that had the horsepower to address—or credibly dismiss—customer needs as they arose. At the time, I felt blessed to be working with Vera's team. And I know even more so today just how lucky I was to have them on my side.

Jake Wilson and I crafted a two-page "heads of agreement"—or term sheet—in which we outlined the business arrangement, intellectual property rights, and security of supply guarantees. Nortel was concerned to be working with a nonprofit like MCNC on their product development and needed to be assured that we had a commercial pathway, that we had plans for a for-profit company, and that we would attract the financial backing to get there.

From the heads of agreement, we went on to draft what is called a "definitive agreement." This is the real deal that takes the terms outlined in the term sheet and creates a binding, legal structure for the deal. It took considerably more wrangling to get the deal past Nortel's lawyers. They initially came back with a legal agreement that looked nothing like the terms Jake and I had drawn up. But Jake and his colleagues were true to their word: They chastised their own lawyers and our final legal agreement was in line with what Jake and I had agreed upon. It was something I was more than happy to sign off on.

As things started to heat up for our MEMS team, it was becoming abundantly clear that this opportunity in optical communications was much larger than anything that could be achieved within a nonprofit like MCNC. Our customer list was growing rapidly, and Nortel was not the only company that expressed concerns about our nonprofit status. Others, like Lucent and OMM, also demanded to see a path towards an independent company with for-profit status. They especially didn't want to be working with a nonprofit when it came time for volume production. They wanted a dedicated company that had the financial resources to scale production and reduce costs.

With all this pressure, it appeared that the mythical "company" Shelby had talked about was at hand. We had world class technology and were licensing other technologies as we needed them. We had an exploding market in optical communications. We had customers that were signing checks and demanding more. We had world class facilities and unique capabilities to execute in almost any facet of MEMS. And most importantly, in Vera, Adam and Matt and the entire MEMS group at MCNC, we had a team that was among the best in the world. This team was almost bursting with desire to form a company. They all recognized that this was their rocketship—their moon shot—and they were not going stand by as it took off into space.

# The Final Touch

While Shelby's vision of spinning out a company was closer than it ever had been, Shelby was not going to be a part of it. Barely a month after my failed trip to Ottawa to see Gregory Hansen, Shelby resigned from his position as President of MCNC and retired.

I thought I had hit my lowest point at MCNC on that flight back from Ottawa, but it was actually losing Shelby that scared me the most. It was because of Shelby that I was even at MCNC. He had given me my dream job and inspired me to take it beyond anything I could have imagined. He was a charismatic leader who understood innovation, encouraged commercialization and had given me opportunities where others had not. His resignation was the heaviest loss for me yet. With the relay failure still resting heavily on my mind, and the Nortel photonics opportunity still nascent, Shelby's resignation increased my sense of impending doom.

In his place, a no-nonsense executive named Jack Phillips took over. Jack had recently retired from IBM in Research Triangle Park and joined the MCNC Board of Directors as Chair. I never spoke to Jack about it, but I am sure he joined MCNC in his retirement to give back to the community. I would guess that he ended up getting a lot more than he bargained for.

With Jack taking over as President, things changed considerably at MCNC. While I loved Shelby, and to this day consider him to have been pivotal to my career, Jack's leadership unequivocally changed MCNC for the better. Jack brought order by focusing on financial planning, discipline, and making sure the details made sense.

I can say today that Jack was the best boss I ever had and that I would work for him again in a heartbeat, if I could. Jack began by instilling order.

While we had many good projects at MCNC, there were too many cooks in the kitchen. Vera's group was actually the least of Jack's problems. Vera had instilled her own brand of discipline in the MEMS group—there was only one cook in that kitchen! But elsewhere, things were a mess and Jack went through it all like a hot knife through butter.

The first thing he did was put out the burning fire that was the network services group. He fired everyone in the gaming network mess including the group of five from the startup team and all ancillary personnel. I was on the block too. Jack was crystal clear: I was to go sit in my office until he figured things out.

By this time, I'd graduated from a cubicle in the fishbowl to one of the smaller offices that ringed its outer edge. I sat for days in boredom and fear, rolling pencils across my desk wondering how my family and I would survive if I was fired. I had railed against the entire network gaming idea, but I had championed Preserve and who knew how that would be perceived?

Fortunately, Jack determined relatively quickly that, while I had my fingers in many pies at MCNC, the networking group was not one of them. The clincher was the risk analysis I had prepared for Shelby that included a financial projection and a memo begging him not pursue the gaming network project. Although I did not get fired, Jack also informed me that things would not be business as usual. "You now only have one job, Jesko. You're going to work with Vera. Anything else is off limits."

Jack always spoke softly, but with an iron will that made it very difficult to argue. Nonetheless, I tried.

"What about Unitive?" I asked, desperate to keep that project. Next to my work with Vera, Unitive kept me most active. And I felt I was very close to getting the deal done with Gabriel Tanner and MST. At the very least I wanted that feather in my cap and I was ready to fight for it.

"No, we'll take care of that without you. Go work with Vera and stay away from everything else."

Jack would say these things kindly, sometimes even with a light a chuckle, as if he knew something you didn't. The room for discussion was zero. When Unitive got funded a short time later, it burned that it had become Jack's deal, when in fact I had worked so hard with Gabriel Tanner on putting the lead investment together.

On the upside, I still had a job and the MEMS group was starting to keep me very busy. At this point, I had initiated the optical switch deal with Nortel and other opportunities were also presenting themselves. Jack's decree to work exclusively with the MEMS team forced me to focus when focus was most needed. In fact, things got so busy that I lobbied for help and, with Jack's backing, hired a young man named Peter Brennan for sales support.

Peter was a real sales professional and took our sales efforts to a whole new level. It's one thing to cut a deal for product development with a customer; it's quite another to translate that into purchase orders, ensure delivery, and monitor payment. Peter did all of that. Between the two of us, the commercial customer base grew rapidly with Peter taking the brunt of the sales work, while I focused on identifying and landing new product development opportunities. We developed aggressive sales projections and consistently hit our monthly targets, much to Jack's delight.

Jack's perspective on saving MCNC was very different from Shelby's, and it was comforting for me. He recognized that doubling or tripling revenue, especially manufacturing revenue, at MCNC was unlikely. He also understood that our manufacturing-oriented endeavors—primarily MEMS and Unitive—were in their infancy and *costing* MCNC money. From a financial perspective, we were doing the opposite of what Shelby set out to do.

Unitive, in particular, was wrapping hundreds and maybe even thousands of dollar bills around every product they shipped out the door. I knew this because I had done a cost analysis on the Unitive production process. It needed much higher volumes to be profitable. The MEMS operation was in much better financial shape, but still had a similar problem. We were growing rapidly and generating strong revenues, but we were losing millions of dollars per year, once you accounted for all the costs. These losses were being carried by MCNC and could not go on indefinitely. Shelby's solution had been to generate more revenue to make up the difference. Jack's solution was to spin these businesses out and let investors carry the losses.

While Unitive was Jack's top priority, with an MST-led investment deal following very quickly after he took over as President, his next most pressing challenge—and opportunity—was the MEMS group. He met with Vera and they formed a new company pretty much overnight. Vera, given twenty-four hours to come up with a name, went home to read her favorite mythology books deep into the night, finally coming up with the name "Cronos". Since Cronos, Cronus, and Kronos were already taken and trademarked as company names, the lawyers asked her to add something descriptive to the name, and so our new company became Cronos Integrated Microsystems.

"Cronos?" I gasped when she told me. "Did you read all the way through that myth? Do you know what Cronos did? He ate his children!"

But Vera just laughed gleefully. She loved that the god Cronos displayed unrelenting power: That's what she wanted her company to do.

Jack met with Vera and me and informed us that he would be hiring a CEO to run the new MEMS company.

"You guys are a great team", Jack told us. "And you've both done wonders, especially you, Vera. But if we're going to go primetime with this, we need someone who has been around the block and you haven't. So, we'll need to find an experienced CEO."

As you might imagine, this did not go over well with either of us, and was much worse for Vera. She was used to being the boss and having complete control over the MEMS work, including all that was to become Cronos. She had borne it, raised it, and named it; and now she was being told to hand it over to someone else. We never spoke directly about the transition and I can only imagine the struggle she went through as she decided whether to hand Cronos off to someone who would become her boss.

Like everyone else, Jack lived in the MCNC fishbowl, so I was able to observe some one-on-one discussions he had with Vera. You didn't have to be a lip reader to get a sense of the conversation—Vera was nothing if not forceful in stating her mind. On the other side of the desk, for all of Jack's kindness and empathy, his words were always said with finality, and in the end, there was very little argument to be had.

I felt for Vera, but I also had my own frustrations with Jack's decision. Of all my projects, Unitive and the MEMS group were where I was having the most influence and emerging success. I was putting good deals together—including the lead investment for Unitive. And I was making sales! I was having success convincing our engineers to bend our technical capabilities to meet customer needs. And I had traction on the customer side, getting them to rethink their needs and accept something we could actually produce. I listened, I cajoled, I charmed, and I pleaded and negotiated until the cauldron of capabilities finally overlapped with the basket of needs. I knew I was successful when money changed hands. It was as simple as that. With all of that effort, we were increasing commercial revenue for the MEMS group on a monthly basis.

*And* I had an *MBA*. I thought all of this meant I should be president of this new company. I couldn't let it ride. Like Vera, I followed up with Jack to make my case, but my results were no different than hers, except that our discussion was much shorter. "You are doing great work, Jesko", Jack told me, killing me with kindness. "You're a catalyst and that's what we need for MEMS. Don't worry, you will be very successful in your career. But right now, we need someone with real operating experience and that's not you".

Jack promised both of us that we would have a say in choosing our new boss, and he stayed true to that promise. We interviewed three candidates:

one who turned us down, one who was clearly inadequate, and one, Brian Novak, who "we" made an offer to.

Jack knew Brian from his IBM days. Brian had been an executive at IBM in charge of a billion-dollar annual budget running IBM's semiconductor fabrication facilities. He was a bull of a man who could be charming at times and an extraordinary bully at others. I was told later that Brian had come out of a management system at IBM that fostered intimidation, and he proved to be an expert at applying pressure.

When it came to operational management, on the other hand, Brian had definitely been around the block. This was the fundamental skill and experience that he brought to the table. Wisely, Jack had picked him for this capability, which was sorely needed on our team. We were a very talented bunch on the MEMS team, but when it came to manufacturing and scaling up, we were novices at best. At that point in my career, operational excellence was not something I would have recognized if it had slapped me in the face. It was an area where I didn't know what I didn't know, and we were very lucky to have Jack on our side, ensuring the proper skillset was being brought to bear in our new startup.

Lastly, Brian was an aggressive negotiator with a deep need to come out on top, no matter what the situation. For the most part, this stood us well, as almost every aspect of our path forward involved negotiation: negotiations with MCNC for resources and intellectual property, negotiations with vendors and customers, negotiations with investors, and negotiations with acquirers. I quickly learned that running a startup means you're negotiating every single day, and it seemed that in Brian we had a homerun hitter. In all cases he took a no-holds-barred, scorched-earth approach to negotiating what was best for him and the company. It's not my preferred approach to negotiation, but for Brian it worked most of the time.

On the other hand, Brian did not know much about MEMS technology and, as I found out over time, he didn't really know much about running a startup, which is a lot different from running a billion-dollar budget at IBM. Fortunately for him—and all of us—he didn't have to run the startup for very long. It was his negotiating skills and his unrelenting drive to succeed that helped win the day for all of us in the end.

Along with Brian, we hired a Chief Financial Officer (CFO), Ron Quinn, and a director of manufacturing, Russel Murphy, both among the best in their fields and two people I am still fortunate to work with to this very day. In the short term, all this hiring caused MCNC to burn even more cash, so Jack went back to the North Carolina legislature and requested a one-year extension on the final $2 million supplement from the State. Because of Jack's towering reputation in the community, the state legislature relented and provided MCNC with this desperately needed lifeline.

In this way, an additional year was added to MCNC's ticking clock, and I breathed a sigh of relief, saying a silent prayer of thanks for my new hero Jack Phillips. He had not only lengthened the runway for us, he ensured we had a fully rounded team with Vera and I well versed in the technology and market, and the new members Brian, Ron, and Russel bringing deep experience in business operations, finance, and manufacturing.

As demand for photonics components took off and our understanding of our value in the market matured, we were finally positioned for success: We had amazing technology and a world-class MEMS engineering team; we were laser focused on a market for photonics that was exploding; we had motivated customers who were giants in the telecommunications industry; we boasted an unmatched ability to fabricate and deliver MEMS devices; and now we had a full-fledged team that could take advantage of it all. We felt unbeatable and began to behave that way.

On the downside, we lacked cash. Money is fuel and we desperately needed funding to fuel the success we knew was within our grasp.

# Cash Is King

Brian Novak loved to say: "Cash is king!" I agree with him.

Cash is the fuel that launches the rocket. It doesn't matter what your capabilities, prospects, and vision for the future are because without cash you are stuck in place.

Getting cash is hard. Very hard. It's the dividing line between *wanting* to be an entrepreneur and *being* an entrepreneur. Of course, there are many entrepreneurs out there who have built successful businesses and even empires without having to raise cash at all. These are smart people with great business concepts and the ability to sell their product or services to make money right from the get-go. These entrepreneurs bootstrap their organization until they can safely take on debt and then expand their operations like any other corporation.

The one issue with bootstrapping is that it generally takes time. These bootstrapped companies are not the rocketships—the unicorns of Silicon Valley—that many technology entrepreneurs aspire to create. Fast-moving technology companies require a lot of cash to get off the ground. The faster they rise, the more money it takes. Paradigm changes do not come cheaply or for free.

To compound the matter, there are not many sources of cash for high-risk startups. Some entrepreneurs tap their own savings or borrow from their family to get started. These sources are rarely enough. Banks are a poor option as they require collateral to cover their loans, which adds even more risk to the entrepreneur's situation. Some entrepreneurs take on other kinds of personal debt, like credit card debt or second mortgages on their homes to finance their vision for a new future. I shudder at the thought.

To me, taking on any kind of personal debt for a venture compounds the risk that the entrepreneur is already exposed to. The risk in a startup is not just financial, there is also another risk that young entrepreneurs often do not consider: It's called career risk. Bob West made that case to me very succinctly before I joined MCNC: "…if you go there and don't pull off a homerun, your career is toast." If I had fully understood those words at the time, I wonder if I would have made the decisions that brought me to MCNC. Sometimes ignorance is bliss!

Today I understand career risk very well. Graduation from high school or university, followed by being CEO of your own company for five years, resulting in failure—or even modest success—is a tough sell when you then try to get a job later on. Corporate hiring managers are looking for a track record of achievement, not a flash-in-the-pan adventure. At that point, unless you are young enough to go back to school to rebrand yourself, your career is now locked into startups. As Bob pointed out, the career risk is very high when you choose to be an entrepreneur.

Now, imagine, on top of all that, you also risk your personal fortune? Or, even worse, you take on life-crushing debt? Now, you not only have to deal with the career risk, but you've also put your financial future and the future of your family at risk. It makes for a great war story for those who win at this game, but it is devastating for those who do not. I know, because I have seen it. I have seen friends and colleagues go down this path and ruin their life because they passionately believed in an entrepreneurial idea but did not understand or manage their financial exposure. Sure, if you have a billion dollars, invest ten million. Heck invest one twenty million! But if you have modest lifesavings, keep them. And for God's sake, avoid debt.

Of course, there is another option that is commonly used by entrepreneurs: You can raise money from friends and family. This is one of the easier routes to getting the cash you need, but this too has its downside. While you are avoiding personal debt, you may be risking family relationships instead. Do your family and friends truly understand the risk they are taking on with their investment? They might simply trust you know what you are doing when they put their money in. Families and friendships have come apart over just these kinds of scenarios and it's a shame.

At the very least, if you ever do take money from family or friends, let them know that they are most likely going to lose it. Then, if they still invest, you can feel comfortable that you have not led them astray.

The best solution to your cash flow problems is to use "other people's money" in your ventures. Find other people, not your family and most preferably sophisticated investors, and convince them to back your venture. The reason you should focus on "sophisticated" investors is because, unlike your mom and dad or neighbor down the street, these investors fully understand the level of risk that they are taking.

Sophisticated investors might be very wealthy individuals called angel investors, who don't mind risking a tiny bit of their wealth on a high-risk scheme backed by a passionate leader. These types of investors are usually good for raising hundreds of thousands of dollars, which may be enough to get a modest venture off the ground.

There are also angel funds, where groups of wealthy individuals pool their resources to make investments in the range of millions of dollars, which is enough to seed a technology venture. More and more angel groups are being formed in the United States and they are responsible for a great number of the very earliest stage investments. Often these angel groups are called networks, because they network people together around one common cause. There is the Chemical Angel Network (CAN) that focuses on early stage chemistry and materials science, the Duke Angel Network (DAN) which focuses on Duke University Alumni and Duke innovations, the Baylor Angel Network led by Baylor undergraduates, and so on.

Angel networks are great sources of funds for early stage investments, but if you want to go primetime that requires venture capital. Venture capital (VC) funds are the fuel for true startup rocketships. Venture capitalists (VCs) help enterprises go from zero to world domination in a few years. They can fund $100 million, or even $1 billion for a revolutionary idea. They can help crush competition by being able to apply more resources faster than anyone else. The important thing to remember is that VCs are not looking for you to build a business as much as they are looking for you to change the world. They want to invest a dollar and make $100 or more! They finance companies that change how humans think and operate. Their money helped shape Yahoo, Apple, Google, Uber, Tesla and many more.

Venture capital can be segregated into two main groups: corporate venture capital and private venture capital. Corporate VCs use company funds to make high risk investments in areas that are of strategic interest to that company. They typically care less about the financial return and much more about maintaining their competitive advantage. For this reason, they tend to be willing to put more money into a company for less ownership stake, supporting higher company valuations, which is good for the entrepreneur. Over the past ten years or so, corporate VCs have become more prevalent and are a major source of funding for many innovative startups.

Private VCs get their money from high net worth individuals and from institutional investors. These groups typically invest a small portion of their available funds and become limited partners—LPs—in a venture capital fund. The LPs pay management fees to venture fund managers who seek out high-risk, high-reward investments with the goal of generating extraordinary returns on the money that has been put into the fund. Private VCs and their LPs are purely interested in financial returns and are ruthless in their efforts, often being called "vulture capitalists." No matter what type of VC you attract, given that venture capitalists are usually the most sophisticated investors, their interest in your deal is an indication you have something of value.

Venture capitalists are very good at what they do because they are industry specialists. They focus on a sector (like healthcare or energy or the automotive sector), they live and breathe it, and most likely know much more about it than even you do as an entrepreneur. That is the upside of pitching to them: They are often the best validation of an emerging business opportunity. On the other hand, their deep sector knowledge combined with their ready access to cash can also make VCs arrogant and dismissive at times, especially if you are pitching them something they don't know. As clever as VCs are, by their very nature, they are still part of the status quo. They are at their very best once they have identified the next big wave and start to surf it. They can be at their very worst when an innovator points to a new wave that has yet to build.

Venture capital funds are further grouped by which stage of the innovation they focus on: seed-, early-, and growth-stage funds. Seed stage is where an entrepreneur has a proof of concept to demonstrate some unique product or service; early stage funds focus on ventures that have prototypes and early customer interactions; and growth stage funds focus on innovations with a well-established product and customer interest with a clear business model that is ready to scale.

It used to be that there were many small venture funds that focused on seed stage ventures, followed by medium-sized firms focused on early and growth stage, and finally, the large firms focused on growth stage and exit of the company. An entrepreneur would work with all three kinds of venture firms, depending on what stage the company was in. In the great recession of 2008, many of the small- and medium-sized firms were wiped out, leaving only the biggest firms like Kleiner-Perkins, NEA, and Kodiak Venture Partners. This consolidation changed the venture landscape considerably and was probably at least some of the impetus for the growth of corporate venture capital. Currently, there appears to be a resurgence of smaller venture firms, but seed capital and early-stage capital can still be very, very hard to get, especially if you are working with new, science-driven innovations.

In addition to venture capitalists, investment bankers also find capital for deals ranging from raising a few million dollars, to selling company, to taking one public for billions of dollars—always getting paid a percentage of the deal to do so.

Encroaching into the seed space and the investment capital space are new crowd-funding platforms. These may be non-equity platforms where people can only pre-purchase a product—Kickstarter and Indiegogo are the most famous—or certain specialized platforms where investors can, with certain constraints, purchase equity in a deal. And most recently blockchain may generate yet another platform—through coin or token offerings—to raise money.

To have a chance of raising money, it is critical the entrepreneur understand the investment capital landscape. It's constantly changing, much like the fashion industry, as investors identify new investment opportunities that are driven by constant changes in demographics, innovation, government policy, environment, economics, and all the other macro-influences that humankind is subject to. What's in fashion one year, may be out of fashion the next, and VCs are like schools of fish in this regard—they follow emerging trends at lightening-speed in a synchronized ensemble where it is hard to spot who is leading and who is following.

Is your head spinning? It should be. When I first started raising money for our ventures at MCNC, I knew none of this and I made a lot of mistakes, mostly because I could not differentiate a real investor from the many charlatans that try to pass themselves off as investors. Now imagine you have the next, game-changing innovation in the palm of your hand. This is your shot. It's taken you years to get here, and all you need is capital to create the next unicorn in the startup world. But where do you turn to for your capital?

In my experience, you won't learn how to raise money in a classroom. Those who have the skills to raise millions of dollars typically don't give classes on the topic. And, even if there are classes, the investment landscape is constantly changing, so what works today, won't necessarily work tomorrow. My entrepreneurship courses in my MBA program didn't come close to preparing me to raise money. At best we were treated to relatively superficial lectures from people who, quite frankly, were not the best in this field.

Raising money requires practice. You have to get out there and do it to learn it. Unfortunately, in order to raise money, you have to have a real deal to sell! You have to have that all important ball to play with. There is no practice ground, unless you are uniquely fortunate to work closely with someone who is raising money, or you are uniquely fortunate to be part of a venture capital firm. Of course, good mentorship helps, but how do you even know if you are getting good mentorship? It's tough when you don't know what you don't know. This puts first-time entrepreneurs in an unenviable situation: They are ripe to be taken advantage of and there are a lot of unscrupulous people around to do so.

My fundraising mistakes started with bad mentorship. By the time I started at MCNC I had a number of mentors. Some I knew as paid consultants, others through classes I took at UNC, and still others through networking in the local entrepreneurial community. They provided me with lots of advice; however, without any experience in raising money I couldn't tell good advice from bad.

My savior in all of this was MCNC. Unlike most other would-be entrepreneurs, I had a job where I *did* get to practice! Unitive was a wonderful learning opportunity. And it wasn't my only one. I helped raise $1 million for another technology in my portfolio: a new design for radio-frequency identification tags. And then there were the other deals like Preserve that never worked out. Shelby put no constraints on me, so I had the wonderful and unique opportunity to go out and try whatever I came up with. This is how I ended up having drinks in Houston with the top investment banker at Alex Brown. This is how I ended up talking to an investment banker in Charlotte, who I mistakenly thought was a venture capitalist. I learned by doing, and only an organization like MCNC could have given me a platform to do so.

Aside from my own circle of mentors, there were lots of people associated with MCNC who were eager to advise me. A number of these were self-proclaimed "venture investors." Some were even on the Board of Directors at MCNC. They drove exotic cars like Porsches and Cadillacs and dressed much better than I did. When we went out to lunch, they picked up the tab and impressed the heck out of me with their knowledge and their war stories. With all this investor horsepower around me, it seemed like all I had to do was put out my hand and I would be done! It seemed that raising money would be so simple: I couldn't comprehend why someone at MCNC had not done this before?

Well, most likely because it was not that simple. It turned out—and it was a rude awakening for me—that a lot of these apparently sophisticated players were not what they professed to be. Some of them were impostors, quacks, and pretenders. Whatever you might call them, they dressed to impress but failed when it counted.

My problem was that I didn't *know* they were imposters—at least not at first. If someone told me they were an investor and they drove a fancy car, that was pretty much all it took for me to treat them like a demigod. But gradually I learned different. I learned that these folks were not the panacea I had hoped for. I idolized Ben Lynch, but he was still human. We're all human. What you have to watch out for is those humans who profess to be much more. Soon I realized that some of the war stories were just a bit too fanciful and oft repeated.

The real learning for me, however, came when rubber met the road. Just like with my customers, I quickly learned to separate fact from fantasy by bluntly asking for a check from investors—or at least proof that a big check could be written. Unfortunately, when it came to a demand for action, the war stories often became muted, the checkbooks turned up empty.

"Well, Jesko, before we can even talk money, we'll need a full business plan."

"Now, wait a second! You said you were ready to invest in this deal!" I might say.

"Of course! But not without a plan!" would be the response.

Or "I can't do the whole deal on my own."

Or "We've just spent out our fund; maybe we can use your deal to help raise the next one!"

Or "There's more risk than I thought here, Jesko. You'll need a volume manufacturing order before I can convince my partners."

On and on. Everyone is looking for an easy score. Everyone is looking for a horse to ride.

A particularly illuminating experience was with an "investor" out of Charlotte, North Carolina that I was introduced to by a person who I thought was an experienced mentor. We met over lunch and the investor invited us to his offices in Charlotte.

"This guy is the real deal," my mentor assured me. "Not like those bozos you're dealing with back at MCNC."

By this time, I had seen my share of "bozos" and was definitely ready to meet a real investor. We drove down to Charlotte and I made my Unitive pitch, which included a request for a two-million-dollar investment. When I finished, the investor lauded my presentation and told me he loved the deal. Then he stood and shook my hand and surprised the heck out of me: "You've got your two million, Jesko," he said.

I was floored.

"You want to do the whole two million?" I asked weakly. Clearly this guy was a horse of a different color. Many of my conversations up to this point had been with people who talked about hundreds of thousands of dollars, not millions. Wow. My mentor had really come through! As we drove home, I was beyond elated.

"You see? That's how it's done, Jesko," my mentor said.

Well, that *was not* how it got done. It turned out that the "investor" ran a brokerage firm. As such, he had access to a database of clients who were "qualified investors." You see, when you are raising money, the term "qualified investor" is very important because it is illegal to solicit investments from unqualified investors. To be a qualified investor you have to be at least somewhat rich—you have to have a certain level of wealth, income, etc. In the United States, the criteria to be a "qualified investor" are actually defined by law. Through the work he did for his clients, this broker had a long list of individuals that he knew would meet these important criteria. In order to make more money, all *he* needed was a product to sell them. As far as he was concerned, Unitive might fit the bill. We were the horse he wanted to ride—I just didn't know it.

Once again, the only barrier to getting the money was that there was no "business plan." With encouragement from the investor, and with a quick $2 million at stake, I took on the task.

Unitive had a draft of a plan, but it turned out to be primarily a technical document. I could use pieces of it, but for the most part I was starting from scratch, in an area I knew very little about. It was very hard work and I still remember sitting in the MCNC fishbowl late at night working on the plan for this investor. It was an eerie feeling—lights were dimmed and not another soul graced the place. I remember my frustration that I was working late into the night while everyone else, including the entire Unitive team, was at home with their families. But I did it because MCNC's clock was ticking and also for my own ego—how I wanted to bring home that two million-dollar prize! The Charlotte "investor" had convinced me that a business plan was all I needed to finalize the deal.

Imagine my disappointment when I discovered that our handshake was not at all what it had seemed. When I think about it, I still feel a bit sick in my stomach even now. I finally delivered the plan, expecting the need for some refinements, but also expecting to be very near to closing the two-million-dollar investment. What I got in return was a contract giving our "investor" the exclusive right to raise $2 million for Unitive, for a tidy sum in his pocket, of course.

It was a terrible deal on so many levels. This broker wanted to raise the money from his clients in relatively small sums of $25,000–$50,000, leaving us with an unwieldy number of 50–60 individual investors to deal with when he was done. He wanted to be paid a lot of money to do this. And, he wanted the exclusive right to do so, essentially blocking us from raising money in any other way. Of course, I turned him down, but what a horrible waste of time.

I had been naive, but nobody had taught me to recognize a real investor. And he wasn't the only one. I had lots of offers to "help" me. What I learned is that everyone was looking for a horse to ride, and they saw me, and the portfolio of technologies at MCNC, as that horse. Well, MCNC had been ridden hard and put away wet once too often. I was starting to get seriously pissed off.

With my Charlotte experience behind me, I became much more discerning. I no longer took potential investors at face value and began to ask pointed questions. Do you manage a fund? How big is the fund? Are you currently investing out of the fund? What size checks do you write? How much follow-on investment (called "dry powder") do you reserve in your deals? What are your current investments? Who do you work with that I might know? Really, it was no different than working with a potential customer. Show me the money. And, if you can't, you're wasting my time.

I also started kicking self-described "helpers" out of MCNC. These were hanger-on, wanna-be investors who, like my Charlotte broker, were trying to exploit us. There was even an MCNC board member in this category who I couldn't kick out, but studiously ignored. I did the same thing on the business development side, where there were a number of people making claims about being able to help us develop or sell products—for a tidy, upfront sum, of course. Out. Out. Out. Surprisingly, Shelby supported me. Secretly, I think he knew there was a bunch of driftwood hanging around and he was happy to see them go.

It was a seminal lesson: Check up on what people are telling you, or "Do your due diligence," as we say in the startup community. Make sure the person across the table from you is real and has value for you. If they won't demonstrate their worth, move on. Today I make these kinds of assessments in minutes and sometimes even seconds.

By the time Gabriel Tanner and MST expressed interest in Unitive, I had learned this lesson. I found out quickly that MST was real, they had money to spend, and they were motivated to spend it. Gabriel was impressed by my no-nonsense approach and treated me as an equal. That's not to say that he didn't know I was green. But green and savvy is a long way from green and stupid.

Gabriel taught me a lot about putting a deal together. He took one look at my business plan and threw it in the garbage—literally—right in front of me. Nevertheless, he treated me with respect and together we set to work to finance Unitive. One of his first moves was to hire an experienced analyst out of Europe who flew over to work with me and the rest of the team at MCNC to put a real (much shorter) business plan together.

The analyst had a whole series of questions, the answers to which he relentlessly pursued throughout the organization. To accommodate him, we set up a small war room next to the fishbowl and it was my job to track down the people the analyst needed to question. Each answer was followed up with independent research, leading to further probing questions. People on the Unitive team soon learned to avoid the analyst like the plague; he was brutal in his questioning and, being somewhat arrogant, tended to laugh at many of our answers. It was painful, but real "due diligence" usually is, especially if you are not prepared for it. On the upside, the result was a fully vetted business analysis supported by a 10-page business plan that actually made sense and would pass muster with any serious investor. Most importantly, it made sense to Gabriel Tanner, who made the decision to invest in Unitive, and when he did, there was no question it was the real deal.

As we began to negotiate terms, I found that every step in the process was an entirely new learning experience for me. I negotiated MST's $6 million lead investment in Unitive entirely by the seat of my pants, with valuation of the company soon being the most pressing issue. Valuation seemed like a black art, even with input from my mentors, so I had to dust off my entrepreneurial finance notes, a topic I *had* been taught something about in business school. Nevertheless, there is a world of difference between a theoretical understanding of terms like pre-money and post-money, and actually negotiating company valuation with a real investor.

To finalize the deal, Shelby had offered up his office and Gabriel and I sat in two comfortable chairs with a coffee table between us. To those on the other side of the glass, inside the fishbowl, it probably looked like a tranquil scene, two men enjoying a chat over morning coffee. But inside the room, it felt very different. At least to me. Inside the room we were two Samurai, facing off, ready to do battle. I'm sure Gabriel Tanner knew he was dealing with a novice and he took full advantage of it.

"So, Jesko, we've done all the hard work," Gabriel started off pleasantly, "We have a good financial plan and we'll need to raise $17 million. I really like this deal, it fits with what I know, and I've decided that MST will lead it with $6 million, so that means we'll have to raise another $11 million from other investors."

I tried not to show it, but I was euphoric. Getting a lead investor in any deal is 80% of the challenge. I can't count how often I have heard: "Yeah, once you have a lead, we'll be willing to put some money in!"

That's because the leader of the round has to do all the hard work. They have to really dig in and evaluate the deal, they have to do all the "due diligence" to make sure that it is a good investment. Then, if they have any credibility—and MST definitely had that—other investors will pretty much fall in line to put their money in under whatever terms the leader negotiated.

One key aspect of leading an investment is "pricing" the deal. That's where you negotiate the price of the shares and the proportion of the company the investors will own. That was the last piece that Gabriel Tanner and I still had to settle that morning.

"Now we just have to agree on a valuation," Gabriel continued. "Have you thought about this?"

There it was: valuation. Crunch time. How much was our beautiful baby—Unitive in this case—worth? It's a very important question: A high valuation meant that the founders (MCNC and the technology team) would gain the most ownership; a low valuation would mean the opposite. My job was to keep the valuation as high as possible.

"Uh…, ah…, yes, well, I have thought about it. It's, ah, it's $40 million," I blustered.

There are many ways to value a company based on its financial performance, but the simplest is to use what are called enterprise value (EV) ratios. For an established company a common approach is to use the price-earnings (P/E) EV ratio: If the company has earned $10 million for the year and its P/E (based on its stock price) is 12, then the company is worth 12 × $10 million, or $120 million. You can also use other "multiples" like the price-EBIT (earnings before income tax) ratio. A common approach to valuing a startup is to take the revenue forecast in the final year of the plan—typical plans are five years—and multiply it by the price-revenue—price/revenue—ratio that is typical for the industry.

To get the price/revenue ratio for your industry, you would look at public companies in your sector and compare their share price to reported sales, and then calculate an average for as many representative companies as you can find. For example, the price/revenue ratio for semiconductor companies is currently around 4, software companies are around 8, and if you want to value a farming business, the ratio is around 1. This data can be found in various places, but one great source is New York University professor Aswath Damodaran who collects and publishes all sorts of valuation data.

Since the valuation you calculate is five years in the future, you have to then calculate the present value of that by discounting it back to the present day. The discount rates (essentially the interest rate that is being used in the calculation) that VCs use is shockingly high at first glance. For an early stage venture, it will be 50–65%! Compare that to a new project in an established corporation, where discount rates are typically 8–15%.

I'd taken the financial plan that Gabriel's analyst had created and used the price/revenue approach to value the company at $40 million. Gabriel just laughed at me.

"That's just silly, Jesko," he said, "You guys are losing money hand over fist, and if I don't save you this whole thing will just go down the drain. There is no way that we could ever convince any investor that they could make money at that valuation…"

Gabriel was making a very good point. We were very, very close to annihilation. MCNC was running out of cash; Unitive was indeed losing a lot of money; and if we didn't get a significant cash infusion—like the $17 million that he was talking about—then the whole thing would die. Gabriel knew it and used it to his advantage, as any VC would.

The other point he was making is that his investment return model—where he calculated the potential return on the $17 million investment—was not showing an adequate return at the $40 million valuation I was proposing. If he could not show other investors a fantastic return—at least 10 times their initial investment—no one would follow MST into the deal.

And so, went the morning. Gabriel and I fought acrimoniously over the valuation of Unitive, finally coming to a bitter compromise of $21 million for the company. We liked each other, but tempers had flared enough to call it a day. As we finally went our separate ways, and I was secretly very pleased with our hard-fought conclusion, only to discover the next day that I had been talking about a pre-money valuation and he had been talking about a post-money valuation. Only an idiot would have let this happen.

The situation was laughable, because it's a *huge* difference. Gabriel was going to lead with $6 million and raise another $11 million from other venture investors, for a total of $17 million going into the company. Our "misunderstanding" had enormous financial consequences.

If the $21 million agreement had been pre-money, then the total value of the company after investment would have been $38 million ($21 + $17), with the investor group owning 45% ($17/$38) and MCNC owning 55% ($21/$38). To me, this was a *great* deal. One that I definitely could be pleased about!

Given that MCNC was providing the people, the equipment, the facilities, the patents and the ongoing contracts for the deal, I thought this was reasonable. But the next day I found out that Gabriel was arguing that the $21 million was post-money! Under this scenario the pre-money valuation was $4 million ($4 + $17 = $21) and the investor group would own 81% ($17/$21) with MCNC owning 19% ($4/$21).

It was an unforgivable negotiation mistake on my part, and I'm guessing that Gabriel knowingly took advantage of me. However, I never got to finish the discussion because at that point Jack Phillips took over and closed the investment very quickly. I have no idea what the final structure was, but I would guess that Gabriel prevailed. Unitive was burning cash and Jack was desperate to move it off the books.

After many months of hard work, it bothered me that I wasn't part of the final Unitive deal. I wanted "credit" for all that I had done, but Jack wasn't the kind of guy you whined to about getting credit. He was teaching me very quickly to focus on teamwork and results. It was a great lesson: If you want to be successful, that is really all that matters.

Not that it was an *easy* lesson. For me, Unitive had turned out much like my experience with Proserve: A lot of hard work ending in little more than a learning experience. But I had to just shrug my shoulders and move on. It made no sense to dwell on something that I could not change, so I put it all behind me and moved forward, focused on the Nortel deal and consumed by MEMS.

# Pitching and Flailing

The good news was that, by the time Jack Phillips kicked me out of the negotiations with Gabriel Tanner, I had made pretty much every mistake in fundraising there was to make, all on MCNC's nickel. How could I possibly ask for more?

It's not often that you get to learn for free, especially when it comes to financing. I was nothing if not a quick learner, and I had learned a great deal from my various failures. Even better, I'd been educated on what a real deal needed to look like from Gabriel and his analyst as they put the Unitive financing together. I had learned what "real" investors looked like and what their expectations might be. And I now understood the basic mechanics of deal structure: what financial projections should look like; how companies were valued by experienced investors; and how dilution could affect ownership. On top of that, I had *almost* closed a deal! While I was no expert by any stretch of imagination, I was now the one-eyed man in the land of the blind when it came to fundraising at MCNC.

In addition to efforts on Unitive, Vera and I had worked to raise money for MEMS under Shelby's supportive leadership. Our initial pitches to potential investors were, in retrospect, quite juvenile and we pretty much got the results you might expect.

Our efforts focused on raising money for the fabrication business. With a revenue of $4.5 million in 1997, Vera's total MEMS business was growing consistently at an average of 40 percent per year. The commercial part of her business—industry customers as opposed to government grants—was growing at 70 percent per year, but it was a pure service business: We either accepted other people's designs or helped them with their design, and then fabricated their products for them. When I first sat down with Vera to discuss financial projections, she estimated that the commercial business could be at $25 million in revenue within five years.

Given the financial and political storm that was brewing at MCNC, we both felt that building a business plan around the commercial fabrication business would be a safe landing spot, protecting our livelihoods and those of the rest of the team.

Vera, being the "Queen of MEMS" was catching the interest of some pretty big names including icons of venture investment like Venrock (invested in Apple) and Greylock Partners (invested in Intel). When her contacts would pass through Raleigh, Vera and I would pitch our plan. But we were way out of our league. These premier investors were looking for unicorns, companies that could be worth a billion dollars or more in a few years, and our plan to reach $25 million in revenue and achieve self-sufficiency wasn't even close to what they were targeting.

Once we included the microrelay product in our plans and increased our projected revenues to close to a hundred million dollars interest grew, but we still weren't big enough to attract the attention of serious venture investors. The drawbacks to our business at that time were numerous: We were a "crazy" nonprofit; we had no business team; we were selling $2 components; and we didn't have an established business model poised for growth. Our current business model was providing fabrication services and no one was interested in that. We had yet to leverage MUMPs, because at that point, we did not fully understand its value. A final drawback was that the bulk of our revenue was still in government-funded programs. When we discussed this with Vera's VC contacts, we soon found out that our government programs were not considered a plus; they were actually viewed as a drag on future commercial activity. Finally, as Bob West had pointed out, MCNC had a terrible reputation for doing business and serious investors were wary.

When Jack came on board, things changed considerably. Although Jack had no connections within the venture world and thought venture capital was all a bit crazy—he had very powerful connections in private equity and high finance. He also had his own professional network which included icons of another kind: business executives in the largest corporations in America.

Jack wasted no time. He needed to get both Unitive and Cronos out the door to ensure MCNC's survival. In addition to bringing in experienced management to run our new startup, within weeks of taking the helm at MCNC, he had potential investors lined up and, much to my relief, looked to me to make the pitches.

It did not take me long to realize Jack was the manager and executive I hoped to be. With Jack in charge, the raging storm that had been MCNC became a calm oasis almost overnight. He knew what he wanted; you knew what he wanted. He was decisive *and* his decisions were clear, and he was so thoughtful and inclusive, you really couldn't argue with much of anything he did. It all made sense. Without a hint of arrogance, he projected a tremendous amount of confidence which made life easier for all of us who reported to him. The almost unbearable stress I had felt in my failure to launch the microrelay with Nortel was a non-issue under Jack's leadership. When he gave me the opportunity to pitch the MEMS business to investors in his network, I felt truly privileged.

The most memorable of our pitches was to Patrick Davis at Pilot Mountain Capital. Patrick had been a very successful dean of a local business school. Prior to that he held executive and board positions with IBM where he was considered one of the key architects of IBM's turn-around in the 1980s. After leaving the business school, Patrick became chairman at Pilot Mountain Capital, which under his guidance became a billion-dollar investment firm. In 1998 Jack and I made the short road trip to meet with Patrick in Chapel Hill.

When we arrived at Patrick's office, we were shown into a small extremely well-appointed conference room exactly as you would expect from a firm that dealt with large investments and wealthy clients. Jack and I sat on one side of the long table and when Patrick came in, he sat opposite us on the other side. Jack and Patrick exchanged some pleasantries about IBM and Jack's new Chevy Yukon and his annual trip to Wyoming. Their discussion was innocuous, and it was brief. Other than saying hello, I said nothing. Finally, Patrick turned his full attention to me and asked me to give my pitch. I remember how direct he was. He wasn't rude, but he also did not beat about the bush. What I remember most were his eyes. I can't swear to it, but I think they were hazel in color. He had a searing gaze and the second he turned his attention on me I felt like a deer in headlights.

I stood and went to the head of the table, with both Jack and Patrick swiveling their chairs to give me their full attention. I gave my pitch, the same as I would any other, but Patrick's unwavering stare will be seared into my mind forever. His piercing eyes drilled into me without ever seeming to blink. It felt like he was peering directly into my soul.

It was unnerving and at the same time exhilarating. Patrick didn't say a word, but I felt like I was being challenged like never before. I loved the fact that this serious and capable person was intently listening to what I had to say, that he might be looking for holes in my pitch, and that he might pounce if I failed in some way. By this time, I'd been living and breathing MEMS for almost two years and I'd had so many ups and downs behind me that I couldn't be shaken.

I was also starting to *believe*! It was the latter half of 1998 and I was seeing serious, consistently increasing commercial interest in our MEMS products and services. I had *paying* customers. This was no longer me trying to sell a deal, this was me preaching the gospel. Nor did I really care if Patrick Davis wanted to invest. He was an icon of industry, the former dean of a prominent business school, and a captain of high finance. I was letting him know I had found a goldmine, success was inevitable, and the train was leaving the station. If he didn't invest, someone else would. When I finished there was silence as I returned to my seat beside Jack. He and Patrick swiveled back to face each other across the table. Their discussion was as surprising as it was short.

"So," Patrick asked Jack, "how much are you going to put into this deal?"

Jack almost choked at the unexpected turn in the conversation, but then he laughed that dry laugh of his.

"Oh, I think I can come up with $50,000 or so."

"Okay. Okay. It's very interesting. I'll put someone on it."

Patrick, it seemed, was a man of few words and rapid decisions, but I wasn't sure what to think. I'd been more than impressed by him and knew having someone of his caliber invest in our deal would bring other investors along, just like Gabriel Tanner had done for Unitive. And it seemed like he had bought into my deal, right there, on the spot. Jack seemed to think this was just how things were done, and I wasn't going to question it. On the other hand, I was suspicious even as I began working with an executive at Pilot Mountain Capital to structure the deal. It was almost too easy.

Structuring financing for a startup is complex at the best of times because there are so many variables that need to be worked out. Any one of these variables can lead to failure during negotiations. The Cronos deal was made more complex because it involved not two, but three parties. In most investment deals there are just two: the company founders negotiating with investors. However, Cronos was a spinout that involved three parties, all of which had to be happy with the deal for it to get done. They included: Jack and the MCNC board who had a fiduciary responsibility to negotiate a good deal for MCNC; Vera Cohen and her team, the founding employees at Cronos; and the investors who wanted adequate control and a good return on their investment.

Putting together a three-party deal is a little like trying to predict a three-body collision in physics. The results of one billiard ball hitting a second is relatively easy to predict using simple Newtonian equations that most people learn in high school. On the other hand, the trajectories of three billiard balls colliding are almost impossible to predict. The same can be said for deals involving three groups of people with varying objectives. The difficulty of closing this kind of deal goes up exponentially.

The Cronos deal was a three-body problem being structured by experienced investors but with relatively inexperienced counterparts at Cronos and MCNC. Jack, for all his years as an executive at IBM, had never put together a venture deal. Of course, he had closed Unitive, but that deal was well underway by the time he came on board. As we worked with the venture community, Jack expressed a number of times to me that he felt the venture capitalists were "nuts."

For better or worse, initially, it was just me and Jack trying to put something together, but soon after our meeting with Patrick Davis, Brian Novak and Ron Quinn joined the Cronos team. Brian had a bit more experience, but his brutal negotiating style made getting to "yes" quite difficult, especially with venture investors who had little patience under any circumstances. The most experienced person at our table was Ron Quinn, and we were fortunate to have him advising Brian as getting investment terms right for all three parties would be very tricky and it was precisely where these kinds of deals tended to go bad.

In forming Cronos, MCNC decided on a 70/30 split where MCNC would own 70 percent of the new company and management and employees would own 30 percent. While some argued that this was too generous for MCNC and not good enough for management and employees, I felt it to be reasonable. After all, MCNC was putting considerable, real assets into the deal and this had to be compensated fairly. On the other hand, the operation could not be run without leadership and engineering from Vera's MEMS group. All of these people had to be incentivized to join Cronos and a 30 percent pool of stock met that bar. From MCNC's perspective, the 70/30 split was a very easy deal to structure: the Board was comfortable with the split, all the assets were theirs and the deal structure was decided unilaterally by MCNC. There was no negotiation.

Once investors got involved, things quickly got much more complicated. First, a valuation had to be agreed upon. The MEMS group had finished 1997 with about $4.5 million in revenue and was tracking to hit $6 million in revenue in 1998. Our target revenue for 1999 was $10 million. As I had done with Gabriel on Unitive, we used the price-revenue EV ratio to establish valuation for the company.

In the case of Cronos, we had data that showed a price/revenue ratio of 4 was reasonable for a MEMS company. We argued the company should be worth $24 million using 1998 revenues of $6 million and assuming we hit our projections of $10 million in 1999, it would soon be worth $40 million! We also looked at projected revenues of the microrelay (still alive thanks to the electrical cross-connect switch application), the emerging optical switch products, and our fabrication services to argue the company would be worth much, much more in the future.

The investors, starting with Pilot Mountain Capital, came back and made counterarguments:

"Most of your revenue right now is government grants! That revenue has nothing to do with your future business. We discount that to zero!"

Or "Your business model is unproven!"

Or "Your projections are optimistic!"

We finally agreed that if MCNC spun out the entire MEMS operation, the resulting company would be worth a post-money valuation of $25 million. We also agreed that the company needed an $8 million investment to cover operating losses over the next two years which determined a pre-money valuation of $17 million. Thankfully, I was much more versed in these issues now, and of course, we also had Ron Quinn who was a seasoned pro. While the valuation was considered reasonable by all concerned, it was the ownership structure that created a fundamental sticking point for the deal.

With $8 million into a company valued at $25 million, the investors owned $8/25 = 32$ percent of the company. By all measures this was a reasonable ownership stake for the investors, and not atypical for a first-round investment. However, the investors had a major concern how the remaining 68 percent of the company was apportioned. Given the initial 70/30 split, MCNC now owned $0.7 \times 68\% = 48$ percent post-investment whereas management and employees owned $0.3 \times 68\% = 20$ percent post-investment. Investors balked at this structure, and MCNC couldn't understand why.

The investors had a strong argument against MCNC's proposed structure: No one would be willing to bet $8 million on a deal where a nonprofit had majority ownership and management and employees only owned 20 percent. This perspective was a very hard pill for Jack and the MCNC Board to swallow.

Another problem lay with Brian's lack of experience running a startup. To be sure, given his IBM career, he brought sorely needed operational experience to the deal. Brian had indeed been "around the block." But for venture capitalists, it was the wrong block. Brian's long history of executive management in a large corporation could actually be considered a negative in an early-stage startup, and raised questions about whether he would be able to manage the constant change and turbulence that is part and parcel of a startup.

Additionally, while Brian was an amazing negotiator, he was used to negotiating from a position of strength at IBM. Quite often, when you are raising money for a startup, this is not the case. In fact, it's usually the opposite: Venture capitalists have the money and startups need it. If you can't respect that, VCs have other opportunities and won't hesitate to move on. Finally, Brian was not great at pitching. He was an inside player, best when he was one-on-one. When he pitched Cronos in front of an audience, he was uncomfortable, and it showed.

I'm not sure which of these issues—ownership or leadership—caused heartburn for Pilot Mountain Capital, but our very promising start soon dissipated into a curt "pass" on the deal. By this time, with Brian on board, I was no longer privy to the negotiations. Nevertheless, the Pilot Mountain Capital negotiation sealed many elements of the deal, including the $25 million valuation, MCNC's preferred ownership structure, and even Jack's $50,000 commitment. These were all set in place and became the basis of our offering to other investors going forward.

Brian also didn't waste any time whipping us into shape. He insisted we put together a detailed, realistic business plan. And with Ron Quinn's involvement, we had a professional financial plan as well. Operationally, Brian cracked the whip too: He carved the organization into engineering and operations and put professional management in charge of both. Vera was designated the Chief Technology Officer, and I was Vice President of Marketing and Business Development.

It was a painful transition for everyone, but there was not much room or even time for discussion. When push came to shove Brian could be a terrible bully, willing to leave a mark and burn bridges if he had to. On the other hand, given the speed at which things were happening, it's probably what the deal needed.

While I had significant differences with Brian's style and ended up having more than one heart-to-heart with him, I had to respect the fact that he never asked anything of anyone that he wouldn't ask of himself. He considered himself a "bull" and loved to drive the organization as hard as he drove himself. At one point, early in 2000 there was a major snowstorm in Raleigh in which two feet of snow fell overnight. It was a crazy scene in a region that rarely saw snow and had no equipment to deal with it. Raleigh took over a week to dig out, but at Cronos we were back at work the next day as Brian and Ron drove the entire team to work in their 4 × 4s through what seemed to be impossible streets.

And that was after Brian had already earned my respect when, in 1999, he was diagnosed with prostate cancer. He went off for treatment for a week or so, then came right back to work. He would get chemotherapy at Duke Hospital in the morning, and then drive directly to work green with nausea and clearly suffering, but never missing a day. To do this while raising money for a startup, with all the pressures that entails, was almost unfathomable to me.

Nevertheless, for some obvious reasons, and perhaps for others that I was not aware of, we struggled mightily through 1998 and into 1999 to raise money. We approached local venture capitalists and attended venture conferences. We flew to California and Boston to meet investors. We pitched to all comers. The end result was consistently negative: a "pass."

It was Vera who came to our rescue.

# Closing Time

While Brian struggled to pitch our deal, Vera was born to it. With her stature in the MEMS industry, she also had connections no one else did. When Vera and I had met with venture capitalists in the early days, our pitch failed not because of her skill, but because we lacked a clear vision for growth, and had no real operational plan to get there.

As we worked with Brian and Ron, we were forced to develop a much better understanding of our approach to the market. By then we also had *real* commercial customers with *orders* who had a clear vision of how our products and services could be of value to them. With their help, we were able to develop a customer-validated model of how our revenues could grow exponentially over time, providing us with the cornerstone of a competent fund-raising campaign.

At the same time Vera developed a clear understanding of our unique competitive advantage. Aside from our rapidly growing patent portfolio, we were recognized as one of the top three MEMS technology groups in the world and had independent studies from our customers (like Nortel) to prove it. All of this was backed up by a realistic operational and financial plan that was based on customer orders and forecasts. None of us could have done it on our own, but as a team we created a story that we all deeply believed in.

Vera didn't need much more than that, and soon brought Intel Capital to the table.

Intel was on its way to becoming the largest venture investor in the United States and Vera had good contacts there, specifically a man by the name of Warren Lee. Warren was the investor who years later in his office on Sand Hill Road would explain to me why it was difficult to deal with universities.

Warren liked Vera and made it clear that he would invest, *if* we could find a lead investor for our deal.

As was the case with Unitive, when putting a deal together, you often find investors interested in putting money into the deal, but not willing to lead. This could be for various reasons: Maybe they like the deal, but feel they are not the best to assess it; maybe they are a corporate investor that has a policy not to take lead positions; maybe they just want someone else to do all the hard work and due diligence putting the deal together. In any case, it's not uncommon to have investors, but no lead to make the deal happen. That being said, to even have interest from Intel was a *huge* step forward that changed how others perceived us. Kudos to Vera.

I was also pursuing connections of my own. Although Jack had bought us extra time with the North Carolina legislature, the cash crunch at MCNC remained very real and was even exacerbated by the extra funds we were spending to spin out Cronos. As the clock ticked deep into 1998, I could literally taste success, but it was mingled with fear as my optimism for our prospects was severely tempered by a deep concern that we might never get there. Could all of this promise end in yet another failure? I feared that I might be destined to always be part of the greatest things that never happened. These concerns lent a certain amount of desperation to my efforts to find an investor who could lead our deal.

I had built my connections in the investment community very carefully, learning to ask the right questions, learning to discard the wannabes, and building a credible reputation with the real players. Bob West was my friend now and he was a credible entree into the local venture investment community. That being said, there still was no local interest in Cronos, with Bob West also joining the long list of investors who turned us down.

Once again, my break came from a totally unexpected direction in the form of an old friend and colleague named Yves Charbonneau.

I met Yves in 1989 at the International Space University in Strasbourg, France. I had applied for and won a summer scholarship to ISU while completing my Ph.D. in Canada. Yves was a vice president at Oerlikon Aerospace in Canada and a huge supporter of ISU. He was also a mentor to me over the summer in Strasbourg, which was how I got to know him.

Quite corpulent and much shorter than me, Yves was a brash French Canadian full of stories of his exploits and capabilities and his reach in the aerospace industry. Much of what he told me I found hard to believe just from the sheer incongruity of the achievements he was claiming. I was particularly distrustful when, one evening, walking back from a bar, he claimed to be a blackbelt in Tae Kwan Do. I couldn't help but snort my derision, as

Yves bragged on and on marching along beside me. I enjoyed his company, but the more I spoke with him the more I saw him as an improbable figure. His stories about connections and conquests were just too fanciful.

In this instance, however, I was taught a quick lesson. Yves, hearing me snort, skipped in front of me and seamlessly performed a roundhouse high kick that whistled marginally over the top of my head. I'd never seen someone so short and so wide move so lightly and so fast. And how was he able to kick that high? It was a tiny proof point that shocked me.

As I started to reassess my perspective, I learned Yves did indeed have connections. As a vice president at Oerlikon Aerospace, he was deeply connected to the Canadian Space program through which he knew many Canadian political leaders. Recitals of his exotic adventures no longer sounded quite so fanciful. He removed all doubt in my mind in a most amazing way.

While at ISU we watched a movie of astronauts performing experiments in microgravity on a KC-135 airplane. Also known as the "vomit comet," this plane flew in huge parabolas to create brief—around 25 seconds—moments of microgravity.

"Man, would I love to fly on that plane!" I told Yves.

"Write a proposal for an experiment, and I'll get you on that plane," he told me.

Once again, I secretly questioned the veracity of his statement: How could he be so sure? On the other hand, by then I was impressed enough by Yves to believe at least half of what he told me. So, I spent a memorable weekend in the Vosges mountains writing a proposal to electrochemically grow crystals in microgravity. We went to the mountains with a large group of students and Yves arranged for me to bring along an Apple Macintosh SE computer. For three days, while my colleagues went hiking, I pounded away on the keyboard.

We had rented an old, decrepit home and I sat in front of a huge French door window overlooking the valley. As I worked feverishly, I missed hanging out with my fellow students and questioned my sanity in believing Yves' boast that he could get me on that plane. On the plus side, the views were amazing. The hills were incredibly steep and in the early morning, while others slept, I would look through the wide-open window, down into clouds that had formed in the morning chill. I was literally sitting on a cloud! It was a scene and a feeling I will never forget.

Six months later I won an unheard of half million-dollar grant from the Canadian government to run a series of experiments on the KC-135. I ended up flying eight campaigns, each one with at least 40 parabolas. I got to experience zero gravity! By then I was a full convert; I believed in Yves Charbonneau.

Later on, I consulted for Yves at Oerlikon Aerospace, but when I moved to the United States and began focusing on my family and my career in North Carolina, Yves and I drifted apart. Oerlikon downsized in Canada and Yves went on to do other things. I was busy and did not keep track.

So, imagine my surprise, when ten years later in the midst of our lackluster fundraising campaign I get a call at MCNC from Yves Charbonneau. How he got my phone number I will never know. I was amazed and pleased to hear from him, not dreaming for a moment that this had anything to do with Cronos. We made small talk, mostly catching up on my career. Glumly, I described to Yves our incredible opportunity with Cronos and our unbelievable inability to raise money.

"Well, I hate to do this to you, Jesko," Yves said with his classic hyperbole. "But this is your *lucky* day." When Yves spoke, he said things with glee. His energy and excitement were contagious, and I had to smile.

"C'mon, Yves, what are you talking about?" I felt like we were back at ISU and Yves was about to sell me something that was impossible to believe but, knowing him, probably true.

"You've been crying into the phone so much, we haven't gotten to what I'm doing! I am an investment advisor at SOFINOV," he told me triumphantly, clearly happy to surprise me.

Investment advisor? My stomach dropped. How many times had I heard that over the past few years? I hated to have to do this to my friend, especially after not talking with him for almost ten years, but I had no time for this.

I felt embarrassed to have to put him off, but this door had to be shut quickly. "Yves, I'm sorry, we don't need an investment advisor. Really, I—".

"Are you kidding me, dumbass? I don't want to advise you, although you guys obviously need it! This is SOFINOV I'm talking about!"

"What the heck is that? SOFINOV?"

"Oh my God, what rock do you live under? It's also called Caisse de dépôt et placement du Québec. But SOFINOV is easier. We manage $50 *billion* of Quebec pensions. *And* we have a new technology fund that invests in deals just like yours. *And* I am a *direct adviser* to the guy who makes the investment decisions!"

Unbelievable, but classic, classic Yves Charbonneau.

"Oh...," my confusion was obvious. But I couldn't help it. When you are talking to Yves, within five minutes you don't know if you are coming or going.

"Have I made your day yet?" he demanded.

Reluctantly, I had to agree. He was at least starting to make my day. Yves hadn't changed a bit.

Even now, I have no idea why Yves called me on that day, how he found my number, or what his real deal was with SOFINOV. I assume that, in his new role as a technology investment advisor, he somehow found out about Cronos and my role in it from the investment community, perhaps even directly from Intel or, even more likely, Nortel. That's how these things happen—there is nothing that the venture community likes to do more than gossip about deals. Once you start to sell a deal, it takes on a life of its own.

What I do know is that, once I got over my surprise, Yves and I were talking deal almost immediately. I was almost giddy with the indulgence of being able to pitch my deal to someone I knew and trusted. It made everything so much easier. I knew Yves so well, I could open up about our business: the good, the bad, and the ugly. Including, of course, our dealings with Nortel and Lucent and some of our other premier customers.

"I love it! I'm in!" Yves told me. "When can you guys get up here?"

Brian and I flew up to Montreal shortly thereafter. We were so desperate for cash that every lead had to be followed. We met Yves in a hotel where Brian gave him the Cronos pitch. It was slightly stilted as usual, but Yves was by then already way ahead of the game. He listened with characteristic impatience and happily needled Brian on his inability to raise money on such a great deal.

"I can't believe you guys have struggled to raise money on this! I don't think you know what you are doing!" Yves exclaimed, rubbing it in. "But, leave it to a pro. I'll help you. I want to do it! I'll pitch it to management here at SOFINOV. They'll invest!"

Brian glowered. He had a huge ego and despised being made fun of. Moreover, he hated the idea that this crazy French Canadian was potentially a gateway to investment. But Brian was desperate too, so he smiled and sucked it up, something I had never seen him do before. Wanting to show that he truly didn't mind the ribbing, Brian made the mistake of inviting Yves to dinner on our tab.

"Hey, Yves, let's go to dinner. Your choice, my treat," Brian said, with feigned friendliness.

I gasped inwardly as Yves' eyes sparkled even brighter. Yves was a true connoisseur of food and wine. I'd eaten some of the best meals in my life with him in France and Germany and Canada, and I knew his tastes were not cheap.

"Can I choose the wine too?" Yves asked, innocently.

Oh boy.

"Of course, Yves!" Brian replied, being a good sport. "We love a good wine!"

I remember the dinner very well. We went to a seafood restaurant where you could choose your meal tableside from a cart of fresh fish, they brought to you. The service is off menu—meaning you have no idea what it costs. Of course, Brian was paying, so this is what Yves went for. The fish were huge, and each one was an individual serving. I chose the smallest one and could still only eat a modest portion of it. Yves also chose the wine, spending a lengthy time discussing options with the sommelier in French. The restaurant knew a mark when they saw one and laid out a feast. The bill for the three of us came to $800. I laughed when I saw it—classic Yves! I wish I could have been in the room when Brian explained that one to Jack, especially considering the cash crunch that had fully pervaded MCNC by that time.

Yves moved quickly and within a few weeks had set up a meeting with his boss who would make the decision to invest. Everything was lined up. SOFINOV had accepted his recommendation to make the lead investment in Cronos. At this point all we needed was the rubber stamp of approval. Yves' boss was very high up in the organization and we would have 45 min with him to finalize the deal. Jack had to be there.

Yves also nixed Brian giving the pitch.

"It's got to be, Jesko," he told Jack. "Just have Jesko pitch it like he pitched it to me over the phone. Don't worry, it's all lined up."

Jack didn't have to think twice to acquiesce to Yves' demands. He was no dummy. He'd seen me pitch to Patrick Davis and others and he'd seen Brian pitch too. He also knew that Yves was my friend. At this point, what Yves wanted Yves got, as evidenced by our $800 dinner!

Jack, Brian, and I flew to Montreal where we met Yves in a gloomy room in a nondescript office building that was part of SOFINOV. Yves' boss arrived late and alone. He was a very stern looking man, who didn't say much. He came in and sat down, and Yves gave me the go ahead to start.

It was evident as I pitched that this was all completely perfunctory: Analyses had already been carried out, recommendations had been provided, and decisions had been made. Where was the pen? Yves, for once, was uncharacteristically reserved.

When I was done, I was asked to leave the room, presumably so the final discussions could be had without my prying eyes and ears. Fine with me. I walked down the hall and down the stairs to the lobby and waited. And waited.

It took much longer than I expected. Yves had assured me that this was simply a rubber stamp. The deal was as good as closed. What on earth could they be talking about? When Jack and Brian finally joined me, Jack looked grim and Brian looked angry. My heart sank as they approached. Neither said a word and we headed outside in silence.

We hailed a taxi and remained in silence until we were well on our way back to the airport. Brian was clearly too angry to speak, and I was afraid to say anything.

"Well, that didn't go as expected," Jack finally said, with his dry chuckle. Brian stewed in the front seat and I don't remember hearing a word from him all the way back to Raleigh.

I'm not sure exactly what happened in the room that day, but my hunch was it had something to do with MCNC's out-sized level of ownership. SOFINOV was okay with everything, they just could not have MCNC, a nonprofit controlled by a somewhat arbitrary board of directors, own a majority share of a company that SOFINOV was investing millions of dollars in. As we worked towards the finish line on the deal, someone had suggested that MCNC bring their ownership share down to match what the financial investors would have after the deal was done. This could be done by giving up a portion of MCNC ownership to other investors—around 20%—and also by increasing the size of the employee pool, since that would be needed for future employees.

I'd had numerous discussions with Yves about this and we thought it was all done, but apparently not. Maybe the MCNC board nixed the idea at the last minute and told Jack that he had to do better. Maybe Jack and Brian didn't respect Yves' position of influence with the decision maker. I knew myself that it was easy to underestimate Yves' authority. In any case, apparently the decision had been made at MCNC to ignore Yves and save the real negotiation for when the SOFINOV decision maker was in the room. Maybe that was why I was asked to leave.

It did not go well. Whatever attempts were made to move the goalposts at the last minute were not received kindly. Yves' boss got really angry and walked out, saying he never wanted to see or hear from MCNC again. Given our increasingly desperate need for cash, it was an almost unfathomable result.

Yves called me the very next day. "What the f---? What kind of idiots do you work for?" Yves yelled in my ear.

"I'm sorry, Yves. I'm sorry! I wasn't even in the room! I had no idea! Believe me, I'm as unhappy as you are. More unhappy!" I was feeling so terrible I couldn't even start to express my remorse.

"God dammit! I look like a f---ing idiot! I backed your deal! We had everything worked out! You won't believe what I just went through! Jesus, Jesko—"

"I swear to God, Yves. Nobody feels worse than I do. I swear, you were our last chance. I can't believe they screwed things up."

In fairness, everybody felt bad about how things had turned out, no one more than Jack. I have to believe that he was under pressure from the Board to pull a move like that. We all knew that things were coming down to the wire and now we had missed our very best chance with SOFINOV. By this time, the transition of people, equipment, and operating space from MCNC to Cronos had occurred. Sure, we were generating revenue, but we were also losing money and these losses were being paid dutifully by the mothership. It was not sustainable. MCNC just could not carry Cronos any longer.

Fortunately for all of us, in spite of his fury, Yves was not easily deterred from anything. He was a magician. He pulled our failed deal that had been burnt to a crisp out of the fire and somehow reconstituted it into a piece of yummy, edible bacon. Yves being Yves—he had a second act. And Yves being Yves—he was going to be dramatic about it.

Having vented to the full extent of his colorful capabilities, he calmly declared, "I have a plan B."

And he did. He had a wonderful, stupendous, amazing plan B. He had a plan B that was even better, much better than plan A.

"SOFINOV doesn't just invest directly in deals, we are also a limited partner in a number of venture firms. We have big money and big influence. One of these venture firms is a group called Spacevest in Virginia. They'll take a hard look at your deal. I've already talked to them."

Classic Yves Charbonneau.

Then he went on to tell me that I was Cinderella and he was my fairy godmother, and I had to agree with him.

Sure enough, it turned out that SOFINOV was a significant limited partner in Spacevest. After our debacle in Montreal, Yves used SOFINOV's leverage to get Spacevest to look at our deal. In the venture world, an introduction is worth gold. It was all we needed. Yves told them that Intel was in, if we could find a lead for the investment. He was also in the unique position of being able to provide insider information, explaining to Spacevest what had happened between SOFINOV and MCNC.

"But, here's the deal, Jesko. And it's so f---ing simple, that even a bunch of dumb southerners like you guys can figure it out. Okay? You just need to take the deal we were going to sign up here with SOFINOV. MCNC has to give up some of their ownership and we've already worked out how to do that. Okay? No bullshit, last minute, surprise negotiations. That's it. Can you guys get that through your thick skulls?"

It was clear, while all agreed on the investment amount of $8 million and the post-money valuation of $25 million, the ownership issue was the sticking point. Under the current structure the investors would own 32%, management and employees 20%, and MCNC 48%. Yves' insistence, and our experience losing the deal with SOFINOV, were confirmation that no investor would be willing to have a nonprofit as the majority shareholder in a deal they were putting $8 million into. Maybe this had been the deal killer all along.

Yves' suggestion was to simply issue more shares to management and employees to change that split. MCNC, on the other hand hated the idea of giving up ownership.

"You need to go tell Jack to fix this!" Yves yelled in my ear. "Tell him if he is willing to accept the deal that he turned down up here with SOFINOV, then Spacevest will lead. You got that? Do I need to write this down?"

"Ah, um," I dithered, trying to think things through. "Okay, but if we work all of it out, why can't we just do it with SOFINOV?"

"Jesus, Jesko! Don't you get it? If I mention MCNC to my boss ever again, he'll castrate me! You guys are *persona non grata* up here, man. Stay out of Canada!"

"Okay, Okay. I'll talk to Jack."

Actually, I first went and talked to Brian. I told him what I had learned, and he agreed that we had a big problem.

"There's no way the MCNC Board is going to give more stock to us. Jack tells me it was a huge fight to get the 70/30 split. Now we're asking MCNC for more. Jack has no room on this. But that's what killed everything with SOFINOV…" Brian looked glum, and that was indeed very rare.

"Okay, but what if we ask MCNC to sell some of their stock?" I asked.

"What?"

"Look, MCNC has to give up some of their share to make this work, right?

"Yeah, I guess so."

"So, let's not ask them to give it away. Let's ask them to sell it. It's common stock, so we'll sell it at some discount to the $1.70 that investors are paying for preferred stock. MCNC needs cash, so if we can put a million dollars in their pockets, they may go for it."

My idea was pretty straightforward. When we first formed Cronos, it was a company on paper only. It had no business and no assets, so it was literally only worth the paper that the stock was printed on—a "paper company." As a result, employees and management (and MCNC) were able to buy stock at one penny. Now, six months later, the deal was starting to come together and the company—after all the transactions with MCNC for patents, equipment, and contracts were completed—would be worth $25 million, which worked out to be $1.70 a share. At this price, investors were buying what is called "preferred stock." As preferred stockholders they held special protections over and above common stockholders like employees and MCNC. Common stock didn't have these preferences, so it was worth much less—at most $0.20. If MCNC was willing, we might be able to sell some of their common stock at some reasonable discount to the preferred price, but still much better than $0.20. Like us, MCNC bought all their stock at a penny so they would make an immediate gain, reduce their ownership, and everyone could be happy.

"Who the hell are you going to get to buy that stock?" Brian asked, sarcastically.

"Are you kidding?" I asked in return.

We were always getting people who had relatively small amounts of money, who wanted to get in on funded deals. This included friends and family, lawyers associated with putting the deal together, even vendors and customers in some cases. If you had a deal coming together with a group of professional investors, especially with a brand name like Intel, then everyone wanted in. Vera alone had enough contacts to buy as much stock as MCNC wanted to sell.

Brian took the proposal to Jack along with the message that, if we could make this work, we would have a new lead investor. It did the trick: MCNC was in. MCNC would end up with slightly more than 30%, but with an immediate return of as much as $1 million. At the same time, the 20% stock pool was increased significantly to provide more stock incentives to future employees being hired into the company. The investors would own 32%. Everyone had what they needed.

Deals require creativity and flexibility and most of all, they require an understanding of the needs of all parties. Making demands and banging fists rarely win the day and ambushing negotiations from a position of weakness is an even worse strategy. You need to understand the other side's motivations and play to that, otherwise deals don't get done.

It's not often in life that you walk off a cliff and then get a do over. But that's exactly what Yves gave us: a do over. And he did it entirely out of passion for the deal. Had the deal gone through SOFINOV, he would have personally benefited. With the deal going through Spacevest, he stood to gain nothing. He backed the deal because he believed in what we were doing.

Now all we needed was our final investor. Spacevest and Intel would put in a total of $6 million, but we still needed a third investor to put up the last $2 million to complete the $8 million deal. It was an excruciating time, but not uncommon when you raise money. With a lead investor, you have most of the investment in place, but you cannot close the deal without all the money. The lead provides a term sheet for the investment that all the followers sign on to. Intel signed up right away, but the term sheet stipulated $8 million and we only had $6 million. If we couldn't get all the money, then the term sheet would be void.

Through my network, we once again brought in a number of local investors and they all turned us down. As before, Vera once again saved the day. Through personal connections, she brought in a family fund that committed the final $2 million.

In retrospect, it's amazing the deal got done. The strikes against us were many given the number of parties involved and the MCNC Board's reluctance to accept the inevitable. Ultimately the investment didn't come from the experienced dealmakers but from the networks of the two relative greenhorns: Vera and myself. I revered Jack, but I was also starting to wonder if his focus on gaining "around the block" experience was the right path. Sure, we were operationally much stronger with the team he had brought in, but of all the things that a startup CEO needs to do, the number one is raise money. In this regard our CEO and MCNC did not deliver, putting a drag on the deal rather than enabling it.

I understand the situation a bit better today. I have put many more deals together since then, including a few more "three-body" financings like the one we did for Cronos. What I have found is that raising money is brutally difficult. There are many dimensions to the challenge, and a CEO has to be attuned to all of them. Raising money is like conducting an orchestra and bringing it to a final crescendo. The one difference is that, in an orchestra, the musicians are reading from a sheet and are motivated to follow the conductor. In financing a deal, it's often the opposite. There are customers, employees, and current shareholders you are trying to please. There are the investors, who are often incredibly savvy, you are trying to attract. You have a technology that is constantly evolving, and not always in your favor. Layered on top of that, you have everchanging market conditions that can crush the best-laid plans.

The CEO is dealing with a deluge of diverging, often hidden motivations under the pressure of running out of cash, with a runway that may be measured in months or even just a few days! I've been there. If this isn't challenging enough, the clincher is that nothing is static: All of these conditions are dynamically changing over the period of six to eighteen months that it takes to raise money. This mostly results in a cacophony of sounds, not beautiful music.

What happened to us as we raised funds for Cronos was fairly typical. Thankfully, in spite of our many, significant challenges, and the many, diverging motivations that existed at MCNC, we pulled through. Between Vera and myself, we had enough connections to put together a wonderful investment group. Between Jack, Brian, Ron, and the rest of the team, we negotiated a creative solution that left everyone wishing they had gotten a little more. A very good deal, all around. On December 7, 1999, our investors wired $8 million to the Cronos bank account, buying in at $1.70 a share.

I bet it's the best investment they ever made.

# Going Large

The biggest optical communications conference in the industry was the Optical Fiber Conference (OFC) held in February each year, typically alternating between the East and the West Coast. Early in 1999 we were not yet funded and had no means to attend the conference, but Jake Wilson at Nortel did. He returned with prophetic news.

"Your world is going to change, Jesko. Lucent gave the keynote at the conference, and basically said that scaling in optical communications won't work without MEMS. I think it's a paradigm changer!"

"Who gave the keynote?"

"Tony Williams. Do you guys know him?"

Tony Williams at Lucent was the architect of the LambdaRouter and a good friend of Vera's. His team had designed the first LambdaRouter chip and we were building it in our facilities. It was a great example of how Vera's MEMS strategy had worked to perfection. As the need for inexpensive, scalable photonics devices grew, Vera's MUMPs program attracted a whole community of early adopters who had small budgets and very large visions for a future full of MEMS optical devices. Tony Williams and his team were one of Vera's very first customers.

"Yeah, I've heard of him. I think Vera knows him too," I replied, nonchalantly.

"Well, Tony is a thought leader on MEMS and photonics, and he made a very compelling case for MEMS and photonics in his keynote at OFC. There is no doubt that you guys are going to get very busy!"

Busy was an understatement. Whatever Tony Williams said at OFC in 1999, it had a profound effect on the engineering community's perception of the value of MEMS in photonics. Month by month interest in MEMS grew. Groups like ours, that were already positioned as MEMS providers, profited handsomely from the increased interest in MEMS. Lucent (a customer) became the de facto leader in MEMS because of its widely hyped LambdaRouter projected to hit the market as a 256-port switch. OMM (a customer) raised $130 million for its 8 × 8 optical switch. New companies like Glimmerglass (a customer), C-Speed (a customer), and Xros (not a customer) raised venture funding overnight. In late 1998, MEMS was an esoteric engineering practice, but by early 2000 there were over 400 optical MEMS companies vying to strike it rich!

Andy Grove, CEO of Intel, defined the new time-space continuum we had entered as "The world now runs on internet time."

If you were caught up in any business that had any connection to the internet, it certainly felt that he could be right: Product development and business deals moved faster on the internet than in the real world. Internet time was heralded as a new economic phenomenon, where value could be created overnight, and riches could be made in months. For a time, it was even true.

As I flew back from Ottawa in early 1998, I didn't know it, but I was about to enter internet time. Like Alice, entering Wonderland by fantastical means, my flight somehow took me through a wormhole into another world, anchored by that fateful call from Jake Wilson. As I showed off my ice-scraper to my wife, eventually laughing with her at what seemed to be another abysmal failure, I was actually standing at the brink of a vortex. I just didn't know it.

In the meantime, even as we were struggling to raise money, our business prospects were beginning to exceed our wildest dreams. Within *weeks* of arriving home from the ice storm in Ottawa, I was licensing technology from Caltech and selling a product development program to Nortel. As we started working with the Nortel photonics group in Ottawa and the United Kingdom, it quickly became clear that selling enabling technology for photonics devices was in a different universe compared to what I had experienced pushing microrelays in a 100-year old industry.

Engineering teams from both Nortel locations (Ottawa and United Kingdom) flew in regularly to meet with us, developing product requirement documents, carrying out product design reviews, and analyzing test results almost overnight. Our MEMS engineering team was creative and knowledgeable—we were experts in MEMS—but we had never developed an actual product before. We learned a lot from Nortel.

To be successful at taking technology innovation to a new product requires a spectrum of engineering skills. The innovation moves from product concept, to proof of concept, to prototype, to product, and then finally to scale up. The skills needed at each stage are not the same: The concept end of the spectrum requires out-of-the box creativity whereas the scale-up end of the spectrum requires conformist discipline. MCNC was not a place for conformist discipline, but our colleagues at Nortel were patient.

Without even realizing how much they were teaching us, Nortel also schooled us on photonics: the most pressing product requirements, the needs in the marketplace, and the trends for the future. It was one of my most valuable learning experiences.

Nortel's United Kingdom team flew direct from Gatwick to Raleigh-Durham. With the six-hour time difference, they would fly out mid-morning their time and arrive in the afternoon our time, driving straight to MCNC from the airport. We would meet in the very room where I first met Shelby at MCNC's Thanksgiving lunch. I remember the CTO of Nortel's photonics division, Jesse Anderson, arriving at MCNC in tremendous back pain from his flight, which he would alleviate by lying flat on his back on one of the large tables. Our team would sit, spread around the room, and our meetings would continue. This was internet time—everything had to be done faster than ever before and there was no room for human frailties or imperfections.

Jesse was a great guy who became our leading light on optical communications devices, networks, and industry trends. At one point he drew out a roadmap for how optical networking had evolved and where it was going. He also explained where the real business opportunities were. I trusted his views more than anyone's. There were many times when I sat with other customers—very prestigious names in the communications industry—and discounted their crazy demands for 4000 port optical switches because it simply did not jibe with Jesse's much more measured analysis of future needs.

"There is huge hype around the very large optical cross-connects," he told me. "But, that's not where our group's interest is. We sell photonic components and are looking for high margin and high volume. There is no volume in large optical cross-connect switches. The world will only need a few of them. The smaller switches, like the $8 \times 8$ and $16 \times 16$ that we're building, is where the volume business will be."

"What about $1 \times 2$'s and $2 \times 2$s?" I asked, hopefully. Those would be so *easy* for us to build, and I was still trying to sell a program. A $1 \times 2$, the simplest of optical switches had one light stream coming in—an input port—and two ports coming out to send a light stream in either of the two directions; a $2 \times 2$ had two input ports and two output ports, so you could send two incoming light streams in either of two directions. I loved the prospect of building these simple devices; I wanted to take baby steps into the photonics wilderness.

"Nah. You're really not going to add value there, Jesko. It's so easy to build those with conventional technology. Do you know how 1 × 2s are built now?"

"No, I can't say I do."

"You buy a $2 relay, rip the cover off and glue a 1 cent mirror to the switching mechanism. Then you seal it in a hermetic package and align the input and output fibers to the mirror. Voila! You have a thousand-dollar product. Pretty much the same for a 2 × 2."

"You're kidding."

"Nope."

I wondered, if one of these simple switches was priced at $1000, what a 16 × 16 switch would bring. If the 16 × 16 switch were created with individual, conventional 1 × 2s, it would require 256 1 × 2 optical switches and cost $256,000 for a single device! Never mind the size and complexity of such a system. No wonder Nortel put down $250,000 so readily for our MEMS switch proposal.

Jesse explained that the real value of MEMS lay in scaling both functionality and volume. As soon as the functionality of the device became complex, like with the larger switches, or volumes got really large, then MEMS was the best approach.

"Like, for example, optical attenuators, those are really high volume," Jesse explained.

Optical attenuator? At that point, I'd never heard of one. But this interaction was typical of the almost casual way Jesse taught us about needs within the photonics industry. It was also emblematic of the speed with which our perspective was changing. Listening to Jesse, within an afternoon I might learn about a new application for our technology; within a day I would talk to Matt to assess if our technology could build it; and within a few weeks we could build it, if we wanted to.

On that day, Jesse explained to me exactly how an optical attenuator worked and why it was so ubiquitous in optical networks. He also explained that if Nortel could come up with something called a *variable* optical attenuator, then he thought the annual production volumes could get into the millions. At the time, optical attenuators were largely static—they could only be set to attenuate one level of power. A variable optical attenuator could be changed dynamically so that it could always respond in real time to whatever was happening on the network.

"JDS Uniphase has a huge cash cow business selling optical attenuators at $800 a pop! Currently these are all static devices that have to be pre-tuned to wherever they are placed in the network. If we could make a *variable* optical attenuator, it could be a huge business. We would have one device that could be put anywhere and then tuned dynamically, online to fit any need."

I was enthralled. "I can think of ten ways we can build a device that cuts the power of an optical beam!"

"No, no. Don't worry about that one, Jesko," Jesse laughed at my eagerness. "We actually have *four* different programs working on the variable optical attenuator in the UK. That's plan A, B, C, and D. We definitely don't need a plan E! You guys stick to the cross-connect switches."

But I had heard enough. What a need! Millions of devices times $800 per device sounded like a great business to me. Clearly Nortel thought so too and with four different development programs to get there, they were signaling both a lack of a current solution and a desperation to find one. Moreover, I *loved* the technology fit. I wasn't kidding when I told Jesse that I thought it would be easy to produce a variable attenuator in MEMS. It was the kind of business I had been looking for—a billion-dollar opportunity to drive a billion-dollar company doing something that was dead easy. The fact that it would be in direct competition with JDS Uniphase's core business was also interesting. Building a business that could threaten the big dog would drive up our company valuation and even spur acquisition.

I immediately wanted to go for it. Who knew if Nortel's first four programs would work? And even if one of them did, it seemed like the kind of product we could do on our own if we had to. The application was so simple that I could think of a number of ways of doing it, the easiest being with our workhorse thermal actuator where it would drive a tiny wedge into the optical beam. It would be like taking a knife edge and dropping it down in front of a pencil flashlight to dim it, but on a micro-scale. What I loved best about this application is that there would be no touching surfaces. No debilitating stiction to keep moving parts stuck together. No micro-welding. And, even as we continued work on Nortel's much more complicated electromagnetic cross-connect switch, in my heart I saw the optical attenuator as being a much easier, and faster, path to product.

Every which way I looked at it, the variable optical attenuator seemed like the perfect device for us, almost made to order for the technology we had already developed. All our microrelay experience and data supported this conclusion. When I asked Matt Steel about it, he agreed.

I had a deep aversion to taking on any kind of development without customer funding. We were always cash poor and our technology risk was so high that pursuing any kind of product development on our own nickel was financial suicide. Cronos simply could not afford it. But the variable optical attenuator was different. The technology risk was so low and the prize was so large, I concluded it would be suicide *not* to pursue it. In all my years at MCNC and Cronos, this was the *only time* I felt this way. And I pitched all of this to Brian Novak. I explained the modest technology risk and the incredible market upside. He listened to my arguments and agreed.

We moved at internet speed, designing and fabricating two versions of the attenuator within weeks. They both worked like a charm the very first time—a testimony to the simplicity of the solution. As we demonstrated the functionality of our first variable attenuators, I knew we had something. Every other product we were working on had complexity after complexity. Stiction problems, alignment problems, scaling problems, and on and on. But the attenuator just worked—right out of the box. Any thoughts of failure were by now far, far behind me.

Meanwhile, MEMS products became a gold rush within the optical communications gold rush. Entrepreneurs and investors raced to take advantage of the technology to serve the insatiable photonics demand. While many new players entered the MEMS race, there were perhaps only four or five companies that benefited. Those that were positioned very early on, well before the hype, suddenly found themselves in exactly the right place at the right time. Cronos was one of them. We were one of the very few in position to ride the monster wave as it built up, passed by, and crashed all in the blink of an eye. The remaining 395-or-so MEMS companies were mostly crushed as the magnificent rogue wave crashed on the rocks, annihilating everything in its path.

For myself, it became the most exhilarating time of my career. I'd slogged it out at Kobe Steel, and then MCNC, with the enduring belief that my skills were meant for something greater than a career in technology management or sales. Picking myself up off the ground numerous times, I convinced myself that each failure was a just a learning experience on the pathway to success. That somehow there was a flipside, an alternate universe to my failures, just beyond the horizon. I knew it was there, I believed it was there, I just could not quite… grasp it.

My belief was so strong that, even as I failed over and over, I could not stop. When I flew back from Ottawa on that fateful day, with a blazing headache, shaking my head, I was really just shaking it at myself. When I laughed with my wife at the ice scraper, I was really just laughing at myself. Why could I not stop this absurd stupidity? Surely, I could go out and get a real job! Why not take the other path, the more traveled one? Why did I not take that path to Buffalo? These were the recriminations that had entered my mind again and again as I bounced from one crazy act to the next. But as the MEMS photonics wave built in 1999, it all finally began to make sense. I felt like I was finally doing what I was born to do.

My quick trip to Caltech to license the perfect MEMS technology for the Nortel optical cross-connect switch, followed by the deal with Nortel to develop their product had felt like a crowning moment. It was the best, most creative deal I had ever put together. I could not imagine doing better. However, it was only the first, fat raindrop in a gathering storm.

My flights to California—primarily Silicon Valley—increased rapidly to the point where I was spending half of my time out there. Half of our customers were from the other 399 venture-backed MEMs startups who, like Lucent, needed our ready-to-go infrastructure to meet the demands of their customers and investors. The other half were established companies like ETEK, SDL, Nortel, Lucent, and many others who needed our engineering capabilities and fabrication infrastructure to develop competitive products. Everyone was a slave to internet time and Cronos was perfectly positioned to deliver to those needs.

More than once, I would be on a call in North Carolina in the morning, on a plane by noon, and in meetings in California that evening. Adrenalin drove me, and it was addictive. Landing in San Jose produced a special kind of buzz that I needed as the frenetic energy of Silicon Valley knocked the air out of my lungs. I was always on—fighting the crowds, fighting for a car, fighting the traffic to get to a customer's office by 7:00 pm, meeting late into the evening with engineers to discuss a new need, a new product, a new purchase order. Then a late dinner meeting or drinks at a bar or a party. Sleep was not a priority.

Silicon Valley didn't sleep and everywhere you went you met other entrepreneurs, investors, and wannabes who were all searching for the same prize. All we could talk about was the communications gold rush and that everything appeared to be turning into gold. Then, perhaps, the redeye back home, or more meetings the next day, and *then* the redeye back home. Work was 24/7 and it fed the rush. Finally, I had dialed into a magnificent trend that VCs were desperate to be part of.

Family and social life suffered, but fortunately my friends and my wife were patient and my children were young. I would drift off to sleep at social events and even at my children's events. We had three kids by then, and my oldest son was especially in need of my time.

At his behest we joined a father-son organization called Indian guides where I proved to be a terrible "chief." Our large group of fathers and sons met once a week at our various homes to discuss progress on completing tasks towards various patches that recognized competence of one form or another. Invariably, we had not had the father-son time to perform any tasks and I often dozed off during meetings, leaving my son to his own devices. I regret very few things from that time, but not being there enough for my son is one of them.

The frenetic pace at Cronos, however, was paying off. In 1999, our revenues jumped to $10 million, from $6 million the year before, and we broke even on a profit basis. Commercial contracts, which had totaled a few hundred thousand dollars in 1996 were now $6 million! Peter Brennan and I were busy, busy, busy. Amazingly, almost all of our commercial contracts were still for prototyping! As I surveyed the multitude of customers that were carrying out product development with us, I imagined even a small portion turning into volume production and started to get a rare feeling of invincibility. The thought of failure was so far in the rearview mirror that it no longer existed. The dreadful fear that failure was just around the corner was magically gone. This *was* going to work!

It now all seemed just a matter of probabilities. While none of the products we were working on were in volume production, the ultimate harbinger of success was the sheer volume of projects. Just statistically, I felt that there had to be a winner in there somewhere! Both Lucent and OMM were starting to reserve capacity for volume production and we were negotiating volume product manufacturing agreements with other companies including Nortel.

Then, finally, our own, proprietary photonics product: the variable optical attenuator. While Jesse had shown us the path, we alone had gone down it: The attenuator was our design, based on our patented actuator, designed and paid for by us. It was our very own, proprietary product. A ball. A ball! A shiny, wonderful, awe-inspiring new ball! Having crashed out miserably in the microrelay game, we were now miraculously poised to conquer in the photonics game. How far we had come since I received that ice scraper from Gregory Hansen. If we hadn't been running our of cash, life would have been perfect.

One of the highlights of my year, besides the deals I was doing, was when Jack pulled me aside for a private discussion. He did not want to meet in his office, which was all glass, but instead asked me to join him in the boardroom, which was closed off. He asked Brian to join us too. At first, I thought I was getting fired. While I could think of no reason for Jack to fire me, I assumed that somehow someone at MCNC had finally managed to drive a knife into my back. But this wasn't the case at all. Jack handed me an envelope, shook my hand, and told me I had been doing a great job. I thanked him, reveling in the praise, accepting what I thought was a letter of commendation.

"Go ahead and open it," Jack said, pointing to the envelope.

"Oh... sure. Okay." I did. It was a check for $25,000. At this point, month by month, my small team was bringing in deal after deal and also consistently meeting very challenging sales projections. I just considered that my job, but Jack chose to recognize my contributions in the most direct possible way. To put this in context, my salary at the time was $70,000. As I saw the number on the check, my jaw dropped, and speechless, I stared at Jack. I knew that MCNC was in a cash crunch, so receiving this bonus was completely beyond belief. I wanted to hug Jack, but refrained.

"Yeah, Jesko, you've been doing a *really* good job!" Jack laughed and patted me on the back, sending me on my way with an admonishment to keep the bonus to myself. No problem there.

When I brought that check home to Monika that evening, we both agreed it was a heck of a lot better than an ice scraper. When things go right; they go right. Just as failure can instantly have you spiraling into the abyss; success fuels euphoria. A $25,000 check out of the blue added to the euphoria. Suddenly things were going well, and they were going well across the board. It seemed like the world was made to be this way. Monika and I didn't just celebrate with a bottle of champagne, I bought a case of it.

This was *before* we funded the company! The cash we raised in December of 1999 when we spun out Cronos was like injecting nitrous oxide into a thousand-horsepower motor—it lifted us into the stratosphere.

While Brian had not been great at raising money, it turned out that he was quite good at spending it. We now had $8 million in the bank and Brian was determined, and experienced enough, to use the money wisely. He made a major investment in marketing. The budgets he proposed were extreme, and as the newly appointed Vice President of Marketing and Business Development, now making $140,000 per year, I voiced my skepticism. "Brian, we're going flat out! Why spend this kind of money on marketing?"

"We don't just need to *be* number one, Jesko. We need to be *seen* as number one. There is a big difference."

"Okay, but $250,000 just to go to the Optical Fiber Conference? It seems excessive. I'm not sure—".

"Well I am!" Brian boomed with the finality of conviction that every word he uttered could never be contradicted. "We're going to be the biggest thing at OFC this year. You're our VP of Marketing, so make it happen or I'll find someone else who will!"

You always knew where you stood with Brian. He prided himself on that.

My budget also included a $15,000 per month expenditure for a marketing communications firm, something else I was skeptical about, but smart enough not to question. There was even money to hire a marketing manager. I was used to making money, not spending it, and felt this was yet another extravagance. However, we ended up making a great hire: Debbie Birch was a true marketing and communications professional with an almost impossible Tennessee twang.

Even though it was my role, I couldn't figure out why Brian needed to invest so much in marketing. Weren't we growing fast enough? We were doing so well, I'd even gotten a bonus. But Brian was adamant and more than happy to ridicule me for wanting to be cautious.

It was a huge learning experience for me. I'd taken marketing classes in business school, but that didn't come close to preparing me for my marketing role at Cronos. Fortunately, Debbie was awesome. As a first step, she helped us hire a marketing communications firm, Brodeur Partners, where I met Corey Parker, an account executive there. Between Debbie, Corey, and all the money we had to spend, I started to see almost immediate changes in how we presented ourselves to the market. It's something called "*positioning*," and I honestly believe that Corey's and Debbie's repositioning of Cronos created more value for our company than anything else we did.

Corey's team began by analyzing key parameters before making any changes: They analyzed how our current customers perceived us, who our target audiences were, and what our messages to these audiences should be. While there were subtle changes in our company operationally—with experienced professionals in charge, our operation became much more disciplined—there were much more dramatic changes in how we presented ourselves to the world.

Vera and I had seen ourselves as a MEMS company. We had the best MEMS engineering and delivery capabilities in the world and were very proud of it. We told everybody so.

Corey, on the other hand, saw us as an "*internet backbone*" company, enabling new technical breakthroughs that were vital to the future of optical communications. It was a brilliant repositioning of Cronos that fit perfectly with what the market wanted to hear. With excellent marketing professionals to guide us, a disciplined program was put in place to hammer home our new persona. By the beginning of 2000, Corey's messaging was being delivered through all available media platforms.

Brian was also very clever in getting out the message. It had always been frustrating that secrecy agreements stopped us from letting the world know that the Lucents, OMMs, Cornings, Nortels of the world were all working with us. It especially grated that Lucent, with its industry leading LambdaRouter, wanted to hide the fact that they were actually building the heart of the system—the MEMS chip with its 256 tiny mirrors—with us. Lucent was particularly aggressive, moving their chips into trial production, and even paying us $10,000 for each week that we cut from our delivery time. We sold a ten-week standard lead time on MUMPs, even though each production cycle was typically a shade over six weeks. This meant we would deliver to Lucent in seven weeks and make a cool $30,000 extra every time we fabricated their devices. I sold the same program to OMM, which is perhaps one of the reasons I got that bonus!

But for all of this activity, for all our customers' desperation to have us deliver faster, more, better, we couldn't tell anyone about it. It grated. Brian tried to renegotiate the secrecy agreements with our customers, but soon realized that it was futile: They simply did not want anyone to know how integral we were to their MEMs success.

Brian, however, was not so easily deterred. His rule was: If you can't beat them, change the rules! He knew there were more subtle ways of communicating our relationships. Everyone (except us) was hyping their efforts. Lucent and OMM were regularly issuing press releases on their dramatic improvements in product development. Improvements they were invariably making with us.

To solve this thorny communications problem, Brian brilliantly had us mimic their press releases every time they came out. One memorable example was when Lucent signed an agreement with us for more (and faster!) production runs. The very next day they announced that they had dramatically increased their capacity to produce "tiny mirrors" for the LambdaRouter without, of course, mentioning Cronos. It was frustrating, to say the least.

The morning the press release was issued; Brian called me into his office.

"Did you see this?" he demanded, waving the press release in my face.

"Ah, no, what's that?" I was busy closing deals and had no time to follow all the crazy press releases that were being issued by our many customers and competitors.

"It's Lucent! They just announced their expansion of chip production without mentioning us!" Brian bellowed, glowering at me as if it was my fault.

"Brian, we've been over this before. We have secrecy agreements—".

"I don't give a damn about those stupid secrecy agreements! We've got to do something! What are we paying all these marketing idiots for!" Brian growled, slamming his fist on his desk.

Brian hated being constrained in any way. On the one hand, he knew as well as I did, we had to be very careful. On the other hand, he was a street fighter, not one to back off under any circumstances, and comfortable bending the rules if it served his purpose. Here, he set out to bend the rules.

"Here's what I want you to do, Jesko. Draft a press release that gives me 'tiny mirrors' in the heading. I want the title to say something about how we are expanding *our* production to meet a growing need for 'tiny mirrors.' Then I want the body of the release to do the same. 'Tiny Mirrors!' Got that?"

Brian was always like this. He had one speed and one direction. He often liked to say that we needed to be "data driven," unless, of course the data conflicted with where he wanted to go. I often suffered silently at his demands, and this was certainly a case in point. What a waste of time! I felt his "tiny mirrors" idea was juvenile, but he was the boss. I dropped everything I was doing, called up Corey, and together we spent the next couple of hours crafting our "tiny mirrors" press release. Brian reviewed it and tweaked it, happy as a kid in a candy store. It went out that afternoon.

Much to my surprise, the "shadow strategy" worked like a charm. People quickly put two and two together and started to see Cronos in a different light. We weren't just MEMS engineers—we really were an "*internet backbone*" company. Cronos *was* in fact enabling new technical breakthroughs that were vital to the future of optical communications. Our efforts to mimic our customers became *proof points* to our messaging.

As reporters and analysts caught on, we were soon fielding questions about our role in producing this chip or that chip. Our pointed responses of "we have secrecy agreements" or "we can't speak to that" or "we can't comment on any relationship with so and so" spoke volumes. The strategy was brilliant.

Vera's presentations and the short courses she taught on MEMS design also changed. We began to pointedly feature many of the iconic images of the day—all of them optical MEMS chips being fabricated by Cronos, but with no direct acknowledgement that this was the case. We never broke a secrecy agreement, but we successfully created a cloud of intrigue in a business environment that was thirsting for winners. Even today, if you search for images of the "LambdaRouter," you will get pictures of the "tiny mirrors" that Cronos fabricated and Lucent made famous, in their quest for market leadership. As we began to link those mirrors to our newly spun-out company Cronos, the world began to catch on.

And it caught on fast. In fact, it caught on much, much faster than we expected. We were funded in December, and by late January we had already fielded two offers for acquisition. One of them, from a company called SDL, was for $150 million, or $9.60 a share! Imagine our investors: They stood the chance to make 6 times their investment in less than two months! To put it into real terms: An investor putting $3 million into Cronos in December would have received around $18 million in January! Imagine how the employees felt; we bought our stock at one penny.

When we founded Cronos, our target for acquisition was *exactly* $150 million. To get an offer for this amount after less than two months of operations as an independent company was mind boggling. But by this time, we were setting our sights much higher. Six times money was not nearly good enough. We all knew that we were on a rocketship that had just left the platform.

We did not set a new target, but we knew in our guts that $150 million was just not enough.

# Chasing the Unicorn

As our marketing efforts accelerated, our main focus was the next Optical Fiber Conference, OFC2000 to be held in Baltimore in early March (just a few months after funding Cronos). Brian was determined to make Cronos the star of the show and was investing unimaginably large amounts to do so. Just the booth for the show, a 100-square-foot structure, cost $75,000! We were also spending enormous sums with Brodeur as we meticulously prepared every detail. We needed slide shows and presentation decks, press releases, product documentation, industry backgrounders, company backgrounders, and executive backgrounders. We lined up interviews with reporters and analysts and new customers. Everything revolved around our new positioning as an internet backbone company, a photonics components leader. The preparation alone was exhausting.

We arrived at OFC2000 with a small team including marketing, sales, and engineering. Each person was scheduled to work the booth at various times during the exhibit. Everything was planned to the last detail, every minute accounted for. We were ready for primetime.

An important aspect of our marketing for OFC was Vera's MEMS short course. The course had started out purely as a technology workshop for product development engineers who wanted to build MEMS devices in our facility. With a new appreciation for a much broader customer base, we modified the focus of the course to greatly simplify the technology portion while expanding our material to all aspects of MEMS, including market research and business impact. This allowed us to target a much larger audience, who themselves might not have a technical role in product development, but who thirsted for information on this new, exploding technical field.

While organizations like Lucent—notably Tony Williams—gave courses right on site at the conference, we had no such cachet. Instead, as we planned to make our mark at OFC, we rented a meeting room at a hotel next door and started to advertise our short course on all things MEMS featuring Vera. The course was to be a cornerstone of our marketing effort at the conference, so I was taken aback when, a week before the OFC, I got a frustrated call from Vera. I was in Boston at a venture conference, walking through a crowded hallway when I picked up the call. At first, I couldn't hear exactly what Vera was saying, but I knew her well enough to recognize that she wasn't pleased. Quickly, I made my way to a quiet corner.

"Can you say that again, Vera?" I asked, doing my best to pinch my other ear closed to hear her.

"There are only five people in the damn course! I'm not wasting my time on five people!"

"Wait, wait, wait… What do you mean five people? What are you talking about?"

"The course you guys set up at OFC! Nobody is signing up! I told you it was a waste of time. Unless you have at least fifteen people signed up, I'm not doing it."

Vera had been a somewhat reluctant contributor to our new course structure for OFC2000. She knew her technical audience very well and hit a home run every time she offered them her MEMS design course. As I recommended including business and marketing in the course, she had her doubts it would play. Nevertheless, she trusted me and was willing to humor us, but now it seemed that she was right. Vera, the Queen of MEMS, wouldn't be caught dead teaching a course to five people! And I knew without Vera we didn't have a course.

"Give me 30 minutes, Vera," I begged. "Let me check into it and I'll get back to you."

Vera agreed, and I immediately called Debbie. "Debbie! What's going on? Do we really only have five people lined up for the course next week?"

"Yep. That's all we have right now!"

"You're kidding! That's crazy. Maybe we're not promoting it right!"

"Maybe…," Debbie twanged. "But to be honest, I think we've gotten the word out. It's just…well, so far, we only have five people. What can I say?"

"Who's on the list?" I asked in desperation.

Debbie read out the names and titles of the people on the list. Four of them meant nothing to me, but the fifth name hit me like a bolt out of the sky: Glenn Dorsey, founder and chief product strategist for JDS Uniphase. As I found out later, he was the 'D' in JDS. It was unbelievable.

JDS Uniphase held a very special place for us. While I had landed about every major account in the optical communications universe, JDSU was not on that list. This was, in fact, somewhat by design. JDSU was the super nova of the optical components industry. They were the darling of Wall Street, soon to be worth an unheard of $100 billion. They were aggressively buying everything in sight, including, ultimately, SDL for a cool $41 billion in *cash*! Early on, I had approached JDS Uniphase to see if they wanted to work with us and had been turned down. At the time, we decided to turn that negative into a positive. We had a plan.

Working with Nortel, our optical attenuator strategy had started to pay huge dividends. Nortel's four different development programs to build a variable optical attenuator had each fallen by the wayside. In contrast, our thermal actuator had proven to be a perfect platform for a variable optical attenuator and our efforts to independently develop the product started to look brilliant.

Nortel had already adopted us as their preferred supplier of MEMS technology. As Jesse Anderson kept us abreast of the problems they were having with their internal programs, I suggested that we could run a few "experiments" to see if we could make a variable optical attenuator for them: for free, of course. As the last of their development programs failed, we already had working devices on the shelf and could, almost overnight, provide a working solution to a desperate customer. I had finally, truly, marvelously matched need to solution!

This is how our thermal actuator, which failed spectacularly as a microrelay for Nortel linecards, now became Plan A for Nortel's variable optical attenuator. We had come full circle in our efforts to commercialize our innovation. Nortel's optical cross-connect switch was also still under development, but it was clear to everyone that the attenuator was the product we all needed right now. It was an amazing lesson on the crazy path that a technology can take on its way from the laboratory to the marketplace. It was also a lesson in addressing customer needs. If we had listened only directly to what Nortel had told us, we would have simply built what they asked for (an optical cross-connect switch) and would never have attempted what they specifically asked us not to do (variable optical attenuator). As it was, by understanding the customer, understanding the technology, understanding the market and its trends, we were able to make great decisions that finally caused the basket of customer needs to overlap with our cauldron of capabilities at an optimal time.

The Nortel collaboration culminated in one of our biggest deals ever when we finally signed off on a manufacturing agreement for optical attenuators in early 2000. Nortel was the archenemy of JDS Uniphase and the optical attenuator business was a JDS Uniphase cash cow. With our newly minted Nortel agreement, Cronos was stepping directly into the JDS Uniphase wheelhouse.

Up until that point we had studiously stayed away from JDS Uniphase, for the simple reason that we wanted JDS Uniphase to acquire us. And the best way to get their attention, was to scare the hell out of them. With our own attenuator product showing great promise and with the JDS Uniphase's archenemy signed as a first customer, it appeared that OFC might be a perfect time to surprise JDS Uniphase with our progress, if I could only figure out a good way to do it.

So, listening to Debbie reading off that miserable list of only five names I could not believe my ears. Wow, this could not have been scripted any better. It appeared we would have the undivided attention of one Glenn Dorsey for the full morning of our short course. But I still needed Vera to make it work.

"Debbie, I don't care if you have to hire drunks off the street, we need another ten people in that room. I'm dead serious, I don't care if you have to pay people. Do it! We need fifteen! Just don't tell Vera. Okay?"

Debbie was a trooper; you never had to tell her things twice, nor did she ever question my crazy requests. She agreed, and I knew it was as good as done. There might be a stench of alcohol in that room, but we would get fifteen people!

With the attendance of fifteen people magically confirmed, I called Vera back.

"Vera, Vera. It's just a misunderstanding. I don't know what Debbie was telling you. I just confirmed it with her. For sure we're gonna get more than fifteen people! Are you kidding? I guarantee it!"

"Alright, Jesko," Vera was mollified, but just. "I swear, though, I'm going to keep checking the list with Debbie and if it's less than fifteen people, I won't be there."

"Don't worry, Vera! It's already done! Are you kidding? People are gonna flock to this course!"

I didn't tell her I was ready to hire actors if I had to.

When we got to OFC, our booth looked magnificent, worth every bit of the $75,000 we paid for it. While it was small by most standards—there were many booths that were the size of a Texas mansion—our company name sign was one of the biggest. Instead of attaching it to the booth as most companies did, Brian had made sure that our sign hung from the ceiling of the conference building. Brian liked things big and audacious. And so, our Cronos sign hovered over our booth, bigger, higher, and more spectacular than any other.

We set everything up the night before and prepared to do battle the next day with a schedule that had two people manning the booth at all times throughout the day.

The next morning, we kicked off our short course well before the conference doors opened. We had timed it to make it easy for people to go from our course to the conference once the doors opened at 10:00 am.

I remember walking through the conference building quite early in the morning. The entire floor looked pristine, with everything in place, but eerily quiet except for a few spots of activity here and there as groups made final preparations. From there, I headed off to the hotel and our short course adjacent to the conference center. When I arrived, Debbie was busy signing people in. By the time Vera showed up the room was packed. It was standing room only, without hiring a single actor or paying of a single homeless person. Vera was pleased. Glenn Dorsey was there, and I was pleased.

We started off the course with the market section and painted a picture that encompassed everything we had learned about MEMS and optical communications over the past year. I used Jesse's description of the evolving optical network and layered in our collective understanding of how MEMS would enable the future of the communications industry.

We showed every publicly available picture of our customers' MEMS chips while stating, without being asked, that we could not comment on whether these were being produced by Cronos or not. When it came to forecasted production volumes, I explained that we also could not comment on the sources of our data, as this was proprietary information. Whose proprietary information? Beyond acknowledging that these were Cronos customers, I could not say. Brian had taught me well.

To top it all off, we then added in details of the variable optical attenuator, proudly acknowledging that this was our own product: A product backed by patents and substantiated with volume manufacturing agreements with market leaders. Discussion of the attenuator included independent market forecasts for attenuators and small-scale switches that made the future of Cronos look very bright indeed.

It is said that you only get the chance to make a first impression once. Every aspect of what we did that day was designed to make a good impression on Glenn Dorsey, to *really* get his attention, and it worked. At the break, he approached me and introduced himself. He told me he could not stay for the second half of the course due to other obligations, but that he was amazed at what he had seen and wondered aloud why he had never heard of Cronos before. He gave me his card and said he would be sure to follow up.

I returned to the OFC exhibition floor just before the doors opened. It was still quiet, and when I joined the team at the booth, everyone was sanguine. The booth was beautifully designed, reflecting all our engineering and production capabilities, telling the story of a company that was at the very core of optical communications. It was our coming out party and for the first time we finally felt like we belonged.

Our plan was that we would all be at the booth when the floor opened. Then staff would take over with two people in the booth at all times while Brian, Vera, and I walked the exhibition floor to check out our competition and meet customers, but remaining available as needed.

It was a fine plan. A reasonable plan under normal circumstances; however, this day turned out to be anything but normal! Once the doors to the floor opened, we entered into a frenzy we could never have imagined. Within minutes hordes of people descended on us. Within half an hour the crowd was at least five people deep, and it stayed that way for the rest of the day. Our biggest challenge was trying to leave the booth! The attention was so insane I wanted to laugh at times. I remember going to get something to eat with Brian and we had to fight our way through the crowd. As we walked away my entire body buzzed and my hands shook. I was high on pure adrenaline. Brian and I turned around and looked back at the booth and had to shake our heads in amazement. The rest of the conference floor did not look this way; Cronos had made its mark.

We made our mark on Glenn Dorsey too. For the rest of the day, waves of JDSU engineers descended upon us, looking at our materials, meeting with our engineers, and asking questions. They observed the frenzy around our booth and walked away impressed. By midafternoon, the JDSU CEO showed up. He sought out Brian and requested a private conversation. At this point, the thought of a private conversation in our booth was laughable, but there was a small storage area in the center not much bigger than a broom closet. Neither man was small, but they managed to squeeze in and close the door for a ten-minute, private conversation.

The JDSU CEO left and Brian rejoined us, uncharacteristically silent, but looking pleased. I learned later that week that an offer to buy the company had been made during that brief discussion: $450 million!

With this, Brian moved very quickly. By Friday of the same week he had set up a telephone auction with Nortel, a west coast company called ETEK, and JDS Uniphase. The Cronos Board flew in for the day, meeting with our local lawyers (Wyrick Robbins) and our west coast lawyer (Benson Mitchel of Wilson Sonsini).

Brian used the Nortel lever to get ETEK engaged and JDS Uniphase even more excited about the deal. Nortel was their most fearsome competitor and they worried about Cronos falling into the hands of the archenemy. Nortel actually dropped out of the proceedings very quickly, leaving ETEK and JDS Uniphase to fight it out. That alone was bizarre as ETEK had very recently been acquired by JDSU in a blockbuster deal, but the deal was under a merger review by the U.S. department of justice and so the two organizations were forbidden to communicate with each other. So, in effect you had one company negotiating against itself. This caused some bad blood later on, but Brian didn't care, he was a street fighter.

Brian and Ron Quinn negotiated all day, and by late afternoon they got an offer of $750 million from JDS Uniphase that ETEK was unwilling to beat. They returned to our conference room where our Board of Directors had sequestered themselves for the day. I was not in the boardroom, but what happened next is one of those stories that has become a small part of Silicon Valley lore.

When Brian and Ron presented the $750 million offer, our investment bankers, whom we had just hired two weeks before, and who stood to make millions of dollars on the deal, argued against taking the offer. They felt that, given a bit of time, they could do better—turn us into a true unicorn with more than a billion-dollar valuation. It was crazy: We were looking at a deal on the table that would take our investor's stock from $1.70 to $50 in less than four months, and our own investments from a penny to $50 in a year, and these two guys wanted more. It was a testimony to the times.

Ben Mitchel, on the other hand, was adamant: "Take the deal!" he roared.

Yes, we were entrepreneurs, but it was finally the moment to take the bird in hand…

Ben is one of the top M&A lawyers in the nation having been involved in some of the biggest deals in Silicon Valley. He is also a super nice guy who comes across as laid back and unassuming. However, in that room on that day, he gave a fiery speech, pounding the table with his fist and exhorting the Board to take the deal. They listened—and agreed on the offer. By the end of the workday, it was agreed: JDS Uniphase would buy Cronos for $50 a share.

Ben and his team papered the deal—prepared all the definitive agreements—over the weekend, which in of itself is hard to imagine, given the hundreds, if not thousands of pages of agreements that needed to be reviewed and signed by all parties. But this was a deal moving on internet time. Sunday night, the deal was fully papered and executed. For $750 million, Cronos was now a division of JDS Uniphase.

It's worthwhile to pause and let that settle in. This was the culmination of the rollercoaster ride that was Cronos. The end result was impossible to predict. We had failed so much, yet we succeeded in the end. We had made good decisions and bad ones, but just enough good ones to prevail. We had embarked on a mission to launch bottle rockets, and here we were planting our flag on the moon after just a few short years.

Was Cronos a unicorn? The simple standard is a startup worth over $1 billion is considered a unicorn. There are very few of those and by that standard Cronos did not quite make it. But, like any metric it does not really tell the whole story. What made Cronos so unique was in fact the return on investment that the deal generated. The deal was completed on March 12, 2000 and announced publicly on April 4, 2000. On that day, anyone who had fully vested shares could sell them. By then, most employees had vested about one third of their stock, but MCNC was fully vested and the MCNC Board sold the entire position ($230 million at the time we closed) almost immediately.

What was MCNC's return? Well, you can calculate it. Like all of us, MCNC bought in at a penny about a year before the company was sold for $50 a share. The return calculation on that investment is 488,399%!

But the real kings were our venture investors, who bought in at $1.70 on December 7, 1999 and were position to sell on April 4, 2000, which was 97 days later. Again, you can calculate the return yourself on a $50 per share sales price. On an annualized basis their return on investment was 3,193,550%.

One nuance to these calculations is that at the time, the stock market was dropping rapidly. On April 4, 2000 the Nasdaq stood at 4149, down 18% from 5049 at its peak on March 10, 2000 when we agreed on a price. This affected the final price on the deal, so the actual price at conversion was somewhat less than the $50 agreed upon on March 12. But even accounting for significant losses in the time between closing the deal and announcing it, the returns for the founders and investors would have been around 400,000% and 1,750,000%, respectively. Crazy.

The outcome was beyond belief, but does this stuff happen by pure, random luck? Some people might look at the Cronos journey and say: "Yes." But I don't think so. Certainly, many pieces that became Cronos coalesced haphazardly in a way that ultimately benefitted the company. However, fundamentally, the core elements of the Cronos story presaged success. It was really ours to screw up, and fortunately we did not.

What were those core elements? One, we had a world-class technology team that was ultimately strengthened by a strong business team. Two, we had a world-class technical capability supported by our own patents and we sought and obtained licenses to key technologies as needed. Three, we focused on real customer needs, as evidenced by their checkbook, and we unabashedly moved away from our own, preconceived ideas to accommodate real customer needs as we found them. Four, we were in a truly exploding market; to be sure, we were blind for a while, but we moved extremely quickly once the blinders came off. Five, we strengthened our ability to execute in technology development by bringing on a team that also gave us operational excellence in product development and manufacturing.

These five core elements created a powerful framework that allowed us to survive, and even thrive, in the turbulence. To this day, these elements—team, technology, market, customers and ability to execute—remain the core metrics that drive any deal I work on. I worry much less about the turbulence and much more about the framework. Having a strong framework in no way guarantees success, but it slants the odds ever so slightly in your favor. In business that's all that counts. And that's all you can hope for when you are an entrepreneur.

We didn't know it at the time, but the rollercoaster was far from over. The markets hit their peak on the Friday we negotiated the purchase, and that Sunday, when we inked the deal with JDS Uniphase, was the very last day before the telecom bubble burst.

On Monday, March 13, 2000, the Nasdaq composite index began to drop. It dropped precipitously, and then tried to come back; then it dropped again, like a rock, the telecom bubble bursting rapidly in a fantastic fashion. Overall the Nasdaq technology company index went from its then historical high of 5049 on March 10, 2000, to eventually bottoming out at 1100 two years later. Companies, like JDS Uniphase, in the telecom space faired much worse. The JDSU stock price dropped from a high of $140 when Cronos was acquired to less than $2 a few years later, never to fully recover.

Unbelievably we sold Cronos in the nick of time. I have a wonderful chart of the Nasdaq from around that time. It looks like Mount Everest. With our financing on December 7, 1999, we parachuted onto Everest within sight of the summit; with our acquisition by JDS Uniphase on March 12, 2000, we were helicoptered out at the very zenith of the Everest peak. Had it taken just a day longer, had Benson Mitchel and his team not worked over the weekend, we would have been in a whole new world. Had we listened to our bankers I very much doubt the deal would have ever gotten done.

Thank you, Ben.

The Nasdaq did not return to its same heights again until a full fifteen years later. As the tech sector suffered a decade-long hangover, many acquisitions on the table before the bubble burst never happened. Very fortunately for us, our timing could quite literally not have been better. To me, the timing of our exit is probably the most magical aspect of the Cronos story.

# Epilogue

As I wrote this book and as I continue to pursue new entrepreneurial opportunities, I sometimes wonder: Is it just me? Do I live in some crazy, chaotic bubble where strange things happen? Or is this truly how entrepreneurship works?

It's a recurring question as I look around at my peers and colleagues and marvel—and envy—that they live such ordered lives. After we sold Cronos, I bought a fancy house in a beautiful neighborhood with expansive manicured lawns and pristine gardens. Everything in the neighborhood was perfect, every tree branch and blade of grass was in its place. Many of the homes were owned by executives in large companies and I envied them. They belonged and I wanted—or thought I wanted—the certainty of life they seemed to have.

After the acquisition, most of the Cronos leadership team left to do other things, but I had a two-year earn out deal that required me to stay with JDS Uniphase for that period. After Brian left, I inherited his position and title within JDS Uniphase: Vice President and General Manager of the MEMS Division. It was a tough job as the gathering storm turned into a hurricane and the telecom industry was obliterated. I reported to my boss in Ottawa and we scrambled to first plug leaks and later deploy life rafts. Forecasts of millions of dollars in orders turned into thousands. Our MEMS revenues dropped from $20 million one year to $4 million the next. Brian, in his final act as GM had worked with a vice president in Ottawa to invest $60 million of JDSU funds into a new manufacturing site in the Research Triangle Park. It was a beautiful facility, right across the road from MCNC, with state-of-the art equipment and world-class staff to run it. The facility needed $45 million in revenue to break even. In one of the hardest and best decisions of my life, I shut the facility down two weeks after taking over from Brian. It was a $50 million write-down that became a rounding error in a year that JDS Uniphase wrote down many billions. I laid off 70 percent of the Cronos team, including long-time friends, as we worked to stem the carnage.

We also ran into other headwinds. Far from being celebrated as a spectacular local success, our $750 million exit was viewed by some with deep suspicion. The MCNC Board of Directors, in particular, were concerned that we had somehow pulled the wool over their eyes. Apparently, the $230 million returned to them in the deal was not enough. Jack's $50,000 investment driven by our early meeting with Patrick Davis was now worth millions and viewed with particular concern, even though the entire Board had signed off on it. Despite approving his investment, The MCNC board apparently never expected him to actually make any money on it! How could such a ragtag team become so successful so quickly? They felt we, and Jack, must have cheated.

In a crazy turn of events, the State Bureau of Investigation was called into investigate the idea we had somehow engineered the whole thing, lining our pockets to MCNC's detriment. I felt terrible for Jack, the true white knight of MCNC who ended up being treated with suspicion by his own Board. Of course, the SBI soon put these silly ideas to rest. After a detailed investigation, and with a short, polite letter, they fully exonerated Jack and the Cronos leadership team, but this could not undo the harm done to Jack's public reputation. MCNC should have put Jack on a pedestal; instead they chose to vilify him. To his credit Jack handled the whole situation amazingly well, with grace and humor, like the true gentleman and leader that he was.

The layoffs were the toughest to deal with and I did my very best to shield my employees, giving long notices and maximum severance wherever I could. The negative local chatter did not impact me much, as I knew it was simply the product of envious or uninformed gossip. Personally, I'd sold my vested JDSU stock as quickly as I could and made millions off of the deal. But still, my biggest challenge was trying to get the rest of my money out of the market as the telecom bubble collapsed. Our deal had been a stock acquisition, trading JDSU stock for Cronos stock, and there were restrictions on how quickly I could sell it. JDSU stock tumbled from $140, to $90, to $75, to $25, to $12 and finally below $2. Cronos was a rocketship no more.

On the other hand, I was a well-paid executive in a very large company, with requests from leadership to become a senior executive in Ottawa. It would be like moving from the minor leagues to the majors. On many levels it was very attractive, just like my offer in Buffalo had seemed the most rational path not too many years ago. On other levels, it scared me to death.

I remember driving to work every day in my new Porsche 911, early in the mornings on empty back roads, with the singular goal of trying to hit at least 100 mph. I was a little depressed. This was it? I was 39 and had caught my unicorn, or at least the closest I would probably ever get to one. I could move into the executive ranks where my talents would allow me to build a lucrative, but more mundane career. All the fears I had when I first joined MCNC, about building a career and truly making a difference were gone. I had confidence that I belonged. But couldn't help asking: Was this really all there was?

But you already know the answer. As much as I tried to go down the more travelled path, it was so clear it was not for me. I wanted to find the next shiny new object, the next opportunity that might rise out of nothingness. Despite knowing the line between entrepreneurial success and failure was razor thin, this was my path. Once again, I found myself looking for something cool, something unknown, something with the opportunity to take me where I had never been before.

Far from avoiding turbulence, I was seeking it out. I'd learned to enjoy the ride along the way.

GPSR Compliance

The European Union's (EU) General Product Safety Regulation (GPSR) is a set of rules that requires consumer products to be safe and our obligations to ensure this.

If you have any concerns about our products, you can contact us on

ProductSafety@springernature.com

In case Publisher is established outside the EU, the EU authorized representative is:

Springer Nature Customer Service Center GmbH
Europaplatz 3
69115 Heidelberg, Germany

www.ingramcontent.com/pod-product-compliance
Lightning Source LLC
LaVergne TN
LVHW010341260326
834688LV00036B/822